Ignorance is a great threat to effective governance and healthy polity. It breeds discrimination, intolerance and prejudice. Ignorance with other social evils, poverty and illiteracy has defied the principle of justice and objectives of law. Alarming consequences have brought the need to address these issues in all forms. The best way to counter the bane of ignorance – is to spread knowledge, for knowledge is the natural enemy of ignorance. The year 2005 has been declared to be the 'YEAR OF JUDICIAL EXCELLENCE' by the Hon'ble Chief Justice of India. Judicial excellence does not merely mean the excellence of the institutions of judiciary but means giving justice to the needy. The book has been dedicated to the creatures because the delayed justice has adversely affected not only the human being but even the environment and its inhabitants.

OUR BEST SELLERS

Come On! Get Set Go — Swati-Sailesh Lodha

This book is a genuine 'mirror' for you to introspect and evaluate yourself. It is not the run-of-the mill stuff dealing with success and personality development. It focusses on "Failure" and its various facets. Read what a failure is, does and think and then refrain from it. Your friend, guide and philosopher is here to motivate you and make you if not "The Best" but "Second to None".

Rs. 195/-

The Secret of Happiness — Jas Mand

Happiness is a state of mind of a human being, which is manifest in a consistent attitude of contentment. There are numerous examples in our daily life which illustrate that individuals with similar outside conditions have different frames of mind and hence varying degrees of happiness. It is not something that exists outside you.

195/-

Secrets of Success — Kapil Kakar

Thoughts originate from mind and by implementing those thoughts we get a result. In this book you will find at length about mind not only scientifically but also what Lord Krishna said about it. The topics covered in this book are the basics of life. If you don't have sound basics then you cannot move ahead in life no matter how much you pray. This book is for people of all age groups as it can help students not only to develop their personality but also handle academic stress in a better way.

95/-

IMPOSSIBLE...POSSIBLE —*Biswaroop Roy Chowdhury*

This book is about change. People by nature are status quoists. It is a state of mind. But those who are able to change, they succeed faster than those who remain tied to their old habits, mindsets and prejudices. This book will tell you how you can change the way you think, act and behave. It requires a little effort. But the results will be phenomenal. The chronic patients can recover, the habitual failures can turn around and the die-hard pessimists can become incorrigible optimists, from the author of Dynamic Memroy Methods.

150/-   125/-

For Trade Enquiries & Catalogue contact
Publishers and Exporters of Indian Books, published more than 1000 titles.

◉ FUSION BOOKS

X-30, Okhla Industrial Area, Phase-II, New Delhi-110020, Phone : 011-51611861, Fax : 011-51611866
E-mail : sales@diamondpublication.com, Website : www.fusionbooks.com

OBJECTION YOUR HONOUR
(All you wanted to know about law)

Nishant Kashyap
Ashutosh Anand

DIAMOND BOOKS

DISCLAIMER

This book is being sold on the condition and understanding that the information contained therein is for guidance and reference only. It is in no way a substitute for the opinion of the Advocates and merely intends to make the prospective client aware of the legal procedures. The answers given to each question have been tried to be made as generalized as possible, however, the same should not be taken to spell out the complete procedure and would definitely vary depending upon the facts of the case and the peculiarity of the circumstances. The authors, publishers and sellers do not owe any responsibility / liability whatsoever for any loss, damage or injury occasioned / sustained by any one on account of action or inaction taken / not taken on the basis of the contents of this book.

ISBN : 81-288-0997-0

© Authors

Publisher
Diamond Pocket Books (P) Ltd.
X-30, Okhla Industrial Area,
Phase-II, New Delhi-110020
Phone : 011-51611861-865
Fax: 011-51611866
E-mail : sales@diamondpublication.com
Website : www.fusionbooks.com

Edition : 2005

Price : 95/-

Printed at : Adarsh Printers, Shahdara, Delhi-32

Objection Your Honour   Rs. 95/-
by Nishant Kashyap & Ashutosh Anand

*All the creatures to whom
Justice has either been delayed or denied.*

---

*All the citizens who aspire to
be legally empowered.*

PREFACE

Now darkness was dispelled, light arose,
Ignorance was dispelled and knowledge arose.
We saw the new way. Unborn is born.

Ignorance is a great threat to effective governance and healthy polity. It breeds discrimination, intolerance and prejudice. Ignorance with other social evils, poverty and illiteracy has defied the principle of justice and objectives of law. Alarming consequences have brought the need to address these issues in all forms.

The best way to counter the bane of ignorance – is to spread knowledge, for knowledge is the natural enemy of ignorance. It promotes understanding, compassion and tolerance. It is the basis on which due respect for laws and legal system can be formed. Spreading knowledge by effective human intervention is bound to harness the power of law to achieve its intended meaning, mandate and manifestations, for law without societal support is impotent.

Dynamic society and ever volatile human behaviour, coupled with its abuse has increased the burden on law. It has become imperative to know the laws, which govern your conduct and approach, know your rights, which you have to assert and know your obligations, which you have to perform.

The year 2005 has been declared to be the 'YEAR OF JUDICIAL EXCELLENCE' by the Hon'ble Chief Justice of India. Judicial excellence does not merely mean the excellence of the institutions of judiciary but means giving justice to the needy.

Indian judicial and legal system is going through an 'acid test' presently. Issue of warrant against the Hon'ble President of India by a Ld. Magistrate of Gujarat, mass strike by judges of Punjab High Court, suspension of a Judge of Delhi High Court on charges of corruption, volte-face by Zahira Shaikh have dented the credentials of these sacrosanct institutions.

These emerging concerns together with the old epidemic of huge pendency of cases, inaccessible and unaffordable quality law professionals, expensive and prolonged litigations have destroyed the fabric of our constitutional principles. A common man who had gone to court to seek justice comes back with a board embossed " JUSTICE DENIED ".

However, our government and judiciary in past two decades have effectively responded to need of time. Enactment of new Arbitration Law, Securitisation Act has given a new dimension to existing legal system. Amendments in Civil Procedure Code and Companies Act will surely go a long way in rendering effective and speedy justice. Liberal interpretation of Art. 21 and recognition of PIL have given more dignified meaning to life and personal liberty.

Specialised courts like Consumer Courts, Family Courts, Debt Recovery Tribunals, and Telecom Regulatory Authorities have been established catering to specific disputes to lessen the burden on the regular courts and to provide speedy justice to litigants.

This book is a humble contribution to further the noble cause of government and judiciary in taking the people from the dungeon of ignorance to temple of light. It has been our endeavour through this book to promote careful assertion of rights and dutiful performance of obligations. It will be worth mentioning here that this book is intended to make the reader legally empowered. A vigilant citizen, who is aware of the applicable law, will certainly assert his right, in case they are infringed. At the same point of time, if one is not aware of his rights, he may lose, to which he was legally entitled.

We have made an attempt through this book to examine and analyse practical issues, which have concern with day-to-day life of a common man, so that they can avoid unnecessary and unwarranted confrontation. We sincerely believe that knowledge provides common man with the necessary strength to counter any infringement and if the needs so arise, the bargaining power to seek effective enforcement.

The book covers important provisions of major laws and has been drafted in lucid language, in question-answer format, which makes reading of complex legal issues, a pleasure. It was not possible to form separate question-answer on every individual issue. The boxes, beside the question-answer, contain, in addition to the Sections and names of Acts which comprise the answer, such other legal provisions too, which are recommended to go through, if a deeper insight on that particular issue is needed. It has been our attempt to address the unfounded bias of a common man against law, legal system and law enforcement authorities. Our effort has been to further the cause of our Constitution intending at social, economical and political justice.

The book has been dedicated to the creatures because the delayed justice has adversely affected not only the human being but even the environment and its inhabitants.

Lot has been talked about the Justice Malimath Committee recmmendations, arguments still continue on need for Judicial Commission and All India Judicial Services, status of undertrial prisoners still sends shivers. All said and done, analytical introspection still leaves many points to ponder. But let's follow the advice of an optimist, " Good days will surely come."

If the reader wishes to know about any other legal issue too, it may be sent on our e-mail id. objectionyourhonour@yahoo.co.in

Equity aids the vigilant, not those who slumber on their rights.

(Vigilantibus non dormientibus aequitas subvenit)

ACKNOWLEDGEMENT

We thank
*Adv. Ram Jethmalani, Dr. S.S. Kushvaha,
Dr. Vidya Yeravdekar, Dr. M.S. Raste, Adv. S.E. Avhad, Mrs.
Nazma Sheikh, Adv. Ravi Bhardwaj, Miss Shabina Rubab, Mr.
Vikas Kr. Srivastava*

&

Faculties of Symbiosis Law College
for their invaluable help
and
special gratitude to our Parents
whose blessings made this endeavour success.

Last but not the least, we are grateful to the **Diamond Group** which established this link between you and us.

CONTENTS

Ch-1: CRIME AND SOCIETY — 19
1. FIR — 19
2. Delay in Lodging FIR — 20
3. Bail — 20
4. Bail as A Matter of Right — 21
5. Anticipatory Bail — 22
6. Arrest Without Warrant — 23
7. Rights of An Arrested Person — 24
8. Confession — 24
9. Self-Incrimination — 25
10. Search Without Warrant — 26
11. Time Limit for Taking Cognizance — 28
12. Abetment — 28
13. Right to Private Defence — 29
14. Culpable Homicide / Murder — 30
15. Indecent Representation of Woman — 31
16. Rape — 32
17. Kidnapping — 33
18. Dowry Death — 34
19. Euthanasia — 35
20. Presumption as to Suicide — 36
21. Sati — 36
22. Paternity of Child — 38
23. Causing Miscarriage — 39
24. Death Due to Negligence — 39
25. Rash and Negligent Driving — 40
26. Ragging — 40
27. Obscene Material — 41

28.	Defamation	42
29.	Medical Negligence (Criminal)	43
30.	Juvenile Justice	44
31.	Probation of Offenders	45
32.	False Complaint	46
33.	Producing False Document in Court	46
34.	Dishonest Misappropriation of Property	47
35.	Superdari	48
36.	Dying Declaration	49
37.	Tape Recorder as Evidence	50
38.	Hostile Witness	51
39.	Expert Opinion	51
40.	Estoppel	52
41.	Organ Transplant	53
42.	Arms Keeping	54
43.	Prostitution	55
	Criminal Courts Hierachy	57

Ch-2: FAMILY — 58

1.	Succession	58
2.	Will-Legal Formalities	59
3.	Will-Requisites	61
4.	Will-Executor-Receiving Benefit	61
5.	Gift	62
6.	Adoption	62
7.	Custody-Muslim	64
8.	Custody-Hindu	64
9.	Remarrying Wife-Muslim Law	64
10.	Marrying Minor	65
11.	Ceremonies of Marriage	65
12.	Prohibited Degrees in Marriage	66
13.	Inter-Religion Marriage	67
14.	Restitution of Conjugal Rights	67
15.	Judicial Separation	67
16.	Divorce - Sikh	68
17.	Divorce -Hindu	70
18.	Talaq-Muslim	70
19.	Talaq -Muslim Female	74

20.	Shuffa	77
21.	Muta Marriage	80
22.	Mahr	81
23.	Hiba	83
24.	Wakf	86
25.	Divorce-Christian	90
26.	Stridhan	90
27.	Recovery of Dowry	91
28.	Marriage Outside India	91
29.	Maintenance	93
30.	Maintenance-Muslim	93
31.	Legitimacy of A Child	94
32.	Homosexuality	94
33.	Marriage Certificate	95
34.	Proof of Marriage	96
35.	Court Marriage	97
36.	Sex Determination	97

Ch-3:	THE PROCEDURE OF COURTS	99
1.	Instituting Suit	99
2.	Suit by Minor	101
3.	Indigent Person	101
4.	Notice to Government	102
5.	Amendment	102
6.	Summon	103
7.	Interim Order	103
8.	Ex-Parte	104
9.	Exemption from Attachment	105
10.	Interpleader Suit	109
11.	Res Judicata	109
12.	Res Subjudice	110
13.	Delay in Suit Disposal	111
14.	Alternative Forum	112
15.	Transfer of Case	112
16.	Mesne Profits	112
17.	Benami Transaction	113

Ch-4: RIGHTS AND LAW — 114

1. Citizenship — 114
2. Birth Certificate — 114
3. Public Interest Litigation — 115
4. Uniform Civil Code — 116
5. Right to Equality -(i) — 117
   Right to Equality -(ii) — 118
6. Right to Property — 118
7. Double Jeopardy — 119
8. Life & Personal Liberty — 119
9. Telephone Tapping — 121
10. Bonded Labour — 123
11. National Flag — 124
12. Contempt of Court — 125
13. Attorney General — 126
14. Difference Between Advocate, Barrister, Attorney, Solicitor — 127
15. Untouchability — 127
16. Advocate Losing Case Willingly — 127
17. Election Irregularities – Voter Card — 128
18. Change in Name — 129
19. Writs — 129
20. Habeas Corpus — 130
21. Mandamus — 131
22. Quo-warranto — 132
23. Prohibition — 133
24. Certiorari — 134
25. Rights of an HIV+ person — 135
26. Disability — 137

Ch-5: OUR ENVIRONMENT — 140

1. Noise Pollution — 140
2. Water and Air Pollution — 140
3. Wildlife — 141
4. Smoking — 143

Ch-6:	**CONTRACTUAL ASPECT**	**145**
1.	Invitation to an Offer	145
2.	Offer-Communication Necessary	145
3.	Cross Offer	146
4.	Revocation of an Offer	147
5.	Opportunity to Review Terms of Contract	147
6.	Capacity to Contract	148
7.	Duty to Speak-Not Always Applicable	148
8.	Restrain of Legal Proceeding	149
9.	Reimbursement of Amount Due by Other Paid by Another Interested Party	150
10.	Agency	150
11.	Minor	151
12.	Insane	151
13.	Consent	151
14.	Deemed Acceptance	152
15.	Restraint in Trade	152
16.	Specific Performance	153
17.	Government Contract – Stamp Duty	153
18.	Sale of Goods	154
19.	Liabilty of Surety for Loan	154
20.	Cheque Bouncing	154
21.	Partnership-Minor	155
22.	Partnership-Unregistered	156
Ch-7:	**LAND AND PROPERTY**	**157**
1.	Adverse Possession	157
2.	Transfer of Property-Destruction	157
3.	Transfer of Property-Sub-lease	158
4.	Transfer of Property - Part Performance	158
5.	Purchase of Land – Clear Title	159
6.	Transfer of Property – Part Performance / Specific Performance	160
7.	Non-registration of a Lease Deed	160
8.	Registration of Sale Deed	161
9.	Acquisition of Properties by an NRI	161
10.	Import of Gold, Silver by an NRI	162
11.	Society Registration	163
12.	Specific Performance	164

13.	Transfer of Property -Standard Rent & Lease	165
14.	Housing Laws -Change in Plan	165

Ch-8: CONSUMER RIGHTS AND TORTIOUS LIABILITY — 167
1. Consumer Rights — 167
2. Medical Negligence — 168
3. Torts — 169

Ch-9: INTELLECTUAL PROPERTY RIGHTS — 170
1. Patent, Design, Trademark — 170
2. Copyright — 172

Ch-10: INFORMATION TECHNOLOGY — 175
1. Hacking — 175
2. Pornography — 177
3. Digital Signature — 178
4. Electronic Contract — 178
5. Cyber Crime — 180

Ch-11: BUSINESS ACTIVITIES — 181
1. Commencing Business — 181
2. Incorporation — 183
3. Memorandum of Association — 183
4. Article of Association — 184
5. Company Shares — 185
6. Debentures — 188
7. Oppression by Majority — 188
8. Merger — 188
9. Fraud — 189
10. Winding up of Company — 190
11. Foreign Investment — 193
12. Trust-Formalities — 194
13. Delegation of Power of a Trustee — 194
14. Trust -Defending the Suit — 195
15. Settlement through Arbitrator — 195

Ch-12: INCOME TAX AND SERVICE TAX — **197**
1. Income Tax — 197
2. Service Tax — 207

Ch-13: WORK AND LAW — **213**
Factories Act — 213
1. Setting Up A Factory — 213
2. Time Frame of Work- General — 215
3. Time Frame of Work- Women and Children — 216

Industrial Disputes Act — 216
4. Closing Industry-Legal Requisites — 216
5. Termination-Wages During Suspension — 217
6. Termination-Remedy — 218
7. Strike — 218
8. Retrenchment — 219
9. Lay-off — 220

Workmen's Compensation Act — 221
10. Compensation — 221
11. Limitation for Filing Claim — 223

Maternity Benefit Act — 223
12. Maternity Benefit — 223

Equal Remuneration Act — 224
13. Prohibition of Discrimination (Men & Women) — 224
14. Leave With Pay — 225

Employee's Provident Funds and Miscellaneous Provisions Act (EPFMP) — 225
15. Contribution by Employer — 225
16. Withdrawal of Provident Fund — 225
17. Pension — 226
18. Applicability-Salary Limit — 227
19. Refund of P.F. on Leaving — 227
20. Applicability- Contractor's Employees — 227
21. Contribution If Not Paid — 228
22. Checking Contribution Paid or Not — 228

Employee's State Insurance Act — 228
23. Leaving Service-Payment of Compulsory Deductions — 228
24. Contribution — 229

25. Benefits	229

Employees Exchange Act
(Compulsory Notification of Vacancies)   231

26. Employment / Vacancy	231

The Payment of Bonus Act   231

27. Bonus	231

Service Matter   232

28. Compassionate Ground	232
29. Suspension	233

Ch-14: SAFETY ON ROAD   234

1. Motor Vehicles Act, 1988 / Central Motor Vehicles Rules, 1989	234
2. Sale-purchase of Vehicle / Transfer / Registration	236
3. Compensation in Case of Accident	237
4. Jurisdiction of Motor Vehicle Tribunal	238
5. Transfer of Vehicle to Other State	238
6. Recovery from Insurance Company	239
7. Hit & Run	239
8. Driving License- Terms	240

Ch-15: RAILWAYS   241

1. Transfer of Ticket to Others	241
2. Circular Journey Tickets	242
3. Booking Luggage	244
4. Ticket Loss-Issuance of Duplicate	245
5. Late Running of Train	247
6. Deficiency in Service	247
7. Missing Onward Train - Refund	248
8. Boarding At Other Station	249
9. Rail Accident - Insurance	250
10. Speedy Disposal - Railway Claim	251

APPENDIX-I	**252**
APPENDIX-II	**265**
About the Authors	**268**

CHAPTER – 1
CRIME AND SOCIETY

FIR

I witnessed commission of a crime and would like to see the criminals punished. I have been told to lodge an FIR but I am afraid of doing so as I hardly know anything about it. Please guide.

F.I.R. stands for First Information Report i.e. information given to the police officer on duty. It may be given either by the aggrieved person himself or any other person in respect to commission of an alleged offence. It can be lodged / given in the police station of the concerned area in whose jurisdiction the offence has occurred. It must be made to the Officer-in-Charge of the police station and if he is not available to the Assistant Sub-Inspector. While lodging an FIR every information relating to the commission of the offence is to be narrated in a sequence to the officer. The officer shall thereafter reduce the same in writing and the person giving it is required to sign on the FIR. The informant is entitled to a free copy of it.

In case the officer refuses to record the same, the information may be sent by post to the Superintendent of Police concerned, who, on being satisfied that such information discloses the commission of a cognizable offence, shall either investigate the case himself or direct an investigation to be made by any police officer subordinate to him, and thus supervise it.

The investigation begins once the FIR is registered and accordingly the charges are framed and after trial, if the accused is found guilty, he is liable to be punished. So you should give whatever information you have to the police, which will help the machinery to proceed further.

DELAY IN LODGING FIR

Some miscreants raped my friend. However, even after 5 days of the incident we haven't reported the matter to the police fearing social outburst, but now seeing her condition her mother wishes to lodge an FIR. Can this be done at such a late stage? Would the delay prove fatal to the case?

As per the law mere delay in lodging an FIR with the police is not necessarily fatal to the prosecution, if the delay can be explained to the satisfaction of the court.

The information is required to be given at the earliest, before the informant's memory fades and in order to prevent any scope of allegation of embellishment.

Courts have held that no duration of time can be fixed as reasonable for lodging an FIR and it depends upon facts of each case.

In your case, as there is mere 5 days delay in filing the FIR, which can reasonably be explained and hence it does not seem that it would anyhow prove fatal for the case.

BAIL

I feel that the police might arrest me. I have heard that after arrest bail can be obtained. What is the procedure for obtaining bail?

Bail is a form of security given for securing the release of an accused and may be coupled with surety.

The offences are classified in two categories:

1... Bailable offences
2... Non - bailable offences

1. BAILABLE OFFENCES

These offences are such in which the accused is entitled to get bail as a matter of right. No application by the accused is required to be made to the court for grant of such and mere filing a bail bond is enough. However the officer / court may in situations permit grant of such with or without sureties.

2. NON-BAILABLE OFFENCES

In these offences, giving bail is a matter of discretion of the court. On an application by the accused the court may grant bail on such terms as it deems fit. However under the law, release of those accused on bail is prohibited who have committed a cognizable offence (an offence in which a police officer may arrest without warrant) and who have already been previously convicted with punishment of death or life imprisonment or imprisonment above 7 years or convicted on two or more occasions of non-bailable and cognizable offences.

Thus for understanding, we can say that, in bailable offences, bail is a rule and jail is an exception, whereas in non-bailable offences jail is a rule and bail is an exception.

In your case as there is no specification about the offence; so it is difficult to say as to whether it is a bailable offence or a non-bailable one.

Hence, on arrest, if the offence is bailable, you are by right entitled to avail bail and otherwise it is the discretion of the court.

You can also seek anticipatory bail from the court to prevent your arrest.

BAIL AS A MATTER OF RIGHT

I have been booked for leaking question papers of an all India entrance exam. It's more than 100 days and I am still in the custody and no chargesheet has yet been prepared. How much is it justified? I am ready to furnish the securities. Can I approach the court to grant me bail?

Your case is a fit one to approach for bail.

There are various circumstances in which the law mandates the release of an accused on bail, and your case too falls in one of them. The various instances are–

A. Where the accused / arrestee is not accused of a non-bailable offence.
B. Where the investigation is not completed within 90 days in case of an offence punishable with death, imprisonment for life or a term not less than 10 years and 60 days in case of other offences.
C. Where detainee or arrested person is under the age of 16 years or a women or infirm.
D. Where the accused is required to be identified by the witnesses during investigation and is entitled to be released on bail and gives an undertaking that he would comply with the directions of the court.
E. Where no reasonable ground exists for believing the accused guilty of non-bailable offence but there are grounds warranting further enquiries.
F. Where the trial by the magistrate of an accused of a non-bailable offence is not completed within 60 days from the first day fixed for taking evidence.
G. Where the court after conclusion of trial but before judgment is of the opinion that reasonable grounds exists believing that the accused is not guilty.

In all these cases the bail can only be given if the accused is ready to furnish bail / security.

ANTICIPATORY BAIL

Mr. X has falsely implicated me in a case. I am a reputed person and if police arrests me, it will tarnish my image and make my business suffer. What should I do?

In situations wherein there is a fear of being arrested, the person may seek anticipatory bail. Anticipatory bail is generally thought of to mean a bail before arrest. Anticipatory bail however means an order directing release of the accused on bail in the event he is to be arrested. The law has envisaged conditions wherein a person might be arrested on a non-bailable offence. Any person having such apprehension may move to the court for grant of anticipatory bail. The person who apprehends that he may be arrested on an accusation of having committed a non-bailable offence may move an anticipatory bail application.

Such application can be made to the High Court or the Court of Session. Registration of an offence is not necessary and reasonable apprehension is enough to seek so. However the accused/petitioner is to make out a special case for the same. Anticipatory bail application can also be made after issuance of process of summon but not after arrest. It is to be noted that in case of offences relating to Schedule Caste Schedule Tribe (Prevention of Atrocities) Act, anticipatory bail application is not maintainable.

ARREST WITHOUT WARRANT

My friend saw a person committing rape. He took hold of the person and kept him in his custody and thereafter called the police. The trial is going on and in the same the defence is alleging that the arrest was made not by the police officer but by my friend. I would like to know whether keeping the accused by my friend in his custody amounts to arrest. How can a common man arrest anybody?

Under the Code of Criminal Procedure all of us are empowered to arrest any offender and there is no need of any warrant of arrest for this. However arrest by a private person can be made only of: -

a. A person committing a non-bailable and cognizable offence in his presence, or;

b. A proclaimed offender.

Such person making an arrest is required to immediately and forthwith hand over the arrested person to the nearest police station and the accused will then be rearrested by the police officer. The police officer is empowered to release the arrested person if he does not find any ground of arrest.

Hence your friend was totally justified and correct in arresting the accused.

RIGHTS OF AN ARRESTED PERSON

I fear that the police might arrest me. I would like to know as to whether the arrested persons have any right and if any, what are they?

The law does provide for rights of an arrested person, these are as follows—

a. Right to be informed of the grounds of arrest.

b. Right to be informed of right to bail, if any.

c. Right to be produced before magistrate without any unnecessary delay i.e. within 24 hours of arrest. Such time shall exclude the time taken in journey from the place of arrest to the magistrate's court.

d. Right of an indigent person to free legal aid.

e. Right to medical examination.

f. Right of information of his arrest to his family member or friend.

g. Right to consult an advocate.

CONFESSION

Police took me in custody in respect of a murder, where I was given third degree treatment and forced to write and sign on a piece of paper that I was one of the gangsters who committed the said murder. Can I deny this in the court of law?

Confession made by an accused is irrelevant if the same is given under inducement, threat or promise.

Confession as recognized under the Indian Evidence Act can only be made before a magistrate and any confession given to any other person is regarded as extra-judicial confession, which is a weak piece of evidence, and needs corroboration for making it admissible.

There are certain procedures which are required to be followed for recording a confession. Before recording the confession, the magistrate shall remove the accused from police custody and take him in judicial custody. The accused is also to be given a minimum of 24 hours time to think over as to whether he is willing to make this confession or not. Thereafter on the next day the magistrate should first of all ascertain that the accused is not under any threat, inducement or promise and should then ask specific questions about the same and only if the accused is willing to confide, should take his confession.

While doing so the magistrate should see that no police officer is present in the room and if the accused demands some more time then he should be duly granted the same.

SELF-INCRIMINATION

The police is threatening me to produce certain documents purported to be in my custody or face dire consequences. I don't know about the whereabouts of the documents but I am sure that they do contain certain facts, which might make me liable for punishment. Isn't there any remedy in law, which can protect me from compulsion in production of the documents?

The law under the Constitution of India does provide protection in such cases and expressly states that no person accused of any offence shall be compelled to be a witness against himself.

However, it is to be noted that such protection is limited only to–

a) A person accused of an offence.
b) Against compulsion 'to be a witness'.
c) Against himself.

Thus protection is available to a person accused in criminal cases and does not extend to parties and witnesses in civil proceedings or proceedings other than criminal. This protection is available from the very stage when formal accusation (like being named in FIR, Complaint) is made against him but is not available when the person is not an accused but is merely interrogated during investigation and protects person from any compulsion.

Compulsion may be mental or physical however for mental compulsion there has to be such extreme act / statement which will make rendering the statement involuntary and therefore an extorted one.

It is also to be noted that such protection is available only in respect to evidences which might make him liable and which are written, made by him.

Thus, an accused cannot seek protection under this in cases of documents which though in his custody are–

a) contains statements of other persons;
b) though written by himself simply shows his handwriting or states facts which do not convey his personal knowledge relating to the charge against him;
c) which may incriminate some other person and not him.

Further, an accused can be compelled to give evidences which are in form of identification like giving thumb impressions, impressions of foot or palm or fingers or a specimen writing or showing part of body, or blood specimen or clothes, etc.

Voluntary statements / confessions or statements made without any compulsion or recorded / obtained without his knowledge are also not protected under this.

Hence, if you have been named in a FIR or a complaint which may lead to a criminal prosecution and the document is one written by you conveying your personal knowledge relating to the charges framed against you, you cannot be compelled to produce the same.

It is worthwhile to mention here that the police can still obtain the document by search and seizure.

SEARCH WITHOUT WARRANT

Recently there have been instances wherein the police entered the house of my neighbour to search without having any warrant. Isn't there any provision in law, which regulates the power of police officers to search without warrant?

The law does prescribe strict conditions while conducting a search without warrant. Generally, a search without warrant is done in cases where there is no time to obtain a search warrant.

However such search has to be conducted by or under a senior police investigating officer.

While conducting a search the following are the requisites so envisaged in the Code of Criminal Procedure–

a. Search can be conducted only by the officer incharge of a police station or any other officer subordinate to him or any officer authorized to investigate.
b. Search cannot be a general one but has to be for a specific thing or a person.
c. The place of search should be within the limits of the police station to which the police officer making the search is attached.
d. The police officer must have reasonable grounds to believe that the thing / person he is searching can be found in the place which he intends to search and it would be too late if he goes to obtain a search warrant. The grounds indicating the necessity of the search shall be recorded along with the things / places required to be searched which should be sent to the magistrate forthwith.

While searching a place the following points have to be kept into consideration–

a. If the place to be searched is closed, the owner or the person incharge should be directed to allow the police officer to enter the same and on failure to do so, an entrance can be made by breaking open a door or a window.
b. When a person is required to be searched, it should be done with strict decency and in case of women, it should be carried out by a lady police officer.
c. Two or more independent and respectable persons of the locality should be present as witness during such search.
d. A list of all such articles seized should be prepared and is to be signed by the witnesses and a copy of the same is to be given to the owner or the possessor.
e. The occupant may be allowed to attend the search.

TIME LIMIT FOR TAKING COGNIZANCE

I have recently received a warrant from a magistrate directing my appearance in respect of a crime alleged to be committed by me 10 years ago. The case diary discloses that cognizance of the said offence was taken recently. Isn't there any provision in law, which can protect me?

The Code of Criminal Procedure restricts the time limit for taking cognizance of an offence by a magistrate. Under the same–

a. If an offence is punishable only with fine, the magistrate is to take cognizance of the same within 6 months.

b. If an offence is punishable with imprisonment upto 1 year, the magistrate is to take cognizance of the same within 1 year.

c. If an offence is punishable with imprisonment for more than 1 year, the magistrate is to take cognizance of the same within 3 years.

However the magistrate is still empowered to take cognizance after the aforesaid limitation if delay is properly explained and it is necessary to do so in the interest of justice.

In this case you can ask for quashing of the said cognizance taken by the magistrate under the aforesaid provision and can even approach the Hon'ble High Court for this relief.

ABETMENT

One of my neighbours, being instigated by my brother, tried to give me a blow by a thick stick (lathi) but accidentally; he hit a friend of mine who was trying to pacify the situation. My neighbour has been arrested but I wish to know as to whether I can make my brother also liable?

Under the Indian Penal Code (IPC), anyone who instigates in commission of an offence would be liable for abetment. The code further provides that in case the act committed is different from that intended by the abettor (your brother here), still the abettor would be liable as the act abetted was likely to cause that effect.

In fact the IPC further punishes the abettor even if the offence, which was instigated for commission, is not committed.

RIGHT TO PRIVATE DEFENCE

My friend who is living beside an area of slum dwellers saw smoke coming out of a hut and assuming it to be fire, pulled down some of the nearby huts, in order to prevent spreading of the same. However it turned out that there was a small fire, which would not have spread. The slum dwellers are now accusing him and have lodged an FIR. Is there any provision in law which might protect him?

Under the Chapter of General Exception in Indian Penal Code the law does recognize some acts as innocent, which under normal circumstances would amount to an offence like–

A. Acts done by a person, who believes him to be bound by law to do so, is protected, if the said act is done under the mistake of fact. Eg. A, a soldier directed by a superior to fire on a mob does so, believing that he is by law, bound to do so. A has committed no offence.

B. A common man arresting another, thinking him to be a proclaimed offender, whereas, he is not. The same is no offence as this is just a mistake of fact, and the person making the arrest thought himself of being governed according to law.

C. An act done without criminal intent or knowledge is no offence if it was lawfully done in a lawful manner and by lawful means with proper care and caution. E.g. an electrician in a factory was authorized to switch on the electric current during particular intervals and before doing so was to ring an alarm. He after ringing the alarm on one such occasion switched on the current. However a person died due to electrocution. A has committed no offence.

D. An act done by a child under the age of 7 years and if the child is of immature understanding, then till the age of 12 years or by a person of unsound mind or an intoxicated person where such intoxication was administered without his knowledge, does not amount to an offence.

E. An act done without consent, but in good faith, like a doctor operating a patient in order to save life, without obtaining his or his family members' consent, but unfortunately the patient dies. The doctor is protected.

F. Act done in private defence by inflicting harm, not more than necessary, does not amount to an offence. E.g. If Mr. X sees Mr. Y coming with a knife and out of fear being killed, takes out his revolver and shoots Mr. Y to death. It is no offence, but if Mr. Y would be carrying a stick, and Mr. X shooting him, would have amounted to crime.

G. Similarly, in case of exercising private defence for protecting one's property, the same extends to any act that is proportionate to the intended harm feared.

H. Right of private defence against an assault and thereby causing harm to an innocent person is protected.

I. An act though causing harm, is done in good faith to prevent some greater harm will not amount to an offence.

In your case if your friend can prove that he had done so in good faith, in order to prevent a greater harm, he would not be liable.

CULPABLE HOMICIDE / MURDER

My neighbour with whom I am not in good terms caught my collar in the market. I too reacted and very soon we indulged in a serious fight, throwing fist and punches on each other. Suddenly someone handed me a knife and, in impulse, I stabbed him. The single stab proved fatal and he died on the spot. I am under arrest for charges of murder. Can I raise the defence that I had no such intention of killing the person and death would never have taken place unless someone had handed me the knife?

Killing a person while being deprived of self-control on account of sudden and grave provocation is not murder but culpable homicide.

What is grave and sudden provocation will depend upon facts of the case. Generally, reacting immediately without thinking of the consequences and without any planning would amount to sudden and grave provocation. For example, if a woman being raped finds a knife or a weapon nearby and stabs him, such would come within the ambit of sudden and grave provocation. However, in the alternative, if after being raped she goes home decides as to the course of action and thereafter kills the rapist, she would not be entitled to plead the defence of sudden and grave provocation.

As in your case the said death was caused on account of provocation on the part of the deceased, you might not be liable for murder, but, the person who handed over the knife to you might be liable for the offence of murder.

The punishment for culpable homicide not amounting to murder is imprisonment upto 10 years and / or fine. For murder the punishment may be even death penalty.

However death penalty is only awarded in 'Rarest of Rare Cases'. Though every murder is brutal but this condition depicts a situation wherein the murder is exceptionally brutal, otherwise the punishment for murder is imprisonment for life and may also include fine.

INDECENT REPRESENTATION OF WOMAN

A local newspaper is publishing an advertisement, which has the photograph of a semi-nude woman. Such publication has become a regular affair and has made reading newspaper quite embarrassing especially in front of the family. Isn't there any law to restrain such publication?

The Indecent Representation of Women (Prohibition) Act prohibits any indecent depiction of woman.

Under the Act, any person who publishes or causes to be published, or arranges to take part in the publication or exhibition or, any advertisement containing indecent representation of women in any form, is punishable on first conviction with imprisonment upto 2 years and with fine upto Rs. 2000/- and on any subsequent conviction, with imprisonment for not less than 6 months which may extend upto 5 years and with fine not less than Rs. 1000/- extending upto Rs. 1,00,000/-.

For the same an FIR can be lodged or a complaint can be made with the magistrate or even the High Court or the Supreme Court can be approached to restrain such activities by way of Public Interest Litigation.

RAPE

1. My maidservant, now 17 years old, is a typical village girl. My neighbour's driver aged 25 years treats her with sweets and also takes her for a drive. I also found out that they have been regularly indulging in physical relationship for more than a year. However, no force whatsoever is involved as the same happens with her consent. I don't want this to continue, as I believe that she is too immature to judge her good or bad. I have tried to stop it but the driver is too rowdy and always has his way. Is there any means of preventing them from continuing the same?

Under the Indian Penal Code, a man is said to commit rape if he has sexual intercourse with a woman without her consent. However, consent becomes immaterial if the woman is less than 16 years of age. Thus, on the date of the incident when the girl had physical relationship with the driver, if she was under 16 years of age, you can file an FIR against the driver for rape. In that case the offence of rape can be made out, as the girl's consent is immaterial. The law believes that a minor is incapable of making sound decisions. So in spite of the fact that she had consented to the sexual act, the person can still be charged with rape, if the other requirements of the section are fulfilled.

2. I am a film producer and met an aspiring actress. I found her beautiful and got attracted to her and even promised to marry. From then we were regularly indulging in physical relationship i.e. for the last 3 years. However, due to some reason I could not sign her in any film. Later, I realized that our taste and nature varies a lot and we would not be able to lead a happy conjugal life and hence I decided not to marry. Now she is accusing me of rape. I have also learnt that if a female subjected to sexual intercourse gives an evidence that it was without her consent, the Court deems

it to be rape. What should I do?

The law does presume a person to commit rape if there is sexual intercourse and the female states that she did not give consent for the same.

In your case if it could be established that at the time of the said intercourse she had given her consent then the law will not presume such.

However you still might be guilty of deception. You can easily rebut the same by bringing material evidences on record showing that there was no deception and you did intend to marry her earlier but could not do so later, on the ground of non-compatibility.

3. I was raped by one of my college friends. My family duly registered a case against him. However later my friend accepting his guilt begged forgiveness and also wished to marry me. Seeing my future and the stakes involved, I feel that he should be given a chance and our family has also consented to this marriage. We now wish to take back the case. What is the procedure for the same?

When a criminal case is lodged, the responsibility of prosecuting the offender is taken over by the State. Generally crimes against human body are considered crimes against the whole society and such are non-compoundable in nature.

Non-compoundable offences means offences, which once lodged, cannot be settled between the parties.

Offence of rape is non-compoundable one and even if you both marry, the said person (your husband) will still be liable for the offence of Rape and will be subjected to the punishment for the same provided the offence is proved in the court of law.

KIDNAPPING

My neighbour's 16 years old son requested my husband to take him to our house. As his parents were not in town and he was alone in the house, we decided to bring him to our place. God knows why our neighbour in the meantime lodged a complaint accusing us of kidnapping their son. Is the complaint legally tenable?

Under the law, kidnapping has 3 essential ingredients–
a. Taking or inducing a minor.
b. Out of the lawful guardianship of such minor.
c. Without the consent of such guardian. (The consent of minor is immaterial.)

As in this case the minor has been taken away from the lawful guardianship of his parents without their consent, you may be liable for the offence of kidnapping which provides for punishment of imprisonment upto 7 years and / or fine.

However, you may plead that there was no taking away of the minor for any ill motive / intention. Moreover you can also plead that at the time when the minor was taken away, he was not under any lawful guardianship and hence there is no offence of kidnapping.

The court after taking into consideration the entire fact may pass an appropriate judgment.

DOWRY DEATH

My daughter was brutally burnt to death by her in laws. What should I do?

As per the Indian Penal Code, if the death of a woman is caused by burns or bodily injury or occurs otherwise than under normal circumstances within 7 years of her marriage and it is shown that soon before her death she was subjected to cruelty or harassment by her husband or in-laws, then such death falls under the category of "dowry death" and all such persons are punishable with imprisonment for a minimum period of 7 years which may extend upto imprisonment for life.

In cases like this, one should immediately inform the police about the death, which will lodge the case under the relevant sections including murder and dowry death.

The law also lays down an obligation upon certain persons to report about the commission of the offence under this Act, viz. —

(1) All officers of Government,
(2) All village officers and such other officers as may be specified by the Collector or the District Magistrate, are to assist the

police in the execution of the provisions of this act or any rule or order made there under. Any person who fails to do so is liable for imprisonment for a term extending to two years and shall also be liable to fine.

EUTHANASIA

My mother is suffering from cancer and the doctors have declared that there is no scope for her survival. We can't see her suffering and even my mother is insisting of dying rather than suffering the pain. When I contacted the doctors, I was told that no drug can be administered to her as such would be murder and is punishable under the law. How can it be so? Isn't there any law which can help us?

Such condition wherein a person is allowed to die to save him from the immense trauma is known as mercy killing euthanasia.

There is no provision in law which recognizes such means of killing. Though in some countries mercy killing is recognized and is allowed like in a state of Belgium, Netherlands, however, the Indian Law bars such type of killing by making it punishable and in fact the Indian Courts have in the year 2001 turned down the requests of the patients right to die. The various offences which punishes such acts are:

Culpable homicide – This offence punishes all such persons who do anything to accelerate the death of a person labouring under disorder, disease or bodily injury with imprisonment for life or imprisonment extending to 10 years, provided the person consents to such and also that the person is above the age of 18 years.

The same may also amount to murder, as it can be argued that the person was, on account of illness, incompetent to give his consent for which the punishment is death or imprisonment for life and thereby making the person liable for death sentence also.

Attempt to commit suicide – Any person who wishes to end his life and does any act in pursuance of that is liable for the offence of attempt to commit suicide punishable with simple imprisonment upto 1 year and / or with fine.

Abetment of suicide – Any person who helps another in committing suicide will be liable for the offence of abetment to suicide

Objection Your Honour

punishable with imprisonment extending to 10 years and fine.

Thus, clearly both - the person who consents to death and the person who does any act in pursuance to causing death - will be liable for punishment.

The purpose behind such policy is the fact that if mercy killing is made legal, it may result in widespread misuse giving rise to innumerable killings. Hence, it's better to prevent such in the general interest of the society.

PRESUMPTION AS TO SUICIDE

Ours is a joint family. My wife committed suicide 6 years after our marriage. We had been living happily but at times used to quarrel, which is normal in every family. The cause of her suicide was basically that she was suffering from an incurable disease and wanted to get rid of the pain more so to ease my burden. Now her mother and father including the police is torturing my family and me by threatening that they would file a case against us on the ground that we had forced her commit suicide. What should I do?

Under the law, if a married woman commits suicide within 7 years of marriage and it can be shown that she had been subjected to cruelty, then the law presumes that her husband or the relatives of her husband have abetted suicide.

In your case burden lies on you to specifically prove the fact that she was not subjected to any cruelty and then only you can escape punishment. Otherwise law will presume you and your family, guilty of the same.

However, even if the court comes to the conclusion that your wife was subjected to cruelty but if you could prove that she committed suicide for some other reason, then the court may refrain from such presumption.

SATI

I was working as a journalist in Rajasthan. I witnessed *Sati* being performed in presence of a large crowd, which

included eminent personalities holding constitutional posts, senior police officials, renowned media persons, etc. In spite of protest by many women organizations and other persons, it was carried out. The police station too was empty to witness the same. What does the law say?

Commission of *Sati* has been strictly prohibited and is a grave offence under the law and any such act depicts the sick mentality of the society.

"*Sati*" means the burning or burying alive of any woman (generally a widow) along with the body of her deceased husband or any other relative or with any article, object or thing associated with the husband or such relative irrespective of whether such burning or burying is claimed to be voluntary on the part of the woman or otherwise.

Under the law any woman who performs *Sati* is liable for punishment of imprisonment for a term, which may extend to one year and / or with fine and any person who, abets the commission of such *Sati*, either directly or indirectly, shall be punishable with death or imprisonment for life and shall also be liable to fine and in case where there is mere attempt to commit *Sati* (i.e. *Sati* has not been committed), then such abettor is liable to imprisonment for life and fine.

It is to be noted that abetment to *Sati* includes-

(a) Inducing a woman to do so irrespective of whether she is in a fit state of mind or otherwise;

(b) Making her believe that its commission would result in some spiritual benefit to her or her deceased husband or relative or the general wellbeing of the family;

(c) Encouraging her to remain fixed in her resolve to commit *Sati* and thus instigating her to commit it;

(d) Participating in the procession by taking her along with the body of her deceased husband or relative to the cremation or burial ground;

(e) Being present at the place where *Sati* is committed as an active participant to such commission or to any ceremony connected with it;

(f) Preventing or obstruction the woman from saving herself from being burnt or buried alive;

(g) Obstructing or interfering with the police in the discharge of its duties of taking any steps to prevent the commission of *Sati*.

The law also punishes persons who indirectly promotes *Sati* by glorification or building temples or the like by providing punishment with imprisonment for a minimum term of one year and extending to seven years and fine which shall not be less than five thousand rupees but which may extend to thirty thousand rupees.

Also, persons who are punished for commission of *Sati* are disqualified from inheriting the property of the person in respect of whom such *Sati* has been committed or the property of any other person of which she would have been entitled to inherit on the death of such person.

PATERNITY OF CHILD

Due to my business I remain out of city, quite often. In the meantime my wife conceived a child. I doubt that the child in the womb is mine. Can I go for a blood test to see whether he is my child or not? What are the legalities involved in this?

A child born during the continuance of a valid marriage or within 280 days of its dissolution, the mother being unmarried, is a conclusive proof that the child is the legitimate son of the husband. The court will refuse to accept any test like blood test or D.N.A. test to disprove his legitimacy / paternity.

However, if the husband can show that at the time when the child could have been conceived, he had no access to wife, then alone the legitimacy / paternity of the child can be disproved. 'No access' here means that he and his wife were living separately and not merely that they had no chance of entering into physical relationship.

So, at the time when your wife conceived the said child, if you and your wife were living together, it is enough to prove that the child so born is yours and the same cannot be disproved.

CAUSING MISCARRIAGE

I had physical relationship with my boyfriend and conceived a child. We went to a doctor for abortion who refused, saying it to be illegal. It is impossible for me to give birth to the child as I will not only have to bear the brunt of my family members but am also liable to be outcasted by friends, family and society. Is it true that the law bars it? Moreover if I manage any doctor to do so and unfortunately be caught then what punishment will I be liable?

The law prohibits any person from causing a woman with a child to miscarry unless done in good faith for the purpose of saving the life of the woman and any person who does so, including the woman bearing the child, is liable to be punished with imprisonment for a term extending to 3 years and / or with fine. And in case the woman is quick with the child, for imprisonment extending to 7 years and with fine.

Further, any act done to prevent the child from being born alive except that done in good faith for the purpose of saving the life of the woman, is liable to be punished with imprisonment extending to 2 years and / or with fine.

The law also prohibits abandonment of a child below the age of 12 years by the parents / guardians and the person doing so is liable for imprisonment extending to 7 yrs and / or fine.

DEATH DUE TO NEGLIGENCE

A bullet, misfired by a police officer, killed my only son of 20 years. Can the officer be made liable for the same?

Yes, the officer can be made liable. The case falls under the heading 'death due to rash and negligent act' as provided in the Indian Penal Code, which is punishable with imprisonment, extending upto two years and / or with fine.

Such acts are those where death has arisen on account of

some rash or negligent mode. Under this provision, rash or negligent act must be the direct or proximate cause of death.

The two essential elements are–
1) Rash or negligent act,
2) Not amounting to culpable homicide.

It does not matter whether the offender is a government employee functioning in any capacity, but if death is occasioned by a rash or negligent manner, then the heirs of the deceased are entitled to compensation.

The court will decide the amount of compensation on various factors, such as your social status, income, the age of the deceased person as well as the age of the dependants and a few other factors.

Even the Government is not immune from it and will be liable for the acts of its servant.

RASH & NEGLIGENT DRIVING

We live in a colony. Some of the youngsters ride their bikes in such rash manner that we fear that they might kill one of us. We have tried to stop them, however, they say that it's none of our business. Doesn't the law provide for safe driving of vehicles?

The Indian Penal Code and the Motor Vehicles Act restrict driving a vehicle dangerously in any public place. Under the same, a person driving a vehicle at a speed which is dangerous to the general public may be liable to undergo imprisonment for a term extending to 6 months and / or with fine extending to Rs. 1000/- on first offence and for each subsequent offence, with imprisonment extending upto 2 years and / or with fine upto Rs. 2000/-. Also, if he contravenes the speed limits, he is liable for fine upto Rs. 400/- on first conviction and upto Rs. 1000/- on subsequent conviction.

RAGGING

I am a fresher in a medical college in Jharkhand and I am being ragged for the last three months, wherein I have

suffered, immense mental and physical trauma. Should I report the matter to the police?

The Hon'ble Supreme Court has recognized the ill effects of ragging and has passed certain observations/guidelines therein, viz.—

1. Acts of indiscipline and misbehaviours of students should be dealt by the institution itself.
2. Unless unavoidable, students should not be subjected to police action.
3. Onus of preventing ragging rests on the institution.
4. Anti-ragging movements to be initiated from the moment admissions are called for - like mentioning the same in the prospectus, obtaining an undertaking during the admission from the students in respect of not indulging in ragging, mentioning strict punishment in form of expulsion, suspension, fine, public apology, withholding benefits like scholarships etc, withholding results etc.
5. Non-curtailment of ragging by the institution will amount to indiscipline on part of the management, which may result in:
   a. U.G.C. / funding committee stopping grants;
   b. Disaffiliation of such institutions.

The institute is to constitute a committee consisting of senior faculty members and responsible seniors to keep a vigil over ragging activities and on receipt of any complaint, the institute is to look into it and after investigation pass the appropriate order.

So you should first make a complain with the institute which is alone empowered to deal with the matter and take necessary steps, including reporting the matter to the police. However, if the institute fails to do so, you can approach the police and at the same time give a representation to the university concerned and may also directly approach the High Court or the even the Supreme Court.

OBSCENE MATERIAL

I live in a colony; a *gumtiwala* has started keeping and selling obscene books, which has started polluting the

environment. How can he be restrained from doing so?

Under the law sale, hiring, distributing, publicly exhibiting, importing-exporting any obscene material is prohibited and the offender is liable for imprisonment extending to 2 years and with fine upto Rs 2000/- in cases of first conviction and on subsequent conviction with imprisonment extending to 5 years and fine upto Rs 5000/-.

Further, any sale, hire, distribution, exhibition or circulation to any person under the age of 21 years makes the person doing so liable for imprisonment extending to 3 years and with fine upto Rs 2000/- in cases of first conviction and on subsequent conviction with imprisonment extending to 7 years and fine upto Rs 5000/-.

Information about the fact of selling obscene books should be reported to the local police station, which will then take suitable action in accordance to law.

DEFAMATION

I am currently facing stiff competition from my colleague for promotion to the position of a manager. Recently, some confidential documents have disappeared from the office. My colleague has asked me if I had taken those. This is absolutely not the case. So far no one knows that my colleague has accused me of taking those documents. Can I file a case for defamation against him?

Defamation is a criminal offence and is punishable with simple imprisonment or with fine. It is to be noted that every act of accusation is not defamation.

Under the Indian Penal Code, whoever, by words either spoken or intended to be read, or by visible representation, makes or publishes any imputation concerning any person intending to harm, or knowing or having reason to believe that such imputation will harm the reputation of such person, is said to defame that person.

However, if the said statements / imputations are true or made in good faith for the protection of the interest of any other person or for the public or are bonafide statements, the same may protect the person accused of defamation. It is immaterial whether the imputation is conveyed obliquely or indirectly, or by way of question, conjecture, exclamation or irony. The gist of the offence of defamation lies in making of the harmful imputation and publishing it, i.e. communicating the same to some other person. What he has said against you may be considered as a defamatory matter / insult, but communicating this matter only to you and not to any third person does not amount to publication and hence would not constitute the offence of defamation.

The law further provides that no imputation is said to harm a person's reputation, unless that imputation, directly or indirectly, in the estimation of others, lowers the moral or intellectual character of that person, or lowers the character of that person in respect of his caste or his calling, or lowers his credit.

Thus for an offence of defamation 3 ingredients have to be satisfied–

1. Making of a defamatory statement.
2. Making it known to at least a third person
3. The statement is such as it lowers or tends to lower the reputation of the person in respect of whom such statement is passed.

In your case as the ingredients are not satisfied for want of making it known to some third person, hence you cannot institute a case of defamation against your colleague. Even if the imputation is published (made known to third person) then also your colleague may escape liability by taking plea that the said statement was made in the interest of the company and to solve the issue of the missing documents. If that is proved to be true, then even a published imputation might not be considered to be defamatory. However, it is to be noted that it is alone not sufficient that the person making the imputation believed in good faith that he was acting for the protection of any such interest.

MEDICAL NEGLIGENCE (CRIMINAL)

My father was operated for respiratory disease but due

to clotting of blood in the respiratory tube, he died. Can I make the doctor criminally liable?

In order to make a doctor criminally liable 'gross negligence' on part of the doctor has to be proved. In your case, it can be done so only by leading 'expert evidence'. In a recent judgment the Hon'ble Supreme Court has very categorically laid down that criminal liability warrants 'gross negligence' on part of the doctor which has to be strictly proved and such proof is more severe than that required for establishing civil liability.

JUVENILE JUSTICE

My servant of 12 years was arrested for keeping country made pistol. I know him since childhood and do believe that he would have done it only on getting lured by some of the miscreants living near our place. I feel that he should be given a chance and not sent to jail. Is there any law, which protects such tender and first time offenders?

The law has made special provision in respect of children below 16 years for male and 18 years for female, committing offences and protects them from being sent to jail by listing Special Trial Procedure for them and providing for an appropriate remedy under the Juvenile Justice Act. Such offenders are called juveniles.

Thus your servant can be protected under the Juvenile Justice Act. First of all, you will have to prove that he is below the said age. If this is done then as per the law, the magistrate is to report the offence involving juveniles to the competent juvenile authority, which is either a juvenile welfare board or a juvenile court. If the juvenile court is satisfied of the offence by the juvenile, it may, depending upon the gravity of the offence and other circumstances, either let off the child after advising or warning him; or release the child on probation of good conduct and place him under the care of the parent, guardian or any fit institution for a period not exceeding three years who will see his good behaviour and wellbeing. Alternatively the juvenile court may order that the child be sent to a special home for a period (in case, where the child is below fourteen), until such time as he ceases to be a juvenile.

The juvenile court further has the discretion to reduce or increase the period of stay depending upon the gravity of offence and circumstances. However, this extended period is not to go beyond two years of the child crossing the juvenile age limit. In addition, there is a possibility of the juvenile being put under the supervision of a probation officer and if the report of the officer on the performance of the child is negative, the child may be sent to the special home.

The law specifically prohibits punishment of juveniles with death sentence or imprisonment or committing to prison in default of payment of fine or in default of furnishing security. In cases of more serious offences and where the child has attained fourteen, the court may order the juvenile to be kept in safe custody. However, such detention shall not exceed the maximum period of imprisonment to which the juvenile could be sentenced for the offence committed.

PROBATION OF OFFENDERS

Due to some family constrains I was forced to commit theft, but was caught. This was my first and only offence. I don't want to go to jail. Isn't there any provision in law that protects persons like me?

Under the Probation of Offenders Act, a court may release certain offenders on probation after giving them a warning. On probation means that the sentence is stayed and the offender is released on condition of good conduct and the court is empowered to call for his presence any day. It is to be noted that the offender is not to be released unless the offender or his surety has fixed place of residence. This act is an overriding enactment over other laws and is applicable to persons found guilty of having committed an offence not punishable with death or imprisonment for life and is applicable for offences in relation to theft, dishonest misappropriation of property possessed by deceased person and cheating including dishonestly inducing any person to deliver a property or with offences in which imprisonment for not more than 2 years is liable to be granted.

Moreover, the Act prohibits imprisonment to a person less than 21 years of age for an offence not punishable with imprisonment for life unless the court is satisfied that such is necessary. However, release of offender on probation cannot be claimed as a matter of right and it is the court's discretion to grant such after taking into consideration the nature of offence, character of offender, effect of offence on society in general, etc.

FALSE COMPLAINT

A person has filed a false complaint against me. Is there any provision in law, which punishes such person?

In case a false complaint is made and the same results in acquittal, the accused is liable under malicious prosecution and also for damages.

Moreover, if the court feels that such complaint was made on unjust and unlawful ground, it may initiate a proceeding against the complainant and in such, the complainant is liable for imprisonment upto 2 years and / or with fine. The punishment is more severe in case the offence charged of had punishment to the tune of death / imprisonment for life or imprisonment for more than 7 years. In such cases the complainant is liable for imprisonment, which may extend to 7 years and / or with fine.

PRODUCING FALSE DOCUMENT IN COURT

My opponent had tried to get me imprisoned by producing false documents to prove my complicity in certain crime. However the learned court rejected the same and acquitted me. Can I file a case against him now, for producing false evidence / document thus misleading the court?

The Indian Penal Code provides for punishment to persons trying to obtain conviction by producing false evidences. Under the law, if the offence for which the false evidence is given is punishable–

a) With death, the person giving false evidence is liable for imprisonment for life or rigorous imprisonment upto 10 years and / or with fine. However, if death sentence has been executed, then such person will be liable for death penalty.

b) With any other term, the person giving false evidence will be liable for the punishment so provided for the offence for which he gave false evidence.

However under the Code of Criminal Procedure, the court concerned is alone empowered to make complaints and institute proceedings against the person giving false evidence and you cannot do so in criminal case except for malicious prosecution.

DISHONEST MISAPPROPRIATION OF PROPERTY

I entrusted a case to an arbitrator. Whenever I inquired about the case, he stated that the matter is pending and is in progress and also kept taking fees for conducting the proceedings. This continued for nearly 2½ years. By chance I got in touch with the opposite party and I was shocked to learn that the case had already been settled about a year back and around Rs 1 crore had been paid for the same in my favour. On contacting the arbitrator, he flatly refused of ever conducting my case. I am in distress and seek immediate help. Can I make the opposite party liable for making payment to the arbitrator, as I fear that the same has been done by them being 'hand in gloves' with the arbitrator? Please advise.

An arbitrator is an agent of the person whose case he is representing in the arbitral proceeding. He is there to see the interest of the principal and any act done by him in his capacity, as an agent would be assumed as if the principal himself has done the said act.

Hence, in your case the opposite party cannot be made liable except in so far that they issued the settled amount to your arbitrator directly which itself is not a substantial ground.

However, if you can prove that they both (the opposite party and the arbitrator) acted fraudulently to deceive you, then a case can be filed against the opposite party also. In the alternative you can sue your arbitrator for the amount paid to him by the opposite party as well as by you as fees with interest and damages by instituting a civil suit and at the same time a criminal case can also be lodged against him. Amongst other grounds he will specifically be liable for Dishonest Misappropriation of Property, Criminal Breach of Trust and Cheating.

Dishonest Misappropriation of Property means a person misappropriating or converting the property of someone else for his own use with dishonest intention.

Criminal Breach of Trust means dishonestly misappropriating the property in violation of the direction.

Cheating means dishonestly inducing any person by deceiving him to do something, which he would in normal circumstances not have done.

Dishonest Misappropriation of Property and Criminal Breach of Trust are non-compoundable offences with punishment for a term which may extend to 3 years and fine, while cheating and dishonestly inducing delivery of property is cognizable, non-bailable and compoundable (with permission of the court only) offences punishable with imprisonment upto 7 years and fine.

SUPERDARI

I intended to sell my bike and for the same gave it to an agency which kept it on display at its premises. However, one day the manager of the agency informed me that the bike was stolen away. I thereafter immediately lodged a complaint with the police in respect of theft of my bike. The police found the bike abandoned at a secluded place after 15 days. On coming to know of this fact, I requested the concerned officers to hand me the bike. However, I was told that I could get the same only with the permission of the court and was further informed that I would not be able to sell the same till the pendency of the case. Is it true?

In case the property forms the subject matter in a criminal proceeding, it is required for proof etc. during the course of the proceedings. In your case, the bike forms the subject matter of the case of theft and also a possible subject matter in respect of an offence, which might have been committed by the thieves with the help of the bike. Hence, the person who is the owner of the same may be allowed to have custody over it. This release is known as *Superdari* and is with a condition that the person shall produce the same before the court as and when directed and cannot dispose it of without the prior permission of the court. So it was totally justified on part of the police officer restricting you, disposing it of.

It is to note here that this provision of obtaining permission is relevant only when the property in question is released by the order of the court and if only a complaint is lodged with the police and no action has been taken on it by the police, then by mere withdrawing of the complaint one is free to do what ever he wishes to do with the property.

DYING DECLARATION

My wife and myself had gone to my in-laws place (my wife's maternal home) where due to a stove blast she suffered severe burnt injuries. Now my in laws have lodged a false complaint against me for murder stating that just before her death she had made a statement in the hospital stating that i had set her on fire. No doubt at the time when the said statement is purported to be made, I had gone to fetch the medicines but I am sure that she could not have made the said statement as it is false. I have been told that such last statement of my wife is capable of convicting me. Is it so? Can't I disprove the same somehow?

Such statement made by a person who is about to die is known as Dying Declaration.

The Law presumes such statements as relevant. However, the court is to apply strictest scrutiny and has to be on guard to ensure that the declaration is not a result of tutoring, prompting or imagination and that the deceased had opportunity to observe and identify the doer and was in a fit mental condition to make the declaration. However, where the dying declaration is suspicious or suffers from infirmity it cannot form the sole basis of conviction and has to be supported by other material evidences.

One has to disprove the said statement by bringing contradictory facts before the court which may include stating that the deceased was not in a position to make the said statement or that the witnesses cannot be trusted as they are related to the deceased etc.

However, it is important to note here that Dying Declaration in some cases is sufficient to prove the case of the prosecution depending upon the contents therein and the mode of giving the statement, the mental condition of the deceased and also the person to whom it is made apart from others.

It is to be noted that statements made at the time of death are in admissible, as evidence in form of Dying Declaration if the person making the same survives i.e. does not die.

TAPE RECORDER AS EVIDENCE

I witnessed a crime and fortunately was having a tape recorder at that time wherein I recorded the arguments between the parties. Is the said-recorded conversation admissible in a court?

The Hon'ble Supreme Court has laid down strict guidelines for the admissibility of tape-recorded conversation as evidence, viz.–

1) Conversation to be relevant to the matter in issue.
2) There should be identification of voice.
3) Accuracy of tape recorder.
4) Eliminating the possibility of erasing the record or tape.

It can also be used to corroborate the evidence given by the witnesses.

It is generally difficult to rely solely on tape-recorded evidence as it can be easily tampered / manipulated, and therefore the court has to exercise more caution before admitting such evidences.

In respect of identification of voice, strict proof is required to determine whether or not it is the voice of the alleged speaker. For making it admissible it is preferred that the tape must be sealed and kept in safe and preferably in official custody. Such evidence is useful not only to corroborate the evidence given by the witness in court but also to contradict the evidences given before the court.

HOSTILE WITNESS

My key witness in a prosecution case has turned hostile. Is there any way by which I can prevent him legally from appearing as a witness in the said case?

It is not uncommon for a witness to turn hostile. A hostile witness is one who makes statements adverse to the party calling and examining him.

The Indian Evidence Act has made a provision to deal with a situation like this. If the court is convinced that a witness has turned hostile it may use its discretion to allow the prosecution to cross-examine such a witness. In this way the party whose witness has turned hostile may be given an opportunity to put questions to the hostile witness to disprove his credibility.

However, it will be worth mentioning here that it is necessary for you to have some material to satisfy the court that your witness is not speaking the truth and needs to be cross-examined.

EXPERT OPINION

I have received a demand notice for payment of a dishonoured cheque amount. On examining the cheque, I found that the said cheque was illegally taken from my possession and the signature therein was a forged one, which does not tally with the signature in my account. I have lodged a criminal case against the person signing it as well as the bank. Now the court has asked me to prove that the said signature is not mine. Can I do so with the help of my wife who is well acquainted with my signature?

In order to prove such, you will have to request the court to seek expert opinion in the matter. An expert under the law is a person who is especially skilled in such a matter being foreign law, science or arts, or in questions as to identity of handwriting, who can give an opinion. The expert need not have been physically present at the time of the incidence, but gives his opinion on the basis of his knowledge and experience. He will basically compare the two signatures - the one on the cheque and the one in the account.

And will give his opinion as to whether the same are of the same person or are different. For this he generally relies upon the amount of pressure exerted by a person on the pen / paper while signing it apart from other considerations like the specific way of writing an alphabet and the curves used, etc. He will also take into consideration the normal deviations likely to occur over a period of time and thereupon give his opinion. Opinions of such experts are relevant and the court will generally consider expert opinions as against other evidences. It was very appropriate on your part of making the bank liable too as such instances can only occur with the connivance of the bank officials. However, you cannot bring your wife to testify unless she is an expert in the field and then also her testimony can be rebutted on the ground of her being an interested witness.

ESTOPPEL

I was in urgent need of money and therefore by falsely representing that the property belonging to my father is mine, sold it for a very meagre amount and executed the sale deed. Now the entire property has actually devolved upon me, on my father's death. Can I set aside the sale deed on the ground that at the relevant time I was not the owner of the same? I am ready to refund the money with interest.

If a person causes another to believe by his own act, declaration or omission a thing or a fact to be true and thereby to act upon such, the law prohibits him or his representative to deny the truth of the same. This is the Doctrine of Estoppel.

As you had intentionally and falsely led the other person to believe that you were the owner and thereby induced him to buy and pay for the property, the law will prohibit you from proving your want of title at the time of execution of the sale deed as a ground of setting aside the same.

ORGAN TRANSPLANT

I am a poor man in dire need of money. I saw an advertisement in a newspaper wherein a patient required a kidney. I wish to donate my kidney and save his life. I contacted the newspaper for the same and they agreed to make me meet the relatives. However I was told that I would not be getting any amount in return as sale or purchase of kidney is illegal. Is it so?

Under the Transplantation of the Human Organs Act, any transfer of a human organ for price is prohibited and any person doing so is liable for punishment.

The law prohibits and punishes persons who–

i. Makes or receives any payment for the supply of, or for an offer to supply, any human organ;

ii. Seeks to find a person willing to supply for payment any human organ;

iii. Offers to supply any human organ for payment;

iv. Initiates or negotiates agreement involving making of payment for the supply of, or for an offer to supply, any human organ;

v. Takes part in management of persons who initiates or negotiates agreement involving making of payment for the supply of, or for an offer to supply, any human organ;

vi. Publishes or distributes any advertisement -

    a) Inviting persons to supply human organ for payment,

    b) Offering to supply human organ for payment;

    c) Indicating that advertiser is willing to negotiate any arrangement to supply of any Human Organ for payment.

Any person who contravenes such is liable for imprisonment for a term which shall not be less than 2 years but which may extend to 7 years and fine not less than Rs. 10,000/- but which may extend to Rs. 20,000/-. However, the court is empowered to grant any punishment less than the same for special and adequate reasons to be recorded in the judgment. The competent authority to try such case is the Metropolitan Magistrate or the Judicial Magistrate First Class (JMFC).

Thus, you cannot demand payment in lieu of your kidney as the same is illegal and you might even be punished for the same.

ARMS KEEPING

I am a leading medical practitioner and am being constantly threatened by some criminals who are demanding 'protection money' from me and threatening that in the event of failure to pay them, they will kill me. Though I have lodged a complaint yet I would like to have a revolver with me. Is it necessary to keep the papers of the licensed revolver always with me?

The law imposes conditions for possession of firearms and ammunitions. A firearm or any other ammunition can only be possessed by a person –

a) who has completed the age of 16 years

b) has not been convicted of an offence involving violence or moral turpitude in which imprisonment is for a term of not less than 6 months, within 5 years of the expiration of the sentence.

c) who has not been ordered to execute a bond in relation to security for keeping peace and good behaviour or any time during the term of the bond.

Such person, except the above, can possess a firearm only under a licence duly granted by the licensing authority, so appointed under the Arms Act. For the grant of licence, a form containing such particulars as prescribed and with such fees is to be submitted to the licensing authority, which is competent to either grant the licence or refuse the same.

In general, a citizen of India, if he satisfies the requisites, is entitled to a smooth bore gun having a barrel of not less than 20 inches in length to keep for protection.

The said license is valid for a period of 3 years and can be renewed. It is advisable to keep the license at all material times and especially when the 'arm' is being carried.

It is to be noted that any person who keeps gun / pistol without license is liable for imprisonment.

PROSTITUTION

I live near a renowned temple. However, just behind the same prostitutes flourishly carry their business. Isn't there any provision in law which can prevent them from doing so, at least near a sacred place?

The law prohibits practising of prostitution within the areas notified in the official gazette and also within a distance of two hundred meters of any place of public religious worship, educational institution, hotel, hospital, nursing home or such other public place of any kind as may be notified in this behalf by the Commissioner of Police or Magistrate in the manner prescribed.

Any person who does so in violation of the same commits an offence, which is a cognizable offence and liable for punishment with imprisonment for a term, which may extend to 3 months. Also, any person who being the keeper, tenant, lessee, occupier or person in charge of any premises, owner, lessor or landlord of any premises of any public place knowingly permits prostitutes, for purposes of their trade to resort to or remain in such place, is liable for punishment with imprisonment for a term extending to three months and / or with fine upto two hundred rupees on first conviction and in the event of a subsequent conviction with imprisonment for a term upto 6 months and also with fine extending to two hundred rupees. Also, if the public place or premise happens to be a hotel, the licence for carrying on the business of such hotel under any law for the time being in force shall also be liable to be suspended for a period of not less than three months and extending to one year.

The law also prohibits seducing or soliciting for purpose of prostitution and punishes such person on first conviction with to be a hotel, the licence for carrying on the business of such hotel under any law for the time being in force shall also be liable to be suspended for a period of not less than three months and extending to one year.

The law also prohibits seducing or soliciting for purpose of prostitution and punishes such person on first conviction with imprisonment for a term upto 6 months and/or with fine extending to Rs. 500/- and in the event of a subsequent conviction, with imprisonment for a term upto 1 year and also with fine which may extend to Rs. 500/-.

In case a man commits the offence of seduction he shall be punishable with imprisonment for a period of not less than seven days but which may extend to three months.

Hence, carrying on prostitution near a temple is prohibited and you can seek interference of the police for preventing the same and on failure on their part you can directly approach the court including the High Court and the Supreme Court.

•••

Hierarchy of Criminal Courts and their powers to pass sentences

SUPREME COURT
(Any sentence authorised by law)

HIGH COURT
(Any sentence authorised by law)

SESSIONS COURT
Sessions Judge, Additional Sessions Judge–any sentence authorised by law; sentence of death is subject to confirmation by High Court)

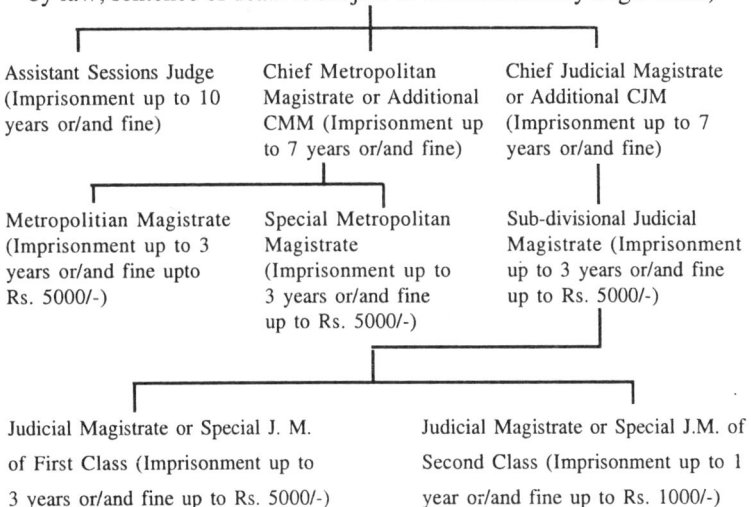

Assistant Sessions Judge (Imprisonment up to 10 years or/and fine)

Chief Metropolitan Magistrate or Additional CMM (Imprisonment up to 7 years or/and fine)

Chief Judicial Magistrate or Additional CJM (Imprisonment up to 7 years or/and fine)

Metropolitian Magistrate (Imprisonment up to 3 years or/and fine upto Rs. 5000/-)

Special Metropolitan Magistrate (Imprisonment up to 3 years or/and fine up to Rs. 5000/-)

Sub-divisional Judicial Magistrate (Imprisonment up to 3 years or/and fine up to Rs. 5000/-)

Judicial Magistrate or Special J. M. of First Class (Imprisonment up to 3 years or/and fine up to Rs. 5000/-)

Judicial Magistrate or Special J.M. of Second Class (Imprisonment up to 1 year or/and fine up to Rs. 1000/-)

Hierarchy of Executive Magistrates

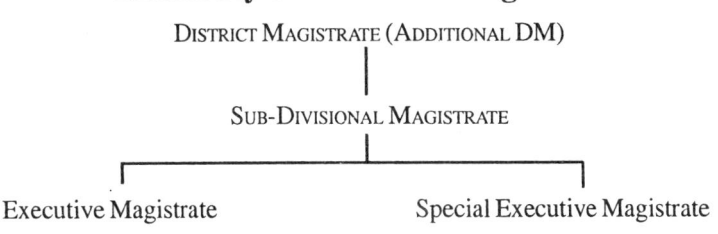

DISTRICT MAGISTRATE (ADDITIONAL DM)

SUB-DIVISIONAL MAGISTRATE

Executive Magistrate

Special Executive Magistrate

Objection Your Honour

CHAPTER – 2
FAMILY

SUCCESSION

I am a Hindu. My father, who died in an accident, had an independent business. Now, my uncle, who was dependant upon my father for his survival and my sister who is married are claiming a share in my father's property. My grandparents are also living with us. Are my uncle, sister and grandparents entitled to a share in the said property?

Under the Hindu Law of Succession, if a person dies intestate, that is, without making a Will, then his property will devolve according to the Hindu Succession Act. According to the same–

1) The property is to be first distributed among the relatives specified in Class-I of the Schedule of the Act. Among the persons so described therein, the son, the daughter, the widow, the mother, children of a pre-deceased son, children of pre-deceased daughter, widow of a pre-deceased son, children of a pre-deceased son of a pre-deceased son, widow of a pre-deceased son of a pre-deceased son are primarily entitled to the property.

Herein, pre-deceased means a situation wherein death of a person occurs before the death of the person whose property is being inherited.

As per the rule provided in the Act, all the above named heirs will equally take one share each, of the property of the intestate.

2) If there is no Class-I heir so mentioned above, then the following person, who comes within Class-II heirs in the order

of preference, will inherit the property, viz.–

a) Father,
b) 1) Son's daughter's children, 2) Brother, 3) Sister.
c) Daughter's children's children.
d) 1) Brother's children, 2) Sister's children.
e) Father's parents
f) 1) Father's widow, 2) Brother's widow.
g) 1) Father's brother, 2) Father's sister
h) Mother's parents.
i) 1) Mother's brother, 2) Mother's sister.

If any person in Class II heir is alive, then the persons below in the order will not inherit the property, e.g. if the father is alive, then the brother of the deceased will not be entitled to any property.

In your case, you, your sister and grandmother are only entitled to claim a share in the property and not your uncle or grandfather. All three of you are entitled to receive one-third share in the property of your father.

(Pre deceased–Son dying during the lifetime of father)

WILL - LEGAL FORMALITIES

I wish to make a will. Kindly guide me as to what are the legal formalities to be complied with while making it.

A will is an instrument by which a person gives directions as to the disposition of the property after his death.

Under the **Hindu Law** every person who is of sound mind and is not a minor can make a will. The person who disposes his property by a will is called a testator. The testator, by signing or fixing his mark makes a will. The mark can also be so affixed by any person acting as per the direction of the maker and doing so in his presence. A will is to be attested by two witnesses, each of whom has seen the testator sign or affix his mark on the will or has seen some other person sign the will in the presence and upon the direction of the testator or has received from the testator a personal acknowledgement of the fact of his signature or mark, or of the signature of such other person. Each of the witnesses shall sign the will in the presence of the testator, but it is not necessary that they should sign in presence of each other. The will can be made in respect of both movable and immovable property.

As a will takes effect only after the death of the maker / testator, it can be revoked at any time by the following ways–

a) By execution of a subsequent will;
b) By declaration of the intention of revoking the will;
c) By destroying the will by burning or tearing or any other mode showing the intention of destruction of the same.

Registration of a will is not compulsory. However, the testator may register the will or deposit the will in a sealed cover with the registrar. There is no time limit for registration. Registering a will is enough proof of the authenticity of the will.

It is to be noted here that will made by Hindus, Jains, Sikhs or Buddhists made with respect to immovable property situated within certain areas like Bengal, Chennai and Mumbai requires a probate of such will to be taken after the testator's death for its execution. A probate is the officially verified copy of a will under the seal of a court together with a certificate to the effect that it has been proved granting the executor the power to administer the estate of the testator.

Under the **Muslim Law** the following needs to be satisfied for a valid will–

1. The testator i.e. the author of the will must be competent to make the will and dispose the property.
2. The legatee i.e. the person to whom the property is given must be competent to take the legacy or bequest.
3. The subject of bequest i.e. the property must be a valid one and capable of being given in bequest.
4. The bequest must be within the limits imposed on the testamentary power of a Muslim i.e. the testator is only empowered to bequeath 1/3rd of the total property owned by him.

For a valid will–

1. The property must be capable of being transferred.
2. The property must be in existence at the time of testator's death. It is not necessary that it should be in existence at the time of making the will.
3. The testator must be the owner of the property.

The Mohammedan Law confers on a testator unfettered right to revoke his will. He may revoke it at any time either by express or implied means.

Thus, primarily the requisites of making a valid will is nearly the same in both Hindu and Muslim Law except that the power of disposing the property by a Muslim is limited to $1/3^{rd}$ of the total property owned by the testator.

WILL – REQUISITES

I have two children living and my husband died long back. My son deserted me and I am being looked after by my daughter. I don't want to transfer any of my husband's property to my son. How can it be done?

Property can be transferred only by the person who is the absolute owner of the same. Hence, if you are not the absolute owner and your husband at the time of his death had not transferred his entire property to you, then you, your son and your daughter, all have equal share over the property and there is no way you can deprive him from the property.

Also, even if he had transferred the said property in your name, but the same was not the self-earned property of your husband but was the ancestral one (inherited from his father or forefathers etc.), your son will still have a right over a share of the said property.

However, you can transfer your share in the said property to your daughter by gift or by making a will.

WILL – EXECUTOR – RECEIVING BENEFIT

I wish to appoint my son to whom I have bequeathed my property as the executor of the will. Can I do so?

Objection Your Honour

An executor is a person to whom the testator has entrusted the execution of his will.

Any person who is of sound mind can be made an executor. He is a legal representative of the testator entitled to represent the estate of the deceased and is empowered to collect the assets, pay the debts and discharge the legacies in the will. Further, he has to provide funds for the performance of funeral ceremonies of the deceased in a manner suitable to his status.

Under the Indian law, an executor is competent to receive benefit in a will. If the will provides any legacy in favour of a person who is also an executor of the will, he shall be entitled to receive his share just as any other person to whom any legacy is bequeathed.

GIFT

I had gifted my entire property to my son. Now he doesn't treat me well, so I would like to revoke the said gift. How can I do so?

The transfer of property by way of gift is the easiest way for transferring any property, leaving negligible chances of challenge to such transfer by the other legal heirs. In case of gift of movable property, the gift is complete once the said property transfers in the possession of the person to whom the gift is intended to be given. If the property transferred is an immovable property, the gift deed is to be executed on a stamp paper, determined by the official market value of the property, and has to be registered.

A gift can be revoked only if–

1. In case of movable property, your son is not in possession of the same.
2. In case of immovable property, the gift deed was not properly stamped nor was it registered.

ADOPTION

I am a woman and I don't intend to marry. However, I

would like to have the pleasure of upbringing a child. I have decided to go for adoption. What are the legal restrictions and the formalities therein?

Adoption is only applicable to Hindus and not to Muslims, Christians, Parsis or others.

Any person, who is of sound mind and is a major, whether male or female, may make a valid adoption. However, if the said person is having a spouse, consent is essential unless and until the spouse has ceased to be Hindu or finally has renounced the world or has been declared unsound by a competent court.

A father, mother or guardian of the child can give, the child for adoption. In case of married persons willing to do so, consent of spouse is again essential but is not needed in cases of disqualification's mentioned earlier. A guardian can only give a child in adoption with the permission of the court, if the child is parentless or the parents are suffering from some disabilities or have abandoned or where his parentage is unknown.

There are certain restrictions even in case of a child to be given in adoption. He / She should be a Hindu, must not have been given in adoption earlier, must not be married unless the custom allows. Moreover the child should not have completed the age of 15 except in few places where custom lifts the age bar, like in Punjab and Mumbai.

If the adoption is of a son, the adoptive father or mother by whom the adoption is made should not have a Hindu son, son's son or son's son's son living at the time of adoption. If the adoption is of a daughter, the adoptive father or mother by whom the adoption is made should not have a Hindu daughter or son's daughter living at the time of adoption. If the adoption is by a male and the person to be adopted is a female, the adoptive father should atleast be twenty-one years older than the person to be adopted. If the adoption is by a female and the person to be adopted is a male, the adoptive mother should at least be twenty-one years older than the person to be adopted.

Though earlier *Datta Homan* was necessary to be performed but now a mere single ceremony of giving and taking is essential.

The registration of such adoption can be done but is not an essential one except in Uttar Pradesh.

Hence, you can easily take a child in adoption subject to the fact that if the child is a male you should be 21 years older to him.

CUSTODY – MUSLIM

I am a follower of the Islamic faith. My husband divorced me a few months earlier. We have a child of 3 years. Please advise as to who would have custody of the child, my divorced husband or me?

As per the Islamic law, the mother is not the natural guardian of a child. But the mother can claim the custody of the child. Under Hanafi law, mother is entitled to custody of a male child till the age of 7, and in case of female child, till attainment of puberty. However, if she remarries, the custody of the child will revert to the father.

CUSTODY – HINDU

We are Hindus and have separated. We have a son out of our relationship. Both of us want to keep the child. Who will have the custody?

There is no hard and fast rule about the custody of the child. But generally in infant stage the custody remains with the mother. The court while deciding the matter of custody takes the welfare of the child at the utmost and sees as to who among the parents will be able to fulfill the child's demand financially and be able to give emotional support. Moreover the custody of the child can shift from mother to father and vice-versa depending upon the circumstances.

REMARRYING WIFE – MUSLIM LAW

I am a Muslim male and gave *talaq* to my wife earlier this year. She is still unmarried and our differences have ended. We wish to marry again. What should I do?

Though in Muslim law, *Talaq* can be given very easily even

without any fault on part of the wife but for remarrying her, there are stringent conditions. First of all she will have to get married to another man and that marriage should be consumated. Then, the said husband should divorce her and then only you can marry her.

MARRYING MINOR

We are Hindu and parents of a 16-year old minor girl. She has married with a neighbour whom she loved, without our consent. Isn't such marriage null and void? Can we lodge a case of rape against the person she has married?

As per the Hindu Marriage Act, at the time of marriage the male should have attained the age of 21 years and the female 18 years. Your daughter's inability to marry will not render the marriage void or voidable. But, the husband, if he is above the age of 18 yrs but below the age of 21 yrs will be liable for imprisonment extending to 15 days and / or with fine extending to Rs. 1000/-. And if he is above 21 yrs of age he is liable for simple imprisonment extending to 3 moths and / or fine. Further all persons who have performed, conducted or directed performance of a child marriage including the parents / guardians (excluding women) of such child who have promoted such or negligently failed in preventing such are liable for imprisonment upto 3 months and / or with fine.

As your daughter is above the age of 16, having sexual intercourse with her consent will not amount to rape.

CEREMONIES OF MARRIAGE

My brother's marriage took place without performance of *vivah-homum* and *saptpadi*. Does it pose any bar in making the marriage valid?

Hindus are spread across the whole country having different customs and rites. Though it is considered in general that a marriage becomes binding as soon as the seventh step is taken in front of the sacred fire by the couple but there is no hard and fast rule prescribed by law and marriage can also be performed in such other form as permissible under the custom in force and the same shall be binding and equally enforceable.

PROHIBITED DEGREES IN MARRIAGE

I am Hindu and my wife expired long back. My only son died in an accident, leaving his wife 3 years earlier. She feels quite insecure and doesn't have any means of livelihood too. In these circumstances I wish to marry my own widowed daughter-in-law so that she can be helpful to me in my old days and at the same time I will be able to fulfil her financial needs too. Is there any legal hurdle in doing so?

This will not be just legally wrong but morally too. According to Hindu Marriage Act, no marriage should take place between parties within prohibited degree of relationship, unless and until customs or the rites allow it. In Tamil Nadu in a particular caste we often see marriages of girl to their maternal uncle.

Prohibited degree relationship means if the parties to the marriage are related in such a manner that–

i) If one is lineal ascendant of other,

ii) If one was the wife or husband of a lineal ascendant or descendant of the other, or

iii) If one was the wife of the brother or of the father's or mother's brother or of the grandfather's or grandmother's or grandmother's brother, or

iv) If two are brother and sister, uncle and niece, aunt and nephew or children of brother and sister or of two brothers or of two sisters.

Others who cannot marry are–

1. Those in half blood, uterine blood and full blood relations, or

2. Persons taken in adoption acquire the same rights and status as the natural one so there cannot be marriage in the adoptive family member with such adopted child.

3. Parties who are bound by illegitimate blood relationship and legitimate relationship.

INTER-RELIGION MARRIAGE

I am a Hindu girl in deep love with a Muslim. We want to marry. Though my parents are liberal one but they fear that the Muslims always have a chance of giving divorce very easily and can also marry another lady too. What should I do?

The best way for you will be marrying under the Special Marriage Act. A marriage solemnized under this Act prohibits a male from subsequently marrying another lady, during the existence of a valid marriage. Moreover, giving divorce under Special Marriage Act is not so easy as that in the Muslim Law. So you and your parents should keep away such worries.

RESTITUTION OF CONJUGAL RIGHTS

I am a Police officer and my duty is such that I have to often return home late at night and be working whole day. My wife has left my place and stays with her father on the sole ground that she finds it difficult to stay with me on account of my job. I find these grounds baseless. Can the law help me to make us live together?

We feel that your wife's decision of not living with you on the mere ground of the nature of job is totally incorrect. The Hindu law has contemplated such situation and provides for 'restitution of conjugal rights'.

If any of the spouse to the marriage defies or neglects or evades his/her obligation of performance of conjugal rights, the aggrieved person may apply to the court for compliance of the same.

Thus as your wife has without reasonable cause withdrawn from your company, you may file a petition in the Civil Court / Family Court for the same and the court on being satisfied may pass a decree in your favour. Moreover, the burden of proving that there exists a reasonable cause for withdrawal from society will lie on your wife.

JUDICIAL SEPARATION

It became difficult for me to live with my husband and

his parents and so I filed a divorce petition. I was told that it would take about a year and half in obtaining divorce. During the pendency of the suit I don't wish to carry the liabilities of being his wife, what should I do?

The law has contemplated situations wherein the parties can live separately. Such is known as Judicial Separation.

Judicial Separation is a separation of husband and wife under orders of court, which puts an end to cohabitation but not to marriage itself. Under the Hindu law, all the grounds of divorce are also the valid grounds for obtaining judicial separation. Either party can make such a petition praying for decree of judicial separation. When such is granted, your marriage will subsist, but there will be no obligation to have cohabitation and further it shall bar the relief for restitution of conjugal right. But the spouses are entitled to claim alimony i.e. maintenance and in case one of the spouse dies without any will before the decree is passed, the other will be entitled to succeed to the property left behind by the intestate spouse. Thus, until you get a decree of divorce, your interest is protected in both the manner i.e. no obligation of a wife but still having all the rights of such.

DIVORCE – SIKH

We are a newly married couple and belong to the Sikh sect. However, I am not happy with my husband and also cannot adjust according to his family and society, which is the present modern day 'high-class society'. I wish to obtain divorce from my husband. What is the procedure for doing so? In the meantime can I be allowed to stay away from him?

Sikhs are governed under the Hindu law and as per the Hindu Marriage Act, a divorce can be obtained on any one of the following grounds—

That the other party—

a. Had voluntary sexual intercourse with any other person than his / her spouse;

b. Has treated the petitioner with cruelty;
c. Has deserted the petitioner for continuous period of not less than 2 yrs immediately before the presentation of the petition;
d. Has ceased to be Hindu by conversion to another religion;
e. Has been incurably of unsound mind or has been suffering continuously or intermittently from mental disorder of such a kind and to such an extent that the petitioner cannot reasonably be expected to live with the respondent;
f. Has been suffering from a virulent and incurable form of leprosy;
g. Has been suffering from veneral disease in a communicable form;
h. Has renounced the world by entering any religious order;
i. Has not been heard of being alive for a period of seven years or more by those persons who would naturally have heard about him, had the person been alive;
j. That there has been no cohabitation between the spouse for one year or more after passing a decree of judicial separation in a proceeding to which they were parties;
k. That there has been no restitution of conjugal rights between the spouse for one year or more after passing a decree of restitution of conjugal rights in a proceeding to which they were parties;
l. That the husband has after the marriage been guilty of rape, sodomy or bestiality (only available to wife);
m. That there has been no cohabitation between the spouse for one year or more after passing a decree of maintenance to the wife (only available to wife);
n. That the marriage was solemnized before the wife attained the age of 15 yrs and had repudiated the marriage after she attained the age of 15 yrs but before she attained the age of 18 yrs (only available to wife).

A divorce case can be instituted in a Family Court or in the absence of such in the Court of Civil Judge Senior Division having jurisdiction over the area where the marriage was solemnized, or where the respondent resides at the time of presentation of the petition or where the parties last resided together. The petition for divorce cannot be presented within one year of the marriage except in cases of exceptional hardship. The court will grant divorce only after it is satisfied of the allegations.

DIVORCE - HINDU

We are Hindus and got married 10 months ago. We have decided to end our marriage by mutual consent. We filed an application for it. What are the related provisions?

The Hindu Marriage Act has made elaborate provisions in respect of divorce by mutual consent. For this, both the spouse may present a petition for dissolution of marriage jointly to the Family Court or the Court of Civil Judge Senior Division having jurisdiction over the area where the marriage was solemnized, or where the parties last resided together. The facts such as living separately for at least a year and that both the parties have mutually agreed that the marriage should be dissolved are essential.

In your case, as only 10 months have elapsed, you should wait for 2 months more, so that the minimum term of 1 year gets completed and then only you can file such petition for divorce effectively. The court will grant divorce not earlier than 6 months from the presentation of the petition and within 18 months, if the same is not withdrawn or the other party has not revoked his consent.

The court may allow the petition to be presented before expiry of one year since the date of marriage, only on the ground that the case is one of the exceptional hardship to the petitioners, or of exceptional depravity on the part of other party.

TALAQ - MUSLIM

I am a Muslim male, I wish to obtain divorce from my wife due to some personal reason and therefore want to know about Talaq with its various forms and procedure?

Under the Muslim law, a husband has greater right to obtain Talaq in comparison with the wife. The various mode of divorce are as such—

By Husband.

Talaq : (Repudiation)

Under the Muslim law Talaq means repudiation or dissolution of marriage tie. In Sunni law the husband who is of sound mind and has attained puberty is competent to give talaq to his wife. It may be either written or oral. There is no particular form for giving Talaq. If the words are clear intention is not necessary but if the words are not clear than intention needs to be proved. Moreover presence of the wife is not necessary while giving talaq. A revocable talaq does not dissolve the marriage till the period of Iddat but an irrevocable talaq dissolves the marriage immediately.

In Shia, law the following conditions required for Talaq :

1. The husband must be of sound mind and has attained puberty.
2. In accordance with the Sunnat.
3. In Arabic term, in the presence of two adult male witnesses.
4. With his own free will.

The 2 forms of Talaq are as followings.

1. Talaq-ul-Sunnat
2. Talaq-ul-Biddat.

1. Talaq-ul-Sunnat is in accordance with the tradition of the Prophet which is again of 2 types.

   i. Ahasan
   ii. Hasan

i. Ahasan is the most approved form of talaq. Ahasan means best or very proper. The requirements of Ahasan are as following:

   a) The Husband must pronounce Talaq in a single sentence.
   b) Talaq must be pronounced when the wife is in the sate of Tuhr or Purity. (Tuhr is the period when the wife is free from the Menstural Course.)
   c) The husband must abstain from intercourse for a period of Iddat which is 3 months. If the marriage is not

consummated or if the wife is old, the condition of Tuhr is not applicable.

The talaq in Ahasan from is revocable during Iddat. Revocation may be implied or expressed Co-habitation with wife is revocation of Talaq. After the Iddat period talaq becomes irrevocable.

ii. Hasan : It means good or proper. Hasan talaq must fulfill the following conditions.

a) There must be three successive pronouncement of talaq.

b) In case of menstruating wife the first pronouncement should be during the first Tuhr, the second must be during second Tuhr, and the third pronouncement, during the third Tuhr, or during the interval of 30 days.

c) Intercourse should not take place during these three periods of Tuhr. Such talaq becomes irrevocable on the third pronouncement.

2. Talaq-ul-Biddat is the disapproved or the sinful way of Talaq. It is recognized only by Hanafis and Shias and the Mallikis do not recognize it. In this form of talaq, three pronouncements are made during a single Tuhr in one sentence, or in three separate sentences. Even a single pronouncement during a Tuhr with clear intention to dissolve the marriage. Talaq becomes irrevocable with the pronouncement. Complete separation takes place and the marriage between the same parties cannot be done unless Halala takes place.

ILA (Vow of Continence) :

If the husband who has attained majority and is of sound mind swears by the God that he will not have sexual intercourse with his wife, it is called ila. Abstaining 4 months from sexual intercourse with the wife, after making ila, dissolves the marriage. Sunni law does not prescribe any legal proceeding.

Ila can be cancelled by either if the husband gets into intercourse with the wife in the said 4 months or by by verbal retraction.

Zihar is a condition when the husband who is sane, adult compares his wife to his mother or any other female within prohibited degree, the wife has the right to refuse herself to him until he has performed penance by–

1) Freeing a slave.
2) Fasting for 2 months.
3) Feeding 60 poor persons.

If penance is not performed by the husband the wife can apply to the Court for divorce. In this such comparison should be to insult the wife and if it was to show respect to the wife penance is not required.

Under Shia Law 2 witnesses must be present when injurious assimination is made. Muta marriage may be dissolved by Zihar. The divorce is not in use.

By Wife– Talaq-e-tafweez : (Delegated Divorce)

In this form of Divorce the husband may either divorce the wife himself or delegate such power to a third party or even to his wife. An agreement can be entered by the husband and the wife that the wife would be at liberty to divorce herself under some specified conditions, provided the conditions are reasonable and are not opposed to public policy. Even such a term that the wife can have divorce if the husband has a second marriage is accepted. While exercising the power of the agreement the wife must establish that the condition under which she has exercised the power, had been fulfilled.

The Talaq takes effect as if the husband has effected it. The Courts declaration is not needed. Thus even in this form of divorce the wife does not do so as she has done it herself but as on behalf of the husband, moreover by delegating the power the divorce the husband is not prevented from exercising Talaq.

By Mutual Consent :

1. Khula (Redemption) means laying down the husbands right and authority over his wife. Divorce by this way is at the instance of the wife on certain consideration over his wife. The essentials of Khula are as following–

    A. The wife must make an offer.

B. The offer must be with some consideration.

C. The offer must be accepted by the husband.

When the husband accepts the offer, the talaq becomes irrevocable and the wife has to observe Iddat.

The property which can be given by the wife can be everything which husband can give as dower. If the wife fails to pay the consideration after divorce, the divorce does not become invalid and the husband has a right to claim the consideration. Under Sunni law the husband must be sane and adult.

Mubarat (Divorce by mutual consent) is a condition when both the parties to the marriage wishes for separation. In such circumstance they can take divorce by mutual consent. Under Shia law, if it becomes impossible for the couple to continue the marriage, it can be dissolved then. Any of the party i.e. husband or the wife may offer to divorce, and it becomes irrevocable after acceptance.

By Judicial Decree: Dissolution of Muslim Marriage Act 1939 dealt in another question.

TALAQ- MUSLIM FEMALE

I am a Muslim woman. My husband accuses me of false charges of adultery and denies paternity of the child. In this circumstance I want to get divorced from him. I have heard that under Muslim law, wife alone is not capable of obtaining divorce if the husband too is not willing. What can I do in such circumstance?

Dissolution of Muslim Marriage Act 1939 provides even the Muslim woman to obtain divorce on various grounds. Your case too falls within one of the criteria, i.e. Lian or false charge of adultery.

Husband who is sane and adult charging falsely, the wife of adultery or denying the paternity of the child, makes the wife is entitled to file a suit for divorce, but if it gets proved to be true in nature, the court will not pass decree in wives favour.

The husband can retract the charge but retraction must be–

1. Bonafide

2. Unconditional

3. Made at or before the commencement of the hearing of the suit.

Such Judicial Separation, due to Lian is irrevocable and is applicable only in case of Sahih marriage and not in Fasid marriage.

The other grounds on which the wife can approach the court are as followings–

1. Absence of Husband

The wife is entitled for divorce if the whereabouts of the husband is not known for 4 years. The decree passed on such a ground will not take effect for a period of 6 months from the date of such decree and if the husband appears in person or through any authorized agent within the said period and satisfies the Court that he is wishes to perform his marital duties, the Court shall set aside the decree.

2. Failure to Maintain

If he husband neglects or fails to provide maintenance to his wife for a period of 2 years the wife can seek divorce. No such ground taken by the husband will be accepted like poverty, ill health, unemployment or personal property of the wife etc.

3. Imprisonment of Husband

If the husband has been sentenced to imprisonment for a period of 7 years or more then in such a circumstance the wife is entitled to divorce but the decree on this ground cannot be passed unless sentence has become final.

4. Failure to perform marital obligation for 3 years.

If the husband fails, performing the marital obligations without reasonable cause for a period of 3 years, the wife can ask for divorce.

5. Impotency of Husband

If the husband is impotent at the time of marriage and continues to be so, the wife is entitled for divorce. Before passing the decree if the husband makes an application the court can make an order requiring the husband to satisfy the court within a period of one year from the date of such order that he is no more impotent and if he satisfies the court, decree cannot be passes on this ground.

6. Insanity, Leprosy and Venereal Disease

If the husband has been insane for a period of 2 or more years or if he is suffering from leprosy or venereal diseases, the wife can claim divorce.

7. Option of Puberty

If the marriage of the girl is contracted by her guardian during her minority, she has a right to repudiate the marriage before attaining the age of 18 years, provided the marriage is not consummated. She can ask for divorce.

8. Cruelty by the husband

A wife can claim divorce if the husband treats her with cruelty. Cruelty includes–

a. Habitual assault or making life miserable by bad conduct even if such conduct does not amount physical ill treatment.

b. Has relations with a woman of ill repute or leads an immoral life, or attempts to force her head an immoral life.

c. Disposes of her property or prevents her from exercising her legal rights over her property.

d. Does not allow her to divorce her religious rights.

e. If he has more than one wife, and does not treat her equally.

The consequences of such marriage are as following–

By such divorce the parties become entitled to contract another marriage. If the marriage was consummated the wife may marry after the completion of her Iddat. If marriage was not consummated the wife may marry after the completion of her Iddat, but if the marriage was not consummated then she is free to marry immediately. If the marriage was consummated and the husband had four wives at the date of divorce, he may marry again after completion of iddat of the divorced wife.

If the marriage was consummated wife is entitled to get whole of the unpaid dower. If the marriage was not consummated, and the amount was specified in the contract, she is entitled to half the dower.

There are no mutual rights of inheritance after divorce.

Cohabitation becomes unlawful.

The wife becomes entitled to maintenance during Iddat of Divorce.

Remarriage between the couple is not lawful unless certain conditions are observed.

SHUFFA

We are 3 brothers. We got our fathers property after his death. It was divided into 3 parts. One of my brother wants to sell off his share to another person. Is there any provision through which we can stop him from doing so as the third party will be some other person.

There is a provision in the Muslim law known as Pre-emption or Shuffa. Right of pre-emption or Shuffa is a right to acquire by compulsory purchase. Main objective is to prevent the introduction of a stranger among co-sharerers and neighbours, so that no inconvinience is caused to them.

Preemption requires three necessary things–

a. Pre-emptor – Owner of immovable property.
b. Sale of certain property, not his own.
c. Pre-emptor must stand in a certain relationship to the vendor in respect of property sold.

Shuffa means adding. It is defined as a right which the owner of certain property possesses to obtain proprietary possession of certain other immovable property not his own. This right is given by law for the quiet enjoyment of the property.

Main intention of the provision of Pre-emption is to lessen the joint owners hardship and inconvinience. Since Muslim law disintegrates the family property, the law of the pre-emption reduces the defects of it to some extent.

The right of pre-emption arises only when sale takes place and is complete;. Sale must be bonafide. It is complete only when the price is paid and possession delivered. Under the Transfer of Property, Sale of immovable property of value Rs. 100/- and

Objection Your Honour

above needs registration. Pre-emption right does not arise in case of Gift, Sadaqah, Waqf, Inheritance, Bequest, Lease or if the property is transferred in lien of Mahr.

There are four grounds on which a claim for pre-emption may be based in India.

a. By State - If there is any Special Act of Legislation relating to pre-emption, it will be governed by it.

b. By Customs – In absence of Statute, it can be claimed on the basis of custom.

c. By Contract – It can be created by Contract and even 2 persons of different religion can enter into a Contract.

d. By Muslim Law – When no custom or statute is there then the right can be claimed under the Muslim law when both the vendee and the vendor are Muslims.

Even the non-muslims are entitled to exercise the right under the following circumstances.

a. Legislation
b. Custom
c. Contract

Following are the persons who can pre-empt.

Under the Sunni Law–

a. Shafi-I-Sharik – Co-sharer in the property.
b. Shafi-I-Khalit – Participator in the immunities. i.e. right of way or discharge of water.
c. Shafi-i-jar – Neighbour, owner of adjoining immovable property.

Shia Law: Right available only in case where there are only two co-sharers in the property.

Shafi Law: Right can only be claimed by co-owner or a co-sharer.

Formalities: The right of pre-emption being a right to interfere with anothers right to sell his property as such it is weak right as per Hedaya and the case law. It is available only upon the full & complete observance of the formalities. Person willing to enforce his right must make three demands after hearing of the sale of the property.

These are known as 3 demands–

a. Talab-i-Mowasibat or Immediate Demand means demand by jumping. The moment the news comes that the property has been sold, he should make an immediate demand. Witnesses are not necessary. Pre-emptor has to be very prompt while making this demand, delay will result in loss of right.

b. Talab-i-Ishhad or Confirmatory demand means the first demand is of no use unless followed by the second demand. Essentials for making it are that the pre-emptor must,

  i. Offer his intentions to exercise his right.

  ii. Make refrences to the first demand.

  iii. Make second demand in presence of atleats 2 witnesses.

First and second demand can be made together if the witnesses are present. Second demand can be made by the messenger of the pre-emptor.

c. Talab-i-Tamleek or Demand for Possession means the Final demand for the enforcement of the claim by instituting a regular suit within the period prescribed by the Indian Limitation Act. I.e. Within 1 year of the purchase.

Right is lost in the following case–

a. Death.
b. If, pre-emptor waves his right in favour of Vendee.
c. Agreeing in the same- Pre-emptor fails to claim his right or fails to perform the demand.
d. Pre-emptor joins with himself as co-plaintiff a person who has no right of Shuffa.
e. He fails in the observance of the formalities.
f. Pre-emptor releases the right for consideration.
g. Pre-emptor transfers the subject of pre-emption to a stranger he transfers his right.

Right is not lost–

a. By the death of the Pre-emptor during the pendancy of the suit.
b. By refusing to buy when the property was offered to him before.
c. Previous notice of sale.

MUTA MARRIAGE

I am a Muslim male, already married. These days my affair is going with a beautiful lady. Both of us agree that we are not made for each other for whole life, but we want to get married for certain specified period. At the same time I don't want to divorce my wife. I have heard some sort of marriage is applicable to Muslims, which gives right to marry only for a short span. What does the law say?

As per your question, we feel that you are willing to know about 'Muta marriage', but this form of marriage is recognized only in Shias. Thus a Shia male has capacity any number of women, who is a Muslim, Christian, Jew or a fire worshipper but not with any other. There is no restriction even in case of Muta marriage of having maximum number of wives, i.e. 4. But a Shia female can contract Muta marriage only with a Muslim male, moreover if the girl is a major, even her guardian cannot object to the marriage, but if the girl is a minor then she can contract such marriage only with the consent of guardian, without which it will be void. The formalities required for Muta marriage is same as in a regular muslim marriage. Condition of Muta marriage should be entered at the time of marriage.

Following are the requisites of a valid Muta marriage–
a. Dower must be specified, otherwise it will be void.
b. The period of marriage must be specified, which can be even a few hours or even years.
c. If no term is specified, the marriage does not become void, but it is implied that the parties intend to go into permanent relationship.
d. In such kind of marriage, no right of mutual inheritance arise,

to the spouse, even if the other dies when Muta marriage is subsisting.

e. The wife is not entitled to maintenance, but if maintenance is stipulated in the marriage contract, she shall be entitled to it, for the whole period of marriage, even if he does not cohabit with her.

f. If the marriage does not gets consummated the wife gets half the dower, but on consummation of marriage, the wife is entitled to full dower.

g. In case the wife leaves the husband in between the contract-marriage, she will be entitled to proportionate dower.

So accordingly you can take your decision.

MAHR

I am a Muslim female from a middle class family. My parents are thinking of my marriage. What can be the appropriate amount of Mahr, which I should demand?

Dower or Marh is a peculiar concept in Muslim Law. It is a sum that is payable by the husband to the wife on marriage, either by agreement or by operation of law, either prompt or deferred. Dower (Mahr) is not a consideration for marriage, but an obligation imposed by law upon husband.

There are 3 main objectives of Mahr–

a. Impose obligation on the husband as a mark of respect to the wife.

b. Check on husband in the use of divorce.

c. Subsistence to the wife after divorce.

Mahr amount can be increased by the husband after the marriage or even wife can forgo the whole amount or some amount with her free consent. Such foregoing of Mahr by wife is known as 'Hiba-e-Mahr'. Since Islam flourished in the middle east countries so the amount for the Mahr is according to the currency prevalent in those countries i.e. – 10 Dishams or 3 Dishams for Hanafi law and Maliki Law but no fixed amount for Shafei as well as Shia Law.

There is a difference between the 2 schools of Muslim Law. There is no limit to the maximum of proper power under Sunni law. Under Shia law maximum amount should not be more than 500 Dishams, the Dower fixed for Prophets Dower Fatima.

There are 2 types of Dower:- Specified and Customry or Proper.

A. Specified Dower: - Amount settled in the marriage in case of minor boy, Mahr specified by guardian is binding on the minor after attaining majority.

Sunni law- Amount not less than 10 Dishams

Maliki Law- Not less than 3 dishams.

Shia Law- Not fixed minimum amount.

2 types of Specified Dower.

1 **Prompt Dower**– Payable immediately after marriage on demand unless aggrieved, does not become deferred after consummation of marriage. The period of limitation for recovering is 3 years, from the demand and refusal.

2. **Deferred Dower**– Payable on dissolution of marriage by death or divorce. If there is any agreement for payment of deferred dower earlier, the agreement is valid and binding. Wife cannot demand deferred dower, she can even forgo the Mahr at her husbands funeral but done with her free consent. Wife's right in the deferred dower after her death is vested on her legal heirs.

If dower not specified specifically as to deferred or prompt then under Shia law the whole amount is treated as prompt. But under Sunni law it is half deferred and half prompt.

B. Customary or proper dower–

Amount is not fixed in the marriage or even if the marriage is contracted on the condition that the wife should not claim any dower, the wife is entitled to what is known as proper dower. This dower is to be settled taking into consideration the following factors.

1. Personal qualification of wife, age, fortune virtue, understanding, beauty.

2. Social position of her father's family.

3. Economic condition of her husband.

Muslim law gives the following rights to a wife or widow to compel her husband to pay dower to her.

A. Refusal to cohabit.

B. Right to dower as debt.

C. Right to retain property of her husband.

If widow is in possession of her husband's property, she can retain it until her dower is paid, but widow must retain possession lawfully without force or fraud, must be in possession of property at her husband's death or divorce. She can only retain the property but cannot become the owner of it or alienate or sell the property.

HIBA

I am a Muslim male and I have a lot of property. I want to make a will and give half of my property as a Gift to a charitable trust and half to my wife. Can I do this?

Muslim law allows a person to lawfully make gift (Hiba) of his property during his lifetime or may transfer it by way of will (effect will take place after death).

The first is called disposition inter-vivos and the other is testamentary disposition.

Hiba-An unconditional trasfer of property, made immediately without any exchange or consideration by one person to another, and accepted by or on behalf of the later.

Muslim law allows a man to give away the whole of his property during life time but only 1/3 by will.

It can be written or oral.

There are 4 essentials of a valid gift.

(a) parties (b) subject (c) extent (d) formalities or mode

(a) Parties – 2 parties required i.e. – Donor who gives the property and Donee who accepts it.

Donor should be major, of sound mind, owner of the property, gift made by him must be free from fraudulent or coercive influences, gift by married woman is a valid gift by Parda Nashien is also valid provided it is not induces by undue influence and the donor understands the transaction. Insolvent person can make a gift provided he has a bonafide intention to give & the act is not merely intended to defraud the Creditors.

A person capable of holding property may be a donnie. Age, sex, creed or religion is no bar. But a donee must be in existence at the time of making of the gift, in case of lunatic or a minor possession is handed to the legal guardian. Gift in favour of an unborn is void but in favour of a Mosque is valid.

(b) subject- Subject of Gift can be anything over which right of property may be exercised or anything which can be reduced into possession. It could be anything which can be designed or termed as mal. Property must be in existence at the time gift is made. If t to be produced in future is void. Subject an be corporal or incorporeal. Former means those things which is in physical existence ie. Money, house where as latter means that which has no physical existence like right to payment of a debt or equity of redemption.

Gift can even be corpus or usufruct. Corpus is the thing itself and usufruct is the befefit or profits of the thing.

Void gift–

a. To an unborn person.
b. Gift of anything to be produced in future.
c. Gift cannot be made on the happening or non-happening of a future uncertain event.
d. In case of Conditional gift- the gift is valid and the condition is void.

For a validity of the gift it is not essential that it should be in writing. If the formalities are not fulfilled, the gift is not valid though made in a prescribed manner as said by the prescribed provisions of Sec 123 of Transfer of Property Act.

(c) formalities or mode: - Act of Gift should fulfill the following 3 conditions–

i. declaration by the donor,
ii. accepted by the donee, &

iii. delivery of possession, by the donor to the donee and taking possession by the donee.

Donor must have a clear and unambiguous intension to make the gift as well as his intention must be bonafide otherwise void. It should be made voluntarily.

Revocation of Gift: - By delivery of possession, the gift is not complete and the donor has unrestricted right to revoke it. According to Muslim Law all voluntary transaction are revocable, hence gifts may also be revoked. The reason for this is that the gift is no gift before delivery of possession and hence, the rules relating to the gift do not apply. After delivery of possession, under Hanafi law there can be decree of the court. Under Shia law it can be revoked by a mere declaration, consent of the donee or decree of the Court is not necessary.

Kinds of Gift–

i. Hiba-bil-iwaz (Gift for consideration) not applicable in India
ii. Hiba-ab-shartual. (Gift with a condition)

   Shart means stipulation or condition. Consideration is expressely stipulated but actual payment is postponed. I waz means consideration. Transaction becomes final immediately on delivery of possession. It is revocable until the iwaz is paid.

iii. Sadaqah: - Gift with religious motive, not revocable. This gift is to get religious merits. It can be made to two or more persons, jointly provided the donees are poor. Delivery of possession is necessary. Express acceptance is not necessary in Hiba.

iv. Ariyat: - Under Muslim law Corpus (property) or usufruct (profits) can be gifted. It means the grant of license by the grantor to take and enjoy the usufruct of a thing is called Ariyat. It should be for a definite period. It is revocable . Donee does not acquire the ownership of the property.

Gift during Marz-ul-Maut (Death-bed transaction)

Marz-ul-Maut means deah-illness. Ilness which causes death. According to Mulla it means a malady which induces and apprehension of death in the person suffering from it and which causes his death. A legator can make a gift during his death illness. A gift nade in Marz-ul-Maut can take effect only as a bequest. Gift made during death is said to be gift-cum-will. So both Muslim law of gift made during death illness it is necessary that the delivery of possession should be made to the donee.

WAKF

I am a Muslim, I don't have any legal descendent, and therefore I wish to give my property for a charitable purpose. Please guide me about Wakf.

Wakf means detention, stoppage or tying up. According to Hanafi School its extinction of proprietor's ownership in the thing dedicated and its detention in such manner that the profits may revert to and be applied for the benefit of mankind. Person creating Wakf is called Wakif. Person to look after wakf property is Mutawalli.

* Wakf Act 1954 means—

"Permanent dedication by a person professing Islam, of any movable or immovable property for any purpose recognized by Muslim law as religious pious or charitable."

Wakf may be in writing or created orally. But there must be an intention to dedicate the property.

* Essentials of Wakf

I. Sunni law: 3 conditions for validity.

1. – A permanent dedication of property and a declaration. May be oral or written.

—Appointment of Mutawalli, or delivery of possession to Mutawalli, not necessary. This view is followed in India.

—Any property used as Wakf property infers legal dedication.

—Wakf of Mosques and graveyards have been considered valid on this ground.

— Perpetuity is another essential condition of Wakf.

2. Wakf can be made of any tangible property, which can be used without consumption, belonging to wakif. The dedicator (major) should be a muslim.

3. Dedication purpose– Religious, pious or charitable. Object must be indicated with reasonable certainty, otherwise void.

II. Shia Law– According to Sharya-ul-Islam

4 Conditions.

1. It must be perpetual.
2. It must be unconditional and absolute.
3. Posession must be given of the property.
4. The wakif should not keep any interest in the dedicated property.

Doctrine of Cypres: - It means, as nearly possible, its applicable to Trust. If from change of circumstances and lapse of time, it has become impossible to apply property in manner directed by the Wakif, the Cout may apply for similar purposes by different Cypres. Wakf once created cannot be revoked nor sold, alienated or transferred. Alienaion except for necessity of the Wakf and without permission of court is void. Wakf property, not liable is for attachment and sale in execution of personal decree against Mutawalli, even rents and profits can't be seized.

Mushaa: - It means undevided share (mushaa) in property.

According to Abu Yusuf: -Created by undivided share in property capable of division, but for Mosque or burial ground such mushaa not valid if property not divided.

According to Imam Mohammad: - Mushaa is not valid where property capable division, because delivery of possession is necessary.

Modes of Creation–

1. By an act inter vivos–

    Abu Yusuf: - Mere declaration is sufficient.

    Imam: - Appointment of Mutawalli and handing over possession to him necessary.

2. **By Will:** -Takes effect after death of Wakif. Its called testamentary Wakf. Only one-third property can be dedicated by will without consent of legal heirs and such Wakf can be revoked.

3. **During Marz-ul-Maut:** - Can be of only one-third property without consent of heirs of wakif.

4. **Long User**

Kinds of Wakf: -

1. **Private Wakf:** - Family Wakf- Wakf-alat-aulad.

It means, a Wakf for settlers own family members and their descendents, which was held void before passing of Mussalman Waqf Vahdat Act 1913.

Sunni Muslim can share income of Wakf by way of maintenance.

2. **Public Wakf:** - (a) Mosques and graveyards: - To consecrate mosque its necessary that–

   i. Building should be separated from other property of the owner.
   ii. A way must be provided for the Mosque.
   iii. Public prayer must be held or possession must be handed over to Mutawalli.

Every Muslim is allowe entry. Private Mosque or Sunni or Shia Mosque is not recognized.

B. Imambara

C. Rauzah and Dargahs

D. **Khanqahs:** - Religious institutuiions where religious instructions are given; of Islam. Its head is Sajjadanashin, who sits on a sajjada prayer mathy. He is teacher of religious doctrine and manager but can act as Mutawalli. Women, Non-Muslims and Minors not valid for the post.

E. Hospitals, Schools and Colleges.

Mutawalli: - Mutawalli is the Manager or Superintendent of Wakf.

Any person–

1. Who is of sound mind.
2. Who has attained the age of majority.
3. Capale of performing functions of Wakf can be appointed as Mutawalli, generally by founder of Wakf at time of creation.

Following persons can be appointed.

a. The founder.
b. Failing him, by executor of the founder
c. By Mutawalli on his death bed.
d. By the Court.

Powers of Mutawali: -

1. Mutawalli can do all acts reasonable and proper for the protection of the property.
2. Employ agents for administration of Wakf.
3. Entitled for remuneration if fixed by the settler. She can apply to Court for the increment of remuneration if less.
4. But cannot alienate except:-
    a. By provisions in the Wakf deed empowering him to do so.
    b. Permission of Court.
    c. Reason of urgent necessity.
5. Cannot lease out agricultural property for more than 3 years and non- agricultural property for more than 1 year.

Can do by permission of the Court–

1. Borrow money.
2. Sell, mortgage or dispose property in any other way.
3. With sufficient funds neglects to repair the property.
4. Knowingly or intentionally causes damage or loss to property.
5. Insolvent

Beneficiary has right to claim accounts. Mutawalli of Public Wakf has to furnish District Court, with all the accounts of Wakf property.

DIVORCE – CHRISTIAN

I am a Christian woman married in 1999. My husband is having an affair with a lady. Though he treats me well but it is difficult for me to live with him in such a condition. I have heard that in Christianity adultery combined with cruelty is a ground for divorce but not mere adultery? Please let me know is there any provision for divorce by mutual consent in Christian Law?

Drastic amendments have been carried out in divorce law for Christians wherein the requirement that women must prove cruelty or desertion on part of their spouse in addition to adultery in order to obtain divorce has been removed. Now, divorce is available to women on the single ground of adultery, cruelty or desertion. Also, the amendment empowers Christian couples who feel that their marriage has failed due to incompatibility and could not be revived to obtain divorce by mutual consent.

Hence, you can obtain divorce from your husband on the sole ground of adultery.

STRIDHAN

My husband's mother is required to undergo an operation and the family property and deposits are insufficient to meet the same. I have certain jewellery gifted to me by my parents at the time of my marriage. Can my husband force me to part with my jewellery for the said operation?

In modern Hindu law, the term *"stridhan"* denotes property acquired or owned by a woman and over which she has absolute control. It includes gifts made by the woman's parents, like the jewellery given at the time of wedding. A Hindu married woman is the absolute owner of her *stridhan* property and can deal with it in any manner she likes without any interference of her husband. Ordinarily, the husband has no right or interest in such property with the sole exception that in times of extreme distress, as in famine, illness or the like, the husband can utilize it. But he is morally bound to restore it or its value when he is able to do so. In your case, as the property needed is to meet the ends of an operation and hence you may have to part with it.

RECOVERY OF DOWRY

My daughter is being treated badly by her husband and cannot live with him any more. She intends to obtain divorce. Can she also recover the amount given to her husband as dowry?

Under the Dowry Prohibition Act, taking or giving dowry is an offence and any person who gives or takes dowry or abets the giving and taking of such dowry is liable to be imprisoned for it. Hence, if any legal action were taken to get back the dowry amount, the person who gave the dowry in the first place would also be liable for conviction.

However, your daughter can recover the same by claiming it as *Stridhan* of which she is the absolute owner. *Stridhan* constitutes of gifts given to the bride (inter alia, by the mother, father, brother and even 'in-laws' of the bride) whether before, during or after marriage and 'which gifts' are specifically meant for her use. It will be open to her to recover the same through the legal process. If her husband or any other member of his family, who are in possession of such property, dishonestly misappropriates or refuses to return the same, they may be liable for punishment for the offence of criminal breach of trust and misappropriation of property under the Indian Penal Code.

MARRIAGE OUTSIDE INDIA

I am an Indian by birth and am residing in Russia for 1 year. I am in love with an Indian girl who too is residing in Russia for more than 6 months. We are both above 22 yrs. and are Hindu by religion. We would like to marry in Russia itself. Please do let us know about the legal procedure involved for the same.

The marriages of Indian citizens outside India are governed by The Foreign Marriage Act, which entitles an Indian citizen, who is not within the territorial limits of India, to marry any person an Indian or a foreigner. The conditions and the procedure therein involved are as under–

1. The parties should not be within the prohibited degrees of relationship as under the personal laws applicable to them and such marriage should not be prohibited under the law of the foreign country.
2. The parties should be competent to marry i.e. should be major, of sound mind and should consent to such marriage.
3. A notice of their intended marriage should be given to a 'Marriage Officer' so appointed by the Central Government in the country of their residence. Generally the diplomatic representatives in the embassy or the high commission are entrusted to act as such.
4. The notice should be in writing and in the form so specified and should be given to the Marriage Officer of the place where the parties have resided for a minimum period of thirty days.
5. The Marriage Officer shall publish a notice of the intended marriage in his own office, the country of their ordinary residence and in India.
6. If no objection is raised within thirty days of the publication, the marriage may be solemnized in the presence of the Marriage Officer and three witnesses within six months.
7. After solemnization of the marriage the same is recorded in the Marriage Certificate book and is to be signed by the parties and the three witnesses. This is conclusive proof of the marriage.

If the Marriage Officer refuses to solemnize the marriage, a representation may be made to the Central Government.

It is to be noted that any person who gets the marriage solemnized by false representation, or by suppressing facts or by practising fraud may be given a punishment for a term ranging from 4 months to 3 years and fine too.

Even marriage solemnized under any other law can be registered under the Foreign Marriage Act.

It is to be noted that the law governing the same will be as per the Special Marriage Act.

MAINTENANCE

I am a Hindu by religion and unable to maintain myself. I have a sole living daughter but she is married and living separately. Can I demand any money from her for my livelihood?

Under the Code of Criminal Procedure, every person who is capable of is liable to maintain–

(a) His wife, unable to maintain herself;

(b) His legitimate or illegitimate minor child, whether married or not, unable to maintain itself;

(c) His legitimate or illegitimate child (not being a married daughter) who has attained majority where such child is by reason of any physical or mental abnormality, or injury unable to maintain itself;

(e) His father or mother, unable to maintain themselves.

Hence, your daughter is certainly liable to maintain you. What amount of maintenance will be payable to you, depends upon the income of your daughter and the number of her dependants and other conditions which the court may deem fit.

MAINTENANCE - MUSLIM

I am a Muslim without any source of income. I have an earning son; can I demand from him some money for my living expenses?

Yes, you can definitely claim maintenance from your son.

According to Muslim law a person not indigent and possessing means of preventing him from accepting alms is bound to maintain following relatives–

1. Wife;
2. Descendants, i.e. children and grand children;
3. Ascendants, i.e. parents and grandparents;
4. Collaterals within prohibited degrees.

Thus your case is a fit one for such claims.

LEGITIMACY OF A CHILD

I am married to a person who was already married to another lady who was alive at the time of our marriage. We have a son out of our marriage. I fear my son being called illegitimate. Is it so? Also, will he have any say in his father's property?

According to the Hindu law, no person who is marrying should have a living spouse. Thus, your marriage has no validity in the eyes of law. So far as the case of your child is concerned, he shall be considered as a legitimate child for all purposes and is even entitled to inherit the property of his father.

HOMOSEXUALITY

We are two females fulfilling each other's physical desires for the last 3 years, and feel quite comfortable about it. Is there any law which can give our relationship a sanction of legal marriage?

Same-sex marriages, which may also be called homosexual marriages, have been accepted in some countries, but are not accepted / admitted in India.

The Hindu Marriage Act, deals with offences like bigamy, polygamy and child marriage, but does not deal with same-sex marriages. The Act does not expressly prohibit or permit marriages between persons of same sex. However, as per the definition of marriage, since marriage cannot take place between persons other than a man and a woman, therefore, even if two women/men have followed the customary rights of marriage, their living together is no marriage and hence they don't have any right which arises out of a valid marriage.

Also, as the Act does not recognize a marriage of the same sex, there is no penalty prescribed in this Act. But, it is noteworthy to mention here that the Indian Penal Code does prohibit having sexual intercourse against the order of nature, and two persons of same sex will be liable to imprisonment for life or imprisonment extending to 10 years and also fine. However, such is capable of being imposed subject to the satisfaction that there is a physical relationship.

MARRIAGE CERTIFICATE

I have been married for 3 years as per the traditional mode. Both of us now plan to settle abroad. I have been told that while procuring visa we have to submit a marriage certificate. Is it so? How can we get the certificate?

It is true that a marriage certificate is an essential requisite for obtaining visa. For obtaining a marriage certificate, the parties to the marriage have to enter the particulars of the marriage in the Hindu Marriage Register so provided for as per the Hindu Marriage Act. The relevant provision for doing so may vary from State to State as the Act enables the State Governments to make its own rules for the purposes of registration of marriages. However, it is relevant to note that registration merely serves as a proof of a Hindu Marriage being solemnized and in case of non-registration it does not affect a valid marriage.

The marriage certificate can be obtained by filling the prescribed form available at a nominal fee with the Registrar and is required to be duly signed by the parties. It is also relevant to note here that the following documents have to be annexed with the form: -

a. Documentary proofs of date of birth of both the parties;
b. A copy of the ration card,
c. Two passport size photographs of the parties,
d. Marriage invitation card, if available,
e. One marriage photograph duly attested by a gazated officer.
f. In case of a divorcee, an attested copy of divorce decree / order and in the case of a widow / widower, death certificate of spouse needs to be filed,
g. Separate affidavits from the husband and wife have to be furnished stating –
   i. Date and place of marriage,
   ii. Date of birth,
   iii. Citizenship,
   iv. Marital status at the time of marriage,

v. Affirmation that the parties are not related to each other within the prohibited degree of relationship as per Hindu Marriage Act.

h. In case of a foreign national, a certificate from the concerned embassy regarding his or her present marital status,

i. In case one of the parties belongs to a religion other than Hindu, Buddhist, Jain and Sikh, a conversion certificate from the priest who solemnized the marriage would be required.

j. If the marriage has been solemnized at a religious place, a certificate from the priest is also required.

Under the Hindu Marriage Act, registration will be done on the next working day. Thereafter, the Registrar on application and on payment of the prescribed fee shall give certified extracts of the same from the Hindu Marriage Register, which we call as Marriage Certificate.

PROOF OF MARRIAGE

My friend, who is a Hindu, is living with a man as wife and husband though there's no legal proof as to their marriage. Now the friend's husband is going out with another girl and I have heard that they intend to marry. Is there any way of stopping the said marriage?

According to the Hindu Marriage Act, a Hindu marriage may be solemnized in accordance with the customary rites and ceremonies of either party thereto. The right so recognized by the Act is *saptpadi*, and only then the marriage becomes complete. It is to be noted that strict proof of the marriage is required and mere living together of a man and woman as husband and wife would not normally give them the status of husband and wife unless there is evidence that they have been living together for years altogether as husband and wife, which may lead to a legal presumption of marriage. However, it is to be noted that it is for the party who claims to have been married to a person to show that he/she was duly married according to the customary rites and ceremonies. The observance of these ceremonies must be specifically pleaded and established by evidences.

Hence, only if your friend can prove that they were married, and then only their marriage may be deemed valid one and she would be able to stop the subsequent marriage.

COURT MARRIAGE

We are of different castes, but belonging to the same religion. Our parents are against our marriage and we do not have the means to go for the elaborate and expensive procedure of marriage. I have heard that couples can also marry in courts. What is the procedure of doing so?

Marriage in courts is termed as court marriages and it is not necessary that the same happens in the court premises, but it signifies that a specially empowered person of the court conducts the marriage. In court marriages, the parties to the marriage will have to get the marriage registered under the Special Marriage Act. According to the same, a prescribed form is to be collected on payment of a nominal fee from the office of the Registrar. On submission of the form, 30 days notice period is given whereafter, the parties to the intended marriage will have to produce legal documents like birth certificate and ration card, which will notify you as a citizen of the country. Then a date for marriage is fixed, which is generally done seeing the convenience of the parties and on the date of marriage both the parties have to go to the office, take oath and sign in a register. Two witnesses are also required to sign the same. This concludes the marriage and a certificate is issued as a proof of marriage.

SEX DETERMINATION

I am a father of two girls and my wife is again pregnant. I don't want to beget any female child so I wish to know the sex of the foetus, but have come to know that the government has prohibited 'sex determination'. Is it true and if caught what is the punishment?

Sex determination of a foetus is prohibited under the Pre-Natal Diagnostic Techniques Act, wherein it has been specifically mentioned that no parental diagnostic techniques including chorionic villi testing or ultra sonography will be carried out for the purpose of determining the sex of the foetus.

However, such diagnostic techniques can be used only in certain specified circumstances like: -

1. If it is threatened that the foetus is having some chromosomal abnormality.
2. If the foetus has the probability of having sex linked diseases.
3. If there is some congenital abnormality in the foetus.
4. If there is chance of having congenital haemoglobinaemia.
5. If there is any genetic metabolic disorder.
6. Any other condition as decided by the Central Committee.

These tests cannot be performed without taking the consent of the mother and explaining fully well the harms and the benefits of the test. The consent must be taken in her language and in writing.

So, in no condition whatsoever the said test can be used for determining the sex of the foetus. The law not only punishes the person conducting the test for this purpose but also the person who seeks such determination by imprisonment which may extend to 3 years and fine upto Rs. 10,000/-.

•••

CHAPTER – 3
THE PROCEDURE OF COURTS

INSTITUTING SUIT

I reside in Pune and entered into a contract with Mr. X, who resides at Bangalore. The documents relating to the Contract were signed into at Calcutta. Mr. X has breached the terms of a contract and I want to initiate proceedings against him. Please suggest me about the place and court for the institution of a suit.

Your case involves two issues to be determined. The first being, the place where you can file your case. The Code of Civil Procedure provides for some options where you can initiate the proceedings. While ascertaining the place for suing one should be very careful because when a case is filed in either of the options provided by the Code the other option to file the same case ceases to exist.

The law governing the movable and immovable properties differs from each other. Your question is silent about the subject matter of the contract. If the contract related to immovable property. In such case the suit should be instituted where the property is situated.

The law governing the wrongs, to person or movable property is almost similar. The suit for compensation for the wrong to the person or movables can be instituted at a place where the wrong was done or where the defendant resides or carries on business or personally works for gain. (Explanation: the word wrong used in this paragraph usually denotes a tort but it sometimes is treated as a breach of contract)

In other suits where the cause of action wholly or in part arose; or the defendant resides or carries on business or personally works for gain.

If there are two or more defendants living in different places, the suit can be instituted at a place where anyone of them resides, carries on business or personally works for gain. In such a case if you chose to file a case in any one court then you should obtain leave of court from the court, which also has jurisdiction over the same subject matter by virtue of any of the circumstances mentioned in this paragraph.

After determining the territorial jurisdiction, the pecuniary jurisdiction of the case should be determined. In our country we have, following Civil Court structure, namely Small Causes Court, Civil Judge Junior Division, Civil Judge Senior Division, Assistant District Judge, Additional District Judge, District Judge. These courts are placed in hierarchy, according to their ascending pecuniary limits to try the case. It is to be noted that every suit shall be instituted in the court of lowest grade competent to try it. The rule laid down is a rule of procedure and does not affect the jurisdiction of the court. Hence, a decree passed by a higher grade cannot be said to be without jurisdiction, but it is merely an irregularity and the decree passed by the court is not a nullity.

So keeping in mind the pecuniary jurisdiction you can ascertain the appropriate court to initiate proceedings.

The legislators of our country have also made provisions for speedy disposal of cases. Alternate Forums or 'Special Courts' are created to deal with certain matters. These courts e.g. Consumer Forum, Family Court, Labour Tribunal etc are constituted to decide matters, which falls under their specific jurisdiction. It would be pertinent to note here that in contact cases an option to chose an adjudging authority is provided to the parties, if the parties have an arbitration clause in their contract. You will have to check for the same in your contract.

After determining the jurisdiction the next step is institution of suit. For this, a plaint i.e. a document which contains the complain / grievance of the party, needs to be drafted in the prescribed format. It is then to be filed along with the prescribed Court fees and the required stamps. Once the plaint is filed the Court Registry gives a number and thereby the suit is instituted.

SUIT BY MINOR

I am a minor belonging to a joint family and my parents are not alive. My relatives are trying to grab / sell the property including my share. I wish to sue and defend my right and title over the said property. Please help.

Under the law minor cannot sue or be sued. However if you wish to establish or defend your title, it can be done with the help of a next friend / guardian.

Thus in such case, you can sue through a next friend. In case a suit is instituted without appointing a next friend the same is liable to be dismissed with costs payable by the concerned advocate.

Further if in any suit the minor is to be made a defendant then the court will appoint a guardian to represent his interests.

INDIGENT PERSON

A suit has been filed against me; I am financially incapable of bearing any litigation expenses. Is there any way that I can be exempted from the fees involved in the suit?

The law deems financially incapable persons as indigent provided–

(1) He does not possess property other than those exempted from attachment to enable him to pay the fees so prescribed,

(2) Where no fee is prescribed he is not entitled to a property worth Rs. 1000/- (Property other than those exempted).

Under the law a person who is financially incapable is given protection in case of institution of a suit. For this the concerned person has to apply to the court for exemption from payment of any court fees. The court may after being satisfied of the bona fide and the genuineness of the application may grant an order exempting from payment of the court fee. Such order does not compulsorily continue till whole of the suit but only till the indigency continues.

In case of defending a suit instituted against an indigent person, the Code of Civil Procedure as well as the Legal Services Authorities Act, prescribes for 'free legal services' for such persons.

NOTICE TO GOVERNMENT

The municipality has ordered demolition of my house for some ulterior motives though I have represented the authorities not to do so. Yet I fear that they will go ahead with it. I wish to file a writ against the same and would like to know whether giving a prior notice to the Government is mandatory as provided in Sec 80 of C.P.C.?

Notice to the Government u/s 80 is an essential condition in case of institution of suits against the government. Writ proceedings are not suits but quite different from it, hence no notice is required in such a situation. However if you wish to institute a suit you will be required to wait for a period of 2 months after serving the notice so that the government can have an opportunity to ascertain their position.

AMENDMENT

I have already filed a written statement in the court along with the affidavit. However, I have come to know of such circumstances, which though favourable to me are completely in contrary to the written statement so submitted. Can I be allowed to replace the earlier written statement with this new one?

A written statement is a pleading submitted before a court of law. The law has contemplated situations wherein there might be need of a party to alter or amend his pleading. For this an application is to be made to the court which may at any stage of the proceedings allow either party to alter or amend the pleadings in such manner and on such terms as may be just, and all such amendments shall be made as may be necessary for the purpose of determining the real questions of controversy (issue) between the parties.

However it is to be noted that the court while granting

permission for amendment will ascertain as to whether in spite of due diligence the party seeking amendment could not have raised the matter before the commencement of the trial. It is to be noted that in a number of cases the courts have refrained from allowing the party to completely alter their stand in an amendment petition.

The term 'pleading' denotes not only a written statement but also a plaint and an affidavit.

SUMMON

I am a plaintiff in a suit and for speedy disposal wishes to have the appearance of the other party. For this I have duly served summons by registered post. However the opposite party has avoided the same. Is there any mode of ensuring his presence in the Court? What if he receives the summons and does not appear even though?

If the other party is purposely avoiding the summons, and the letter is returned to you with the said remark, then it will be deemed service of summons.

The court may in the alternative direct you to serve summons via registered post with AD at his permanent address or his last known place of residence or where he carries out his business. The court may also direct for affixing of the notice at his permanent place of residence. The last resort for service of summons is getting it published in a local newspaper of the place where he resides. If in spite of these he does not turn up then this will amount to deemed service of summons and the court will proceed ex-parte.

However, if his presence is very essential for the disposal of the suit and the court is of the opinion that he has absconded or is about to abscond or has disposed of or removed any property from the local limits of the jurisdiction of the court, the court may issue a warrant of arrest or an attachment order in respect to the property belonging to the said person and described by the plaintiff.

INTERIM ORDER

My brother is in possession of a property leased out on

rent, which my father has gifted to me. Now I have instituted a suit against my brother claiming title over the same. Can I restrain him from receiving rents and at the same time seek directions from the court ordering the tenant to deposit rent in the court during pendency of the suit.

An injunction can be sought from the court restraining your brother from receiving the rent.

However for the same the court will ensure appearance of your brother and only after hearing the parties and keeping in view the balance of convenience and the flexibility of the relief, depending upon the facts and circumstances of the case, may grant such order as it deems fit during the pendency of the suit.

In your case as the ownership over the said property is in dispute and if the rent is being paid to him, you will suffer immense hardship therefore balance of convenience lies in your favour. The Court may grant such injunction for such period as it deems fit.

EX-PARTE

The advocate who was conducting my case in the lower court was also practising in the appellate court. So I decided to authorize him to appear and defend my case in the appellate court even. He duly appeared and filed the *Vakalatnama* and received a copy of the memo of appeal. However thereafter he failed to appear on the relevant dates and ultimately the court adjudicated the matter 'ex-parte'. What can I do to have my case re-heard, as the said decision was not on account of any fault of mine but on the sole negligence of the advocate concerned?

An advocate is an agent of the party and any act done or any statement made by him within the limits of the authority given to him are deemed to be the acts and statements of the principal i.e. the party who has engaged him.

Hence, whatever is the consequence of the proceedings the same is binding upon the parties and the party cannot simply disown the acts of the advocate, be it negligence or misrepresentation or otherwise.

However, in certain situations the court may, in the interest of justice, set aside the dismissal order or an exparte decree notwithstanding the negligence and / or misdemeanor of the advocate, especially when the client is an innocent / illiterate litigant.

The Hon'ble Supreme Court has laid down certain guidelines while setting aside the exparte decree on case of negligence or misrepresentation, viz, the tenure of the litigation, the party's co-operation with the court throughout its pendency i.e. the intention of the defaulting party, whether there were any deliberate efforts to delay the proceedings, the background of the defaulting party and its competency to follow the court proceeding in order to protect his interests are some of the considerations that are required to be paid attention to while setting aside the said decree. For setting aside the said ex-parte decree, a petition to the effect may be filed either before the same court or the appellate court, or even before the Hon'ble High Court which has the power to try such under the power of superintendence so given to it under the Constitution of India.

EXEMPTION FROM ATTACHMENT

A decree has been passed against me for payment of the due amount so owed by me. However, I am a retired person and living on pension which is barely sufficient for my own survival. The creditor has threatened me of obtaining an order of attachment of my pension for satisfaction of his debt. Isn't there any safeguard under the law, which can prevent him from doing so which will ultimately put me in a starving situation?

Having a debt, which is legally payable, ought to be settled and the law does provide for attachment of the property of the debtor, if he fails to pay the same.

However, the law recognizes certain essentials of life, which cannot be attached.

According to the Code of Civil Procedure:

(1) The following property is liable to attachment and sale in execution of a decree, namely,

a. Lands, houses or other buildings,
b. Goods,
c. Money, banknotes, cheques, bills of exchange, hundis, promissory notes, government securities, bonds or other securities for money, debts, shares in corporation and,
d. All other saleable property, movable or immovable, belonging to the judgment-debtor, or over which, he has a disposing power which he may exercise for his own benefit, whether the same is held in the name of the judgment-debtor or by another person in trust for him or on his behalf,

(2) However, the following are liable not to be attachment or sold in execution of a decree, namely,

(a) The necessary wearing-apparel, cooking vessels, beds and bedding of the judgment-debtor, his wife and children, and such personal ornaments as, in accordance with religious usage, cannot be parted with by any woman;

(b) Tools of artisans and where the judgment-debtor is an agriculturist, his instruments of husbandry and such cattle and seed-grain as may, in the opinion of the court, be necessary to enable him to earn his livelihood, and such portion of agricultural produce or of any class of agricultural produce as may have been declared to be free from liability under the provisions of law;

(c) Houses and other buildings (with the materials and the sites thereof and the land immediately appurtenant thereto and necessary for their enjoyment) belonging to an agriculturist or a labourer or a domestic servant] and occupied by him;

(d) Books of account;

(e) A mere right to sue for damages;

(f) Any right of personal service;

(g) Stipends and gratuities allowed to pensioners of the government [or of a local authority or of any other employer] or payable out of any service pension fund notified in the official gazette by the Central Government or the State Government in this behalf, and political pension;

(h) The wages of labourers and domestic servants, whether payable in money or in kind;

(i) Salary to the extent of [the first (one thousand rupees) and two third of the remainder] in execution of any decree other than a decree for maintenance.

Provided that where any part of such portion of the salary as is liable to attachment has been under attachment, whether continuously or intermittently, for a total period of twenty-four months, such portion shall be exempt from attachment until the expiry of a further period of twelve months, and, where such attachment has been made in execution of one and the same decree, shall, after the attachment has continued for a total period of twenty-four months, be finally exempt from attachment in execution of that decree.

(ia) $1/3^{rd}$ of the salary in execution of any decree for maintenance;

(j) The pay and allowances of persons to whom the Air Force Act or the Army Act or the Navy Act applies;

(k) All compulsory deposits and other sums in or derived from any fund to which the Provident funds Act, 1925, for the time being applies in so far as they are declared by the said Act not to be liable to attachment;

(ka) All deposits and other sums in or derived from any fund to which the Public Provident Fund Act, 1968 for the time being applies in so far as they are declared by the said Act as not to be liable to attachment;

(kb) All moneys payable under a policy of insurance on the life of the judgment-debtor;

- (kc) The interest of a lessee of a residential building to which the provisions of law for the time being in force relating to control of rents and accommodation apply;
- (l) Any allowance forming part of the emoluments of any servant of the Government or of any servant of a railway company or local authority which the appropriate Government may by notification in the official gazette declare to be exempt from attachment, and any subsistence grant for allowance made to any such servant while under suspension;
- (m) An expectancy of succession by survivorship or other merely contingent or possible right or interest;
- (n) A right to future maintenance;
- (o) Any allowance declared by any Indian law to be exempt from liability to attachment or sale in execution of a decree; and
- (p) Where the judgment-debtor is a person liable for the payment of land-revenue; any movable property which, under any law for the time being applicable to him, is exempt from sale for the recovery of an arrears of such revenue.

It is to be noted that the moneys payable in relation to the matters mentioned in clauses (g), (h), (i), (ia), (j), (1) and (o) are exempt from attachment or sale, whether before or after they are actually payable, and, in the case of salary, the attachable portion thereof is liable to attachment, whether before or after it is actually payable.

The term 'salary' as referred to in clauses (1) and (ia) means the total monthly emoluments, excluding any allowance declared exempt from attachment under the provisions of clause (1) derived by a person from his employment whether on duty or on leave.

The term "wages" includes bonus, and labourer" includes a skilled / unskilled or semi-skilled labourer.

As the said properties are specifically exempted from attachment, any contract to the contrary will be void and not enforceable.

Thus, under the CPC and under the Public Provident Fund Act, 1968, the provident fund is exempted from attachment. Further, according to the Pensions Act of 1971, no pension granted or continued by government on account of past services and no money due or becoming due on account of any such pension or allowance shall be liable to seizure, attachments or sequestration by process of any court for any demand by a creditor against the pensioner or in satisfaction of a decree or order of any such court.

Hence, as your pension, stipend and gratuity are exempted from attachment, the same cannot be attached, you need not fear.

INTERPLEADER SUIT

A property has been mortgaged to me and the title deeds of the same are lying in my possession. Two brothers are claiming the whole property and both are ready to pay the debt. To whom should I give the title deed?

Since the title deed is lying in your possession and you cannot ascertain the true owner and giving the same to the wrong owner might make you liable, hence the appropriate mode would be to institute an Interpleader Suit.

Interpleader Suit means a situation wherein the plaintiff has got no interest in the suit matter, except than charges or the costs and the real dispute is between the defendants.

The court in such a proceeding being satisfied, dismiss the plaintiff i.e. you from the suit after awarding the necessary costs.

RES JUDICATA

A judgment was passed 10 years ago in my favour in a land dispute between my brother and me. I have come to know that he has again instituted a suit in respect of the same matter in another court. Isn't there any way by which I can stop him or will I have to fight the lengthy legal battle again?

If the said second suit, is in form of an appeal made before a higher court, then the only remedy is to defend your case in the appellate court by pleading that the appeal is time-barred under the Law of Limitation apart from other grounds of defence.

However, if the second suit is not an appeal but a separate (new) suit then in such a situation and under the law, re-agitation of the same matter is prohibited. The principles of Res judicata will come into play, which expressly debars any court from trying any suit, which has already been decided in a former suit in respect of the same matter and in respect of the same parties, by a competent court.

RES SUBJUDICE

Courts take a long time in disposal of suits. I wish to institute a suit in respect of a land dispute. However, the said land is situated in one place while the defendant is residing in other place. Can I file the case in both the courts and if so which courts decision shall be binding on me.

The law prohibits institution of two simultaneous suits in different courts. If a suit has already been instituted in one court and if another suit is instituted in a different court under the same law, in respect of the same subject matter and between the same parties, then the court will refrain from entertaining the second suit on the ground that the matter is already pending before another competent court. This principle is called as Res-subjudice.

Hence, you cannot file two simultaneous suits in different courts.

In your case as the subject matter is immovable property, the appropriate court is the court having territorial jurisdiction over the place where the immovable property or the land is situated.

It is noteworthy to mention here that there may be instances when two cases are filed pertaining to the same matter and between the same parties.

However, if they are being filed under different law, then the cause of action becomes different and hence the principle of res judicata or ressubjudice will not be applicable and such cases are permissible.

For example, in a case of medical negligence, a suit for claiming damages / compensation can be filed along with a criminal case for punishing the negligent doctor and any of the principle of res judicata or res subjudice will not apply.

DELAY IN SUIT DISPOSAL

I have heard that suits take a lot of time for disposal, I would like to know as to why does such a delay happens?

No doubt suits take a long time in disposal. The main reasons behind these are: -

a. Less number of courts,
b. Less number of judges,
c. Large number of suits pending (Approx 3 crore in various courts in India),
d. Procedural / technical delays like–
   1. Defect in filing a plaint,
   2. Delay in issuance of summons, may be because of wrong address of parties or on account of delay in dispatching summons or other party avoiding summon, etc.,
   3. Delay and non-appearance of parties purposefully or due to ignorance,
   4. Delay in filing replies by the opposite party purposefully or due to ignorance,
   5. Delay and non-appearance of witnesses / production of evidences on account of delay in service of summons or the witnesses being not interested in coming or the evidences may not be easily forthcoming or other like matters.
   6. Hearing / argument taking long time and the advocate or the court seeking / granting adjournments.
   7. Passing of judgment by the court may be delayed on some consideration or the other of the judge.

Apart from these, long dates are given which is the prime cause of this long delay. Adjournments too are major reason. However this delay has been tried to be curtailed by way of major amendments in the Code of Civil Procedure wherein summons can now be served by courier even. It has also limited the maximum number of adjournments, which can now be granted only thrice. Various fast track courts and tribunals have been constituted. Judgments too are required to be passed within 1 month from the date the judgment is reserved.

ALTERNATIVE FORUM

I am a holder of a dishonoured cheque and have instituted a case under the Negotiable Instrument Act 1881. Can I also institute another suit in a Civil Court for recovery of the amount?

No doubt the Negotiable Instrument Act has provided special trial / punishment for cases concerning dishonour of cheques. However, it is to be noted that the punishment so provided is imprisonment upto 2 years and / or fine upto twice the amount of the cheque. There is no provision of re-imbursement / payment of the dishonoured amount and hence the provisions of res judicata would not be affected and a suit for recovery of the amount can be filed.

TRANSFER OF CASE

I feel that the judge trying my case is biased against me and would like to change the court. How can I do so?

If you have a strong notion supported with some basis then you can approach the appellate court by making an application for transfer of the suit or any proceeding. The High Court or the District Court is competent to withdraw the suit to itself and thereby dispose it of, or may transfer it to some other court or re-transfer it to the court from which it was withdrawn.

MESNE PROFITS

I had leased out my agricultural land for a period of 10 years with a clause that after the expiry of the said period the land will revert to me and tenancy will terminate. However

the tenancy has continued for 10 years and 6 months. During the last 6 months the tenant has cultivated Indigo and has sold it for a huge profit and is only giving me the 6 months rent. Am I not entitled to part of profit made by him as he has illegally cultivated the same?

Subject to the State Land Laws, if a person makes any profit from a property to which he is in wrongful possession, the said profit is known as Mesne Profit and the owner of the property is liable to recover the same.

In your case once the tenancy expires, and if the law does not prescribe continuance of tenancy, then the tenant was in wrongful possession of the land for the last 6 months and therefore under the Code of Civil Procedure you are entitled to the whole of the profits so made by the tenant excluding the personal expenses which he has incurred over the cultivation.

BENAMI TRANSACTION

I have heard that I cannot purchase land beyond a specified limit. Is it true? What if I purchase the said land in the name of one of my friend whom I trust?

It is absolutely true that lands can only be purchased to a specified limit known as ceiling limit. The limit depends from state to state and you cannot hold any excess land. Also the law prohibits purchase of land in some other person's name. Though in your case it will be difficult to prove that you have purchased the land in your friend's name. Such transactions are called as *Benami* transactions and are prohibited.

•••

Objection Your Honour

CHAPTER – 4
RIGHTS AND LAW

CITIZENSHIP

I am working in an I.T. sector in an MNC. My company is sending me to U.S for training. There is a possibility that I might be provided a job there itself for a long period. Will I lose the citizenship of India in such circumstances?

Citizenship is acquired either by birth or parentage or by registration. A person once a citizen of India continues to be such till he renounces it or it gets terminated on account of voluntarily acquiring citizenship of some other country or where he is deprived of such by the order of the Central Government. Living for prolonged period in a foreign country would not amount to termination of citizenship.

Hence you need not worry of losing the same. It is to be noted that if you acquire the citizenship of another country, then your Indian citizenship shall itself get terminated, as the Indian law does not recognize dual citizenship.

BIRTH CERTIFICATE

My birth date has been wrongly recorded in the municipal records due to which I am now facing trouble in filling out forms of various entrance examinations. Is there any way by which I can get the same corrected?

The entry so recorded in the register of the births and deaths is deemed to be correct and genuine. However, the Registration of Births and Deaths Act lays down procedure for correction of an entry wrongly recorded in the register.

If the wrong entry is on account of a clerical error occasioned by mistake in wrongly entering the date in the register as against the date in the form and is brought immediately to the notice of the Registrar, i.e. within one year of the date so recorded as birth date, the Registrar or any person so authorized by the Commissioner of the municipal corporation may correct the entry by drawing a line across the original entry and writing the correct entry above it and initialize the same. However in case of the same being brought to notice after one year, sanction of the commissioner is necessary.

In cases where the entry so recorded is incorrect on account of error of fact, the Registrar may correct the same by making the correct entry in the margin without any alteration in the original entry and the same shall be initialized and the date of correction be recorded therein. However, the same is regulated by the rules so made by the State Government in this behalf, which basically warrants a declaration on oath to be given by two credible witnesses having knowledge of the case before a magistrate and the magistrate certifies the same being given in his presence.

PUBLIC INTEREST LITIGATION

These days the term PIL is widely used in newspapers. What is it?

The term PIL stands for Public Interest Litigation, which clearly symbolizes a case filed not for self-interest but in the interest of society or a section thereof. There is no compulsion that it should be filed by an advocate only. It is not even necessary that the person filing PIL is to be resident of such place. Recently we witnessed students in Maharashtra filing such cases in Bombay High Court for compulsory helmet usage, restricting pornographic and gambling sites on net, appointment of adjudicating officer under the Information Technology Act, etc.

Thus, we see that the scope of PIL is too broad and can cover anything and everything, which involves well-being of the general mass. We have witnessed a number of such PILs for protection of environment, prevention of terrorism, protection of human rights, protesting against the wrong policies of the government or in the interest of weaker section of the society, like scheduled castes or tribal people, womenfolk, children etc.

Another important aspect of such sort of litigation is that it can be only filed against the government and not against a private party, although the private party can be made a respondent along with the government. We have even witnessed judges accepting mere letters, newspaper reports, articles, etc. as PILs. However, it is the discretion of the court whether to accept such letters as PIL or to discard them. It is to be noted that in case of letters, the same is required to be addressed to the court and not to any particular judge. PILs can also be initiated suo-motto by the courts. No PILs can be filed in a court other than the High Court (under Article 226 of the Constitution of India) or the Supreme Court (under Article 32 of the Constitution of India). A copy of the petition is required to be served to the Government in advance before filing a PIL. When approaching the High Court, the petitioner should file the petition in 2 sets and while approaching the Supreme Court, 5 sets of the petition has to be filed. The other respondents are served with the copy when the notice is issued to them thereon.

UNIFORM CIVIL CODE

There is a vast discrimination between the laws so prevalent in the country. Why can't we have a uniform law governing all the religions?

The Constitution of India lays down a duty upon the Central Government to strive for a uniform civil code. Our country consists of various religious and linguistic people having their own peculiar culture and mode of religious practices. Ours is a democratic country and gives every citizen right to practise and profess religion of his choice. This fundamental right to practice and profess the religion of ones own choice is the main hurdle in having a uniform code in respect of family and religious matters which thereby has affected disparity amongst various religious people in every walk of life.

Having a uniform civil code would have both its positive and negative aspects. A die-hard religious follower would never like to have any restriction upon his way of practising religion. Also, no political party can go for such drastic changes, as it will definitely have a negative impact upon its vote bank esp. in respect of the persons whose religious practices are grossly affected.

It is to be noted that the courts have now adopted the principle of judicial activism and thereby have tried to remove some disparity amongst the various religions, like the judgment of the Bombay High Court while dealing with S. 10 of the Indian Divorce Act, wherein the provision that a Christian wife had to prove adultery along with cruelty or desertion while seeking a divorce, was struck down on the ground that it violates the Fundamental Right of Christian women to live with human dignity under Article 21 of the Constitution

However, this is merely a tip of the iceberg and it will definitely take a long way, as the Hon'ble Supreme Court is itself reluctant to tread this path, which is evident from its observation, "Uniform law for all persons may be desirable. But its enactment in one go may be counterproductive to the unity of the nation." Also, let's take for example that we are to have a uniform law of marriage, then which community will denounce its religious practices and whether we will be ready to accept any other form of marriage, which is not prescribed by our religious text.

RIGHT TO EQUALITY

I. I appeared for an all India entrance examination where total number of seats was 80. My rank was 70th but I was shocked to note that my name was not there in the list of selected candidates. On contacting the management, I was told that the selection was zonewise and they had to select 20 candidates from each zone. Is it fair?

The Constitution of India recognizes equality before law as a Fundamental Right of every citizen. Since all the candidates appeared in an all India level entrance examination, they were to be treated on equal footing and selecting candidates by categorizing

Objection Your Honour

them zone wise would be unconstitutional. You can challenge the same by approaching the Hon'ble High Court or the Hon'ble Supreme Court.

II. I am working in a public sector undertaking. There was a senior post lying vacant for a long time in our department. One of my colleague, who was in fact junior to me approached the Hon'ble High Court for promotion and was granted the same, while I was more eligible for the post. Now it's too embarrassing for me to work under my own junior. How just is it?

The Constitution of India recognizes equality before law and equal protection in matters of opportunity in the public employment.

In your case as you both were entitled for the same and you being senior should have got preference. You can challenge the same by filing a writ petition under Article 226 before the Hon'ble High Court or under Article 32 before the Hon'ble Supreme Court and the said promotion is liable to be cancelled, as this discrimination was illegal and the direction of the Hon'ble High Court may be set aside.

RIGHT TO PROPERTY

I have come to know that the Government is going to acquire our ancestral land for constructing a hospital. Can I stop the government from acquiring the said land, as it is violative of my right to hold property?

Rights are basically of two types - Fundamental Rights, which are the basic-natural-human rights recognized by the Constitution of India, and Legal Rights, which are granted to us under the law. Fundamental Rights cannot be curtailed except according to the restrictions so imposed in the Constitution of India while the Legal Rights can be withdrawn any time according to the will of the authorities concerned.

Initially, Right to Property was a Fundamental Right. However, as acquiring of property needed by the Government to boost land reforms proved to be a troublesome task, the Government opted to withdraw the same from the Fundamental Rights so guaranteed and made it a Legal Right. This enabled the Government to acquire any property for public purpose and pay such sum as it deems fit 'by authority of law'. The Government is capable of acquiring any property under the Land Acquisition Act and may pay such amount in lieu of compensation as it deems fit.

Thus, there is no way of stopping the government from acquiring the land. However, if the government has acquired a land for a specified purpose and the said land is not being used for the same, then the erstwhile owner of the same may file a suit / writ petition for recovery of the said land.

DOUBLE JEOPARDY

I have been prosecuted under the Departmental Proceeding and thereafter dismissed from service. The department has also lodged a criminal case against me. I have heard that no person can be prosecuted and punished twice for the same offence. As I have already been prosecuted and punished whereby I have been dismissed from the job, is the subsequent prosecution before a Criminal Court valid?

No person can be prosecuted and punished after he has earlier been punished for the same offence, which is better known as Double Jeopardy, and the law prohibits it. However in your case it will not be applicable, as prosecution has to be understood in the light of prosecution before the Criminal Court and under the law, prosecution does not cover departmental proceedings. Hence you cannot avail of this protection.

LIFE AND PERSONAL LIBERTY

I have heard that people having any problem or whose rights are violated can seek protection from the court by invoking Article 21. Please throw some light in this respect.

The Hon'ble High Court and the Hon'ble Supreme Court, while exercising their power conferred under Article 226 and 32 of Constitution of India respectively, have widened the scope of

Article 21 to touch every nook and corner of one's life.

Article 21 reads as "No person shall be deprived of his life or personal liberty except according to procedure established by law".

The courts while interpreting life / personal liberty has interpreted it to such an extent so as to include the following rights–

1. Right to speedy trial.
2. Right of a HIV person to be considered for employment.
3. Right of an indigent person to be released on bail when there is no substantial risk of his absconding.
4. Right to be entitled to get compensation for the wrongs occasioned by the executives like in cases of custodial death, etc.
5. Right to be freed when there is inordinate delay on part of the State in bringing an accused to trial if there is no fault on the part of the accused.
6. Right to healthy environment including pollution free water and air, protection against hazardous industries, etc.
7. Right to fair trial and a fair, reasonable and just procedure.
8. Right to health.
9. Right of an accused not to be handcuffed and put to bar-fetters except under exceptional circumstances.
10. Right to livelihood.
11. Right to timely treatment in government hospitals.
12. Right to privacy.
13. Right to live with human dignity.
14. Right to free education upto 14 years of age.
15. Right of succession of women especially the Scheduled Tribe ladies.
16. Right to be given an opportunity of hearing.
17. Right to be released of an under trial prisoner after his confinement in jail exceeds the maximum term so provided for the offence.

18. Right of rehabilitation to a bonded labour.
19. Right to information.
20. Right to shelter.

If any of the aforesaid rights or if one's right to life or personal liberty is being infringed by State machineries, then one can seek assistance of the High Court by approaching it under Article 226 and the Supreme Court under Article 32. However, this remedy is limited only in case of violation of Fundamental Right by the State machinery.

It is worthwhile to mention here that approaching the High Court is much easier and cheaper. Moreover the High Court is competent to try matters related to violation of Legal Right including the Fundamental Right.

TELEPHONE TAPPING

I often hear strange noises in my telephone when I am talking to a specified person. On enquiring I came to know that there is surveillance over me and there is every possibility of my telephone being tapped. I am not into any criminal activities and don't fear my telephone being tapped but I fear about my privacy. Don't I have the Right to Privacy?

The Telegraph Act permits interception of messages (what we call tapping) in certain cases wherein there is an apparent –

1. Occurrence of any public emergency; or
2. In the interest of public safety.

Interception of a message cannot be occasioned on any other ground even if the authority is satisfied of the necessity for doing it.

The Hon'ble Supreme Court has laid down guidelines in which interception of telephone can be done, which are as follows:

1. First of all a competent authority who is either the Home Secretary of the Central Government or the State Government is only empowered to pass an order of interception. However, such power can be delegated to any officer of the Home Department not below the rank of the Joint Secretary.

2. The competent authority is to do so after satisfying itself of the necessity or the expediency to do so –
    i. In the interest of the sovereignty and integrity of the nation; or
    ii. For the security of the State; or
    iii. To protect the friendly relations with other sovereign states; or
    iv. In the public order; or
    v. For preventing incitement to the commission of an offence.

However, it is to be noted that before satisfying itself on these grounds, the authority has to satisfy itself that there is an apparent occurrence of any public emergency or the same is required in the interest of public safety. If these grounds cannot be satisfied then the authority is not competent to issue any interception order.

3. A copy of the order directing interception is to be sent to the review committee within a week of the passage of the order.
4. Before passing of the order, the authority is to ascertain the possibility of acquiring information from other means.
5. The interception order should be for interception of communication between specific addresses, which shall be specified in the order.
6. The interception order will cease to have effect after 2 months from the date of passage unless extended. However, the total duration of the order should not be more than 6 months.
7. The Authority issuing the order is to maintain–
    a) The intercepted communications;
    b) The extent to which material is disclosed
    c) The number of persons and their identity to whom the material is disclosed.
    d) The extent to which the material is copied
    e) The number of copies so made.
8. The use of the materials is to be limited to the minimum,

which is necessary.

9. Copy is to be destroyed where retention no longer necessary.
10. A review committee consisting of the Cabinet Secretary, Law Secretary and Secretary, Telecommunications is to be constituted at the Central Government level. For State government, it will consist of Chief Secretary, Law Secretary and another member other than Home Secretary who are to be appointed by the State Government.
11. The review committee is on its own empowered to investigate within 2 months of the order, the fact as to whether the order is relevant and legal.
12. If the committee comes to the conclusion that there is contravention, it is to direct destruction of the materials and if no contravention, the committee is to record its findings to that effect.

So you should not worry if your activities are legal, as the interception has to be carried out between specified addresses and the same is not to be disclosed. However, if you feel that the guidelines so stated above are not being followed or you are being unnecessarily harassed, you can make a representation to the review committee or you can even directly approach the High Court or the Supreme Court claiming infringement of your Fundamental Right of privacy and right to speech and expression.

BONDED LABOUR

My friend's father had taken a loan from the local zamindar but failed to repay him within the stipulated period. Thereafter my friend was forced to work for him without any wages and is working there since a long time. I do think that the loan amount ought to be cleared by now and would like to free him. What can I do?

Such type of forced labour is known as Bonded Labour and is prohibited under the Bonded Labour System (Abolition) Act.

Bonded Labour System means the system of forced labour in which a debtor enters or is presumed to have entered into an

agreement with the creditor that–
a) He or his family member would work for the creditor either without wages or with nominal wages, or
b) Would not move freely, or
c) Would not sell or appropriate any property belonging to him or his dependants.

Any person who is working as a bonded labourer is, as per the provisions of the Act, freed and is discharged from all obligations and such debt or liability to pay such debt would stand extinguished. Further, all property mortgaged / sold in pursuance to such bonded debt to the creditor is liable to be returned to the bonded labourer. Also, bonded labourer is not liable to be evicted from the premises, which he was occupying in consideration for the bonded labour and if he is removed from such, the bonded labourer is liable to be reinstated to such. The Act punishes every person who compels another to render any bonded labour or advances any amount as bonded debt with imprisonment upto 3 years and with fine upto Rs. 2000/-

Thus, clearly irrespective of the fact that the amount be satisfied or not, your friend is liable to be freed and if he has been forced to work after the date of the commencement of the Act i.e. 25/10/1975, the zamindar is liable for the above punishments. The competent authority is the District Magistrate who is competent to free and abolish such practices and if he fails to do so, the High Court or the Supreme Court can be approached for such relief.

NATIONAL FLAG

I am a fashion designer and would like to promote national feeling/unity using the National Flag in my products. Would I be violating any law while doing so?

No doubt while living in a democratic country one would like to inculcate patriotism amongst fellow countrymen, but the same ought to be done within the boundaries of law.

Under the Constitution of India, all citizens have a duty to respect its ideals and institutions, the National Flag and the National

Anthem. Further, the Prevention of Insults to National Honour Act prohibits all persons from burning, mutilating, defacing, defiling, disfiguring, destroying, trampling upon or otherwise bringing into contempt, whether by words, either spoken or written or by acts, the National Flag or any part thereof in any public place within public view and any person who does so is liable to be punished. Also, according to the Flag Code, guidelines have been prescribed wherein it has categorically been mentioned, "the Tiranga must not be used as a portion of a costume or uniform of any description". However, it is worthwhile to mention here that the said Flag Code is not a law but a mere executive direction and hence no contravention thereof is liable for punishment subject to the said act not contravening the Emblems Act and the Prevention of Insults to National Honour Act.

I do respect your sentiments but the same will not be permissible as per the law.

CONTEMPT OF COURT

I feel that the recent decision given by the Hon'ble Supreme Court is not socially and morally correct. Can I present my bona fide comment including criticism or will it amount to Contempt of Court?

Presenting a bona fide comment including criticism would not amount to Contempt of Court unless the same is done with malice or in order to defame or disrepute the judiciary. Judiciary is the pillar of the administration of justice, having enormous responsibility of protecting the citizens and for the same the citizens must have faith in it. Therefore anything which tends to cause the citizen to lose faith over it or its functioning will seriously impair its functioning. According to an old saying, "you can criticize the judgment but not the judge."

Under the Contempt of Courts Act, nothing shall be deemed to be contempt in connection with any civil or criminal proceeding which is not pending at the time of publication of the alleged matter / article. Further a person shall not be guilty of contempt of court for publishing any fair comment on the merits of any case, which has been heard and finally decided. However, if it transgresses the limits of fair and bona fide criticism, it will definitely amount to contempt of court.

It is also to be noted that no court can initiate any proceeding of contempt, either on its own motion or otherwise, after the expiry of a period of one year from the date on which the contempt is alleged to have been committed.

Thus presenting your bona fide view on a judgment would not amount to contempt unless you transgress the limits, which may make you liable for the same.

ATTORNEY GENERAL

What is the duty of the Attorney General?

The Attorney General is regarded as the chief law officer of the country. His office is created under the Constitution of India and is appointed by the President. The minimum qualification required for becoming The Attorney General is that as required for appointment of a Judge of the Hon'ble Supreme Court of India. He holds office during the pleasure of the President and his function includes–

a) To give legal advice to the Government of India, on matters referred to him by the President of India.

b) To perform such other duties of legal character which the President may assign. The President has assigned him the duty to appear on behalf of Government of India in all the cases in which the Government of India is concerned and to represent it in any reference made by the President to the Hon'ble Supreme Court.

c) He has the 'right of audience' in all Courts in India.

d) He has also right to speak and take part in the proceedings of either House of Parliament but he is not entitled to vote.

Similarly the Governor of the State appoints Advocate General who has qualification as required to be appointed a Judge of the Hon'ble High Court to represent and advise the State Government in all legal matters.

DIFFERENCE BETWEEN ADVOCATE, BARRISTER, ATTORNEY AND SOLICITOR

What is the difference between an advocate, barrister, solicitor and an attorney?

In India the term literally means the same and is the expression used for the person who holds a law degree and is enrolled with the State Bar Council to assist, defend, plead or prosecute for others in the legal aspect before the court. However in some High Courts like Mumbai, the barrister is a person who has to pass an exam to this effect.

UNTOUCHABILITY

There's a temple built by my friend, which is within his boundary. However the same is open to every person except the Harijans. I have heard that there can be no restriction on the right to worship in a temple. Is it true?

As per the facts stated, it seems that your friend is practising untouchability, which is prohibited under law. Though the said temple appears to be a private one and if only limited persons are allowed to worship there, it would not become a public temple. Moreover what persons are to be allowed and what are not to be allowed is within your friend's sole discretion. However such should not be against the provisions of the Constitution.

In this case your friend can impose restriction of use of the temple for friends, family or whomsoever he wishes, but if he does so on the basis of discrimination on caste, he will be violating the provisions of law and liable for strict punishment.

ADVOCATE LOSING CASE WILLINGLY

I lost the case as my advocate did not raise certain facts, which were very crucial and would definitely have turned the decision in my favour. During the course of the proceeding, I also felt that the advocate might have tied up with the opposition. What can I do?

If you strongly feel that your advocate has lost the case purposely, then a complaint can be made to the Disciplinary Committee of the State Bar Council which shall fix a date for hearing of the case and issue notice to the concerned advocate and the Advocate General of the State. After hearing them, the committee may either dismiss the complaint or let off the Advocate with a warning or suspend him for such period as it deems fit or may even remove his name from the State advocate roll. It is to be noted here that the finding in the disciplinary proceeding is sustained by a higher degree of proof than that required in civil suits.

In respect to the case, which is lost, you can approach the appellate or the Hon'ble High Court under Civil Review and place your grounds, for setting aside the order and retrial of the matter. The court may, if it feels fit, pass such order as it deems necessary.

ELECTION IRREGULARITIES - VOTER CARD

Our elections are nearby and I have just received my voter card, which has gross mistake in regard to my name and sex. My actual name is Namit, whereas in the voter card, it's printed as Namita and in spite of me being a male I have been declared to be a female. Will I be able to cast vote now?

The election office / machinery has to arrange for a large number of voters in a very short period and such clerical errors cannot be ruled out. We would suggest you to first approach the appropriate authority concerned for election in your constituency to have it rectified. Generally the Sub-Divisional Officer or the District Magistrate is empowered to do so.

Even if it is not possible to do so, still your right to franchise (to cast vote) cannot be snatched, merely due to some printing error. You can at the time of election carry some other identification proof like driving license, ration card or I-Card issued by your employer etc. along with the said voter card to prove your identity to the poling officer who is authorized to permit you to cast vote after ascertaining your identity.

CHANGE IN NAME

I have recently married and wish to keep the title of my husband. What is the procedure of changing name?

In general a woman after marriage wishes to keep the husband's last name. Under law, for the change of name, an affidavit swearing the same has to be executed and notarized by a notary officer. The same also needs to be published in a local newspaper, which would ascertain that every person would come to know the change of name. A copy of the affidavit along with an application to this effect is to be given to all machineries like bank, L.I.C., employer's etc including the municipality, which will after verification carry out the necessary changes.

WRITS

Many a time I have observed a prayer in the pleadings, requesting the court for issuance of an appropriate writ. What is a Writ?

A Writ is a written command or a formal order issued by a court directing someone to do or refrain from doing an act specified therein. The power to issue a Writ vests only in the Supreme Court and the High Court. No other court in India is capable of granting Writs.

As mentioned in Art 32 and Art 226 of the Constitution, Writs are of 5 kinds, i.e.–

1. Writ of Habeas Corpus
2. Writ of Mandamus
3. Writ of Prohibition
4. Writ of Quo Warranto
5. Writ of Certiorari

Generally a Writ of Habeas Corpus is granted to produce a person detained illegally before the court. A Writ of Mandamus is issued directing or prohibiting an authority to do or from doing something. Writ of Prohibition and Certiorari are granted against an inferior judicial authority. In Prohibition, the inferior authority is prohibited from going on with the proceedings while Certiorari is an order correcting the order of the inferior authority. Writ of Quo Warranto is a question posed by the court to an authority holding a public post to show his authority under which he is holding that post.

HABEAS CORPUS

My brother was arrested by the police but has not been produced in the court yet. When I went to inquire about him, the police constable assaulted me brutally and threatened me of dire consequences if I ever stated that they had ever arrested my brother. I have come to know that they are trying to make him accept responsibility of a certain crime, which he has not committed. I have approached the higher officials including the politicians, but in vain. What should I do to get my brother released from these brutal beings?

As per the facts stated above, it seems that the police is illegally detaining your brother. Under the Constitution of India, which is the mother of all enactments, no person is to be detained illegally and if so detained any person interested in him has the right to approach the High Court or the Supreme Court for issuance of a Writ of Habeas Corpus. Habeas Corpus means bringing the body.

The Supreme Court or High Court is competent to issue the Writ of Habeas Corpus in the following circumstances;

1. Where detention is prima facie illegal, i.e. there is no law to support the detention;

2. Where the detention is made under some provision of law and the provision is unconstitutional and has been challenged,

3. Where the detention is not in consonance with the procedure established by law.

Vide this writ, the court orders the person or authority or the Government who has detained any person violating his constitutional or some material legal right, to bring such person before such court.

A petition of habeas corpus may be filed by the detained person himself or by somebody else who is either related or has an interest in him. An Advocate holding a power of attorney (*Vakalatnama*) may also file such petition in his behalf.

However, if a person other than a detainee is filing the petition, the petitioner has to state reasons as to why the detainee could not make the petition with affidavit himself.

It is to be noted that even a letter sent by the detainee to the court may be taken as a writ petition for habeas corpus. Also, a pending prosecution in some case is no bar to issue the Writ of Habeas Corpus.

MANDAMUS

Due to slackness of the municipality, our entire locality is strewn with garbage, which has given rise to various water and air born diseases. We have contacted the municipal authorities for removal of the same; however, they are showing total disregard to our sufferings, which has made living here a hell. Can we somehow compel the municipality to perform its duty and remove the garbage?

Right to a healthy environment has been recognized as a Fundamental Right under Article 21 and if any person is deprived of such due to State inaction / action, he can approach the High Court or the Supreme Court by filing a Writ petition or a Public Interest Litigation claiming issuance of a Writ of Mandamus directing upon the concerned authority to perform its duty.

A Writ of Mandamus is a command / an order to the government, authority, corporation, to do or to forbear from doing something, which he is legally bound to do or not to do and is either violating or evading it.

Any person, whose right is directly affected by the non-performance or violation of a legal duty, can apply for issuance of the writ of mandamus.

A writ of mandamus will lie against a person who holds a public office, public body, or corporation, or an inferior court or a tribunal. But it does not lie against a private person. The following conditions must be satisfied for issuance of the Writ of Mandamus.

(1) The respondent must be duty bound to perform some act, which is of public nature, and not merely some contractual obligations. Also, such duty should not be directory in nature i.e. the respondent should not have the option of not doing it;

(2) That the respondent is either not performing the duty or violating the law which mandates it to perform such duty;

(3) That on consequence of such violation or evasion, a legal right or the constitutional right of the petitioner is being infringed;

(4) That there exists no alternative remedy, which is swift and efficacious. Mere existence of an alternative remedy is no bar for issuance of a writ of mandamus.

Hence, you can approach the High Court or the Supreme Court for issuance of such Writ wherein the Court may issue a command upon the municipality to perform its duty and thereby remove the garbage from your area. Such can be done even by filing a Public Interest Litigation.

QUO WARRANTO

By a recent notification, one person who did not have any qualification for appointment as a Vice-chancellor in the university was appointed therein. No doubt the government has the power to appoint any person, but such appointment will grossly affect the working of the university. Can I challenge the said appointment even though I am not a contestant to that post?

You can challenge the said appointment by filing a writ petition in the High Court or the Supreme Court, praying for issuance of a Writ of Quo Warranto.

A Writ of Quo Warranto is issued where a person holds some independent public office without a constitutional or legal authority. This writ is in the form of a question asked to the respondent as to what is his authority to hold such post/office. On issuance of such writ, the respondent has to show his authority or title to the office in question. The following conditions are to be satisfied before issuance of a Writ of Quo Warranto, viz–

(1) The office is a public office;
(2) The person holding or appointed for such office is not legally qualified or such appointment is unauthorized under the law or the Constitution;
(3) The office under challenge must be of substantial character;
(4) The respondent must have assumed the office. A mere proposal for appointment or the appointment order itself will be premature for issuance of a writ of quo-warranto.
(5) The respondent should continue to be in office and should not have left the same.

Any person interested in the office can challenge the same and it is not necessary that he should be personally interested in that. Generally such writs are preferred against an executive action appointing a public officer.

PROHIBITION

A suit has been instituted against me in respect of title of an immovable property. However, neither do I reside there nor is the suit property situated within the territorial jurisdiction of that Court. I did bring the said fact to the notice of the court, but it did not give an ear to my plea, and is going ahead with the proceeding. Is there any alternative and efficacious remedy to prevent such wrong exercise of jurisdiction?

Such wrong exercise of jurisdiction can be prevented in the most efficacious manner by approaching the High Court of the State or even the Supreme Court. Such can be done so by seeking a Writ of Prohibition. A Writ of Prohibition may be issued against a subordinate court or tribunal or other authority for restraining it from exercising jurisdiction which it does not legally or constitutionally possess, or for an act which the court or the tribunal is doing beyond or in excess of its jurisdiction.

The following are the essentials for issuance of a Writ of Prohibition, viz–
(1) The Writ of Prohibition can be issued when the respondent is exercising a judicial or a quasi-judicial authority;
(2) Such judicial or quasi-judicial authority has assumed jurisdiction in excess than bestowed upon it;
(3) Proceedings relevant to the challenge must be pending before such judicial or quasi judicial authority;
(4) There should be no concealment or mis-statement of any fact;
(5) There should not exist any alternative remedy except in the case of usurpation of jurisdiction in which existence of alternative remedy is no bar for the writ petition.

It is to be noted that only a person whose legal or constitutional right is violated can apply for issue of a writ of prohibition. Hence, you can institute a Writ proceeding seeking an intervention from the court and also restrain such inferior court from continuing with the proceedings.

CERTIORARI

A criminal case was instituted against us. However, no cognizance was taken for more than 10 years from the date of the alleged incident. The judge refused to accept this plea and instead passed an order against us. In the said order, I have been directed to be imprisoned and am likely to be arrested any day. Is there any speedy and efficacious way by which I can avoid the same?

Imprisonment can be avoided by approaching the Hon'ble High Court or even the Supreme Court by way of filing a Writ petition praying for issuance of a Writ of Certiorari. A Writ of Certiorari can be issued to a subordinate court or a quasi-judicial tribunal or authority for quashing any order or proceeding, which is beyond or without jurisdiction or in the wrongful exercise of jurisdiction or in disobedience of some constitutional mandate.

A writ of certiorari can be issued on the following grounds–

(1) that there is an apparent error on the record.
(2) that there is absence or excess of jurisdiction or failure to exercise jurisdiction.
(3) that there is illegal exercise of jurisdiction.
(4) that there is some disregard for applying the rules of natural justice.
(5) that there is no alternate or efficacious remedy.

Such writ is generally issued to–
a) correct errors of jurisdiction;
b) correct the violation of the principles of natural justice, gross errors of law or wrongful exercise of jurisdiction;
c) call for records of the lower court in order to correct the errors apparent on the face of it.

It is to be noted that only persons whose legal or constitutional right is violated can file a Writ Petition for praying issuance of a Writ of Certiorari.

Hence, you can file a writ petition challenging the said decision and praying for quashing the said judgment.

RIGHTS OF AN HIV + PERSON

I have been declared HIV positive. However, this fact was communicated by the hospital to my employer who dismissed me from service on this sole ground. Don't the HIV positive patients have any right?

The three epidemics sweeping across the whole world today are of HIV infection, of AIDS and of stigmatization and discrimination against people with HIV/AIDS. In your case no doubt such disclosure was gross violation to the duty of confidentiality liable to be maintained by the hospital. However, if the hospital can prove that it had done so in the greater public interest, it can escape liability. Further, your employer was unjustified in dismissing you from service on this sole ground if you were medically fit for available, appropriate work and, hence, you are entitled to claim reinstatement.

The law does recognize certain rights of HIV infected persons, viz–

(1) Right to be informed about his status;

(2) Right to autonomy i.e. self-determination;

(3) Right not to be forced to undergo mandatory / compulsory testing for HIV blood test etc;

(4) Right to medical treatment, nursing care and use of the appropriate diagnostic equipment;

(5) Right to die without pain and with dignity;

(6) Right not to be discriminated, i.e. workers who are infected should be treated in like manner as a worker who is ill;

(7) Right not to be stigmatized / discriminated by co-workers, union, employers or clients;

(8) Right not to have pre-employment testing or screening of candidates either, directly or indirectly, during selection;

(9) Right to confidentiality, i.e. the HIV status of the person should be kept confidential and not to be disclosed unless to prevent a greater and imminent harm;

(10) Right not to be terminated from services on this sole ground till the person is medically fit for available, appropriate work;

(11) Right of no deductions in benefits to which they are entitled except the legal deductions permissible in law;

(12) Right of access to appropriate counselling and referral courses dealing with HIV.

(13) Right not to be unnecessarily quarantined.

(14) Right not to be forced in involuntary participation in vaccine trials.

(15) Right to move within the country, including the right to choose or transfer residence.

(16) Right to access to the education system and educational privileges and opportunities, which are available to the rest of the community.

If any of the above-mentioned rights is violated, apart from the relief of approaching the appropriate court including the Supreme Court, the High Court or the Consumer Foras, the National Human Rights Commission may also be approached. You can even approach the State Human Rights Commission, if constituted, in the state. The complaint can be given in writing, addressed to the President / Chairman or any of the members of the commission. Moreover neither a lawyer is required nor any fee is payable on any complain to the commission. The other modes of making complain are by telegraphic message or a fax. On receiving a complaint the commission takes decision whether the complain should be investigated or not. The commission may direct the Government / authority to report in such matter. The commission has power to afford personal hearing and examine the witnesses and there may be even a visit on the spot by any of its official. Sometimes the commission even takes cases in its own hand suo-motto, i.e. taking cognizance itself on coming to know any violation of human rights published in a newspaper or likes.

DISABILITY

I had applied for a government job. However my candidature was rejected on the sole ground that my legs were amputated. No doubt this is true but the same in no way was a requirement for the job for which I had applied. Is 100% physical fitness necessary for government jobs? Is there any law that can help people like me to join the mainstream?

It was totally unjustified of rejecting your candidature if your imparity was not likely to affect the job. You can claim employment by approaching the High Court or even the Supreme Court and the Court after being satisfied is empowered to grant a direction to consider your candidature.

It is to be noted that except in certain cases like those for employment in Armed Forces, a person cannot be deprived of employment on the sole ground that he is impaired / disabled, if he can perform the said work in the same manner as a normal person can. In fact, a law known as Persons with Disabilities (Equal

Opportunities, Protection of Rights and Full Participation) Act (The Disabilities Act) has been enacted with the prime objective of promoting and ensuring equality and full participation of persons with disabilities. The Disabilities Act aims to protect and promote the economic and social rights of people with disabilities. However, disability here means disability as in the medical terms and not the common perception of disability. Further a National Trust for Welfare of Persons with Autism, Cerebral Palsy, Mental Retardation and Multiple Disabilities Act is enacted to fulfil a common demand of families that seek protection for their severely disabled. The specific objectives of this Act are:

1. To enable and empower persons with disabilities to live as independently and as fully as possible in the society;

2. To promote measures for the care and protection of persons with disabilities in the event of death of their parent or guardian; and

3. To extend support to registered organisations to provide need-based services during the period of crisis in the families of disabled persons.

The Act mandates the creation of a Local Level Committee (LLC) comprising of a District Magistrate along with one representative from a registered organisation and one person with disability. The LLC is also empowered to decide upon applications for legal guardianship. Also, duties of such guardians have been dealt to in the Act. The overall supervision of this Act is vested with a National Trust Board appointed through a democratic process by registered organisations of parents and others providing services to the disabled people. The government has also contributed Rs. 1 billion in the trust fund and the interest earned is used to support its activities.

Another Act known as the Rehabilitation Council of India Act, has been enacted whose main function is:

a) Standardising training courses and prescribing minimum standards of education and training of various categories for professionals dealing with people with disabilities;

b) Regulating these standards in all training institutions uniformly throughout the country;

c) Promoting research in rehabilitation and special education;
d) Maintaining a Central Rehabilitation Register for registration of professionals.

Thus, the Government of India has established elaborate provisions to deal with this segment - the segment of the differentially-abled and - any person who is so can contact the authorities for needful action. Also, reservation in employment has been provided to these people.

•••

CHAPTER – 5
OUR ENVIRONMENT

NOISE POLLUTION

There is a temple adjacent to my house and religious functions are a regular feature. The management of the temple has installed loudspeakers to spread the preaching and prayers. Though I do respect their sentiments but the same has snatched our peace. Can anything be done to prevent it?

Noise pollution is a big disturbance and the law has laid down strict regulations to deal with it. Under the Noise Pollution (Regulation & Control) Rules, the sound level in residential area is limited to 55 dB during daytime and 45 dB during night. And if the noise level increases by a margin of 10 dB, one has a right to make a complaint in respect to the same before the magistrate or the police or any other official so appointed. The concerned authority is empowered to investigate the complaint and on finding the complaint genuine, may either order for prohibition or regulation of the noise. One can also approach the civil court for injunction, restraining / regulating such noise levels. A criminal case can also be lodged as noise pollution is regarded as a public nuisance and the same is duly punishable.

WATER AND AIR POLLUTION

I have been running a hospital in my locality for some time now. Recently a factory has sprung up in the area discharging the liquids through a hole dug up in the ground and is also emitting smoke. This has resulted in the ground

water being polluted, from which I derive and fulfil the water necessity. The polluting of the water and the air has not only affected the environment but my business too, as the patients have stopped coming. Is there any mode of preventing the pollution and also how can I recover the loss caused to me?

If the said factory is emitting / discharging pollutants in the natural resources and the air and thereby polluting the same then a complain in respect of the same may be made to the Central Pollution Control Board (if any constituted) or to the State Pollution Control Board (if any constituted) or to the Effluent Board (if any constituted). However in absence of any, an application to this effect may be made to the municipal authority concerned and if they fail to act then the Hon'ble High Court may be approached for issuance of a Writ of Mandamus directing the municipal authority to do the needful with a further direction upon the factory concerned to stop discharging the pollutants without treatment and against the rules made in this behalf.

In respect of recovering the loss so caused, you can do so by instituting a Civil Suit for Tortuous Liability under the heading of damages in lieu of public nuisance. However for the same you will have to prove public nuisance and the compensation if awarded might be quite meager seeing the present scenario. But it is doubtful that any damages might be paid to you on account of loss sustained by you. For the same you will have to supply necessary documentary proofs supporting the averment and establishing your claim for loss occasioned to you on account of the said pollution.

WILDLIFE

I live near Crawford Market in Mumbai. One can see tiny birds caged in small iron boxes, and being sold purchased openly. Moreover it's surprising to see people eager to know their fate through a fortune-teller carrying a parrot who is caged and upon instructions picking up a card. I wish to protect these innocent birds but don't know as to what can I do. Please help.

We are pleased to see your love towards birds and zeal to work for their interest. The Wildlife Protection Act makes it illegal to catch, keep, kill, buy or sell or even damaging nests of all birds of indigenous species. Further the Convention of International Trade in Endangered Species restricts trade of foreign birds, which is very much applicable in India as India is one of its signatories. Prevention of Cruelty towards Animals Act protects animals and birds from any cruel behaviour. Thus it is illegal to keep any birds in captivity, with the only exception being lovebirds and blue rock pigeons. Moreover as you referred about fortune-tellers, we would like to clarify that the green birds used by them are mistakenly understood as parrots, whereas in reality they are parakeets. Generally the offences related to animals and birds are cognizable in nature and can make one liable for imprisonment of a term upto 5 years and heavy fine.

Some of the other acts recognized, as offences are as below–

- Colouring feathers of birds to make them more attractive.
- Cutting feathers which amounts to maiming.
- Training any birds for fights.
- Organizing fights of animals and birds like cockfighting.
- Showing caged birds in ads, movies or serials.
- Organizing bird release ceremonies to mark occasions where the birds have been procured by sale.
- Organizing circuses by obtaining any animals from the wild.
- Destroying the nests.
- Possessing any wild animal, its parts or any article made from its parts.
- Commerce or trade in any wild animal, their parts or articles made from their parts including ivory.
- Possessing Shahtoosh Shawl if they are not registered, showing proof of purchase before 1972 i.e. enactment of Wildlife Protection Act.
- Possessing peacock feathers without having a certificate from the CWW to establish that such have naturally shed and not

been obtained by harming or killing the bird.
- Peacocks farming or rearing or held in captivity.
- Farmers using electrified fences to deter wild animals.

Thus, if you find any of these offences or the like being committed, you can register an FIR with the police and if the police machinery does not work then you can simultaneously file a PIL in either the High Court or the Supreme Court. You may also take help of various NGOs working in this regard.

SMOKING

While smoking in a park, one of the senior citizens interrupted me and told that the Hon'ble Supreme Court has banned smoking. How is it possible, as cigarettes are not only being advertised but also being sold openly?

Smoking in public place is banned not only by a decision of the court but also by a recent central enactment, which expressly bans smoking in public places.

A 'public place' under the Act means "any place to which the public have access, whether as of right or not". Public places would include auditorium, hospital buildings, health institutions, amusement centres, restaurants, public offices, court buildings, educational institutions, libraries, public conveyances and the like, which are visited by the general public.

The Act further lays down punishment in form of fine of Rs. 200/- for any contravention of the same. Also, any direct and indirect advertisement of cigarettes and other tobacco products in print, electronic and outdoor media (hoardings) is banned and so is sponsorship and promotion of cigarette and other tobacco products. Tobacco products include cigarettes, cigars, cheroots, beedis, cigarette tobacco, pipe tobacco, hookah tobacco, chewing tobacco, snuff, pan masala or any chewing material having tobacco as one of the ingredients, *gutkha* and tooth powder containing tobacco.

Any advertisement in contravention of the same is punishable with two years imprisonment and / or with a fine up to Rs 1,000 and in the case of second or subsequent conviction, imprisonment for a term of five years with a fine of Rs 5,000/-.

The Act also prohibits the sale of cigarette and other tobacco products to a person below the age of 18 years. The owner/manager of a place where tobacco products are sold, are mandated, under the Act, to display a board at a conspicuous place in the local language a prohibition/warning that "sale of cigarette and other tobacco products to persons below 18 years in punishable offence".

Hence, the said statement of the senior citizen was totally justified and if caught smoking you are liable to pay fine of Rs. 200/-.

•••

CHAPTER-6
CONTRACTUAL ASPECT

INVITATION TO AN OFFER
I saw a *salwar kurta* displayed in a showcase, bearing a price tag of Rs. 700/- and promised my girlfriend to gift her the same. Astonisingly, the shopkeeper refused to sell it on the displayed price. I was very disappointed of not fulfilling my promise made to my girlfriend. Can't I force him legally to sell it on the displayed price?

In legal terms a contract is complete once the offer is accepted. One might think that the price tag displayed is an offer of the shopkeeper to sell the goods at the quoted price. However, this is not true in the eyes of law, and the said price tag constitutes mere 'an invitation to offer'. A prospective customer, acting upon the said invitation, makes his offer to buy the goods at the quoted price, which the shopkeeper may accept or refuse.

Hence, it is basically the customer who makes the offer and the shopkeeper who accepts it. So, the shopkeeper is totally justified in refusing to accept your offer on the displayed price.

OFFER - COMMUNICATION NECESSARY
A lad of 6 years was roaming in a suspicious manner. On enquiring he revealed that he is the son of a big businessman and has run away from home. I took him to his home and handed him to his parents. Now I have come to know that his father had kept a reward of Rs. 50,000/- to the person who brings his child back or gives any information of his whereabouts. On claiming the same, the miser

Objection Your Honour

businessman refused to give me the reward. Can I approach the court for the same?

No doubt you have done a noble work in taking the child to his parents' place and you need to be appreciated for it. But as far as claiming the reward, we are afraid that it would not be possible.

Under the Indian Contract Act, no doubt the businessman's proposal to reward can be said to be an offer to the general world. However, it becomes binding when any person accepts the same by doing an act in pursuance of the offer, i.e. the person doing the act has done so with the knowledge of the offer.

In your case as you were not aware of the said proposal so there is no scope of your accepting it even though you have done some act for which the said offer was made. Hence, you cannot claim the award you being unaware of the same.

CROSS OFFER

We are retailers of food grains and purchase it from a wholeseller. By postal letter, we offered the wholeseller to send us 100 quintals of rice of certain variety @ 20 per/kg. On the same day I received an offer from the same wholeseller, willing to sell us the same variety of rice @ 20 per/kg. Presuming that there was no need to give acceptance again, as even the wholeseller would have got our letter, we did not have any further communication till it came to our knowledge that they refused to perform the same. What should I do? Please suggest.

It seems that your's and the wholeseller's letters were sent without you both being aware of each other's letter. Such offers whose terms are same and sent by both the parties of the contract are deemed as 'Cross offer'.

So in this case, the wholeseller sending you a letter even of the same terms and conditions will not amount to an acceptance but it is merely an offer from his side and as neither party has accepted the offer, hence there is no concluded contract and no bindingness.

Thus, you can neither sue the wholeseller for damages nor claim specific performance of the said contract.

REVOCATION OF AN OFFER

I had sent my acceptance in respect to a certain offer. However, due to some reason I sent my revocation for the same, which reached the other party before my letter of acceptance. However, the second letter was not considered and the other party purposely went on to perform the contract and I was asked to pay the consideration amount. Am I liable to do so in spite of my revocation of acceptance?

Yours is a case of revocation of an acceptance. In our opinion the 2nd letter of yours should have been taken into consideration by which you clearly revoked the acceptance as it reached them before the first one was accepted. Hence, there was no concluded contract and you can very well deny your liability to pay any amount, which will be just and proper in respect to the facts and circumstance of the case.

OPPORTUNITY TO REVIEW TERMS OF CONTRACT

I deposited a bag in a locker of a hotel. On asking for it I was told that the hotel staff had somehow misplaced it. On demanding compensation for it, I was shocked to note that I could get only Rs. 1000/- for the same, whereas my bag contained valuables like camera, digital diary and a watch, worth a minimum of Rs. 10,000/-. This fact was even known to the hotel staff as they had seen me keeping the said contents in the bag before handing it over to them. On arguing the manager showed me the 'reverse side' of the token, which I was given as a receipt on account of depositing the bag, wherein the hotel acknowledged a limited liability of Rs. 1000/-. Seeing the circumstances I accepted the same under protest. Can anything be done in this regard?

You are entitled to claim the full amount of Rs. 10,000/- that will indemnify your loss. As per the Law of Contract there should be a reasonable notice of the contractual terms in order to make it binding. In your case you must have gone to the hotel, then presented the bag to be kept in safe custody, and paid the consideration on which they must have issued you the receipt. If this was the thing we believe that you never had an opportunity to review the terms and conditions, which was not even printed on the front side. The situation could have been in favour of the hotel management, if they would have orally made you aware of the condition or would have had a notice to this effect displayed at the counter or would in any other way render you time to think over the terms. However, it is upon you to prove that the bag did contain the said valuable documents in order to claim compensation for it, if admissible. Further as you have accepted the said amount under protest, the Doctrine of Estoppel would not bar you from claiming the unpaid amount. According to this doctrine, if one does a particular act or states a particular fact, he is prohibited from disowning it.

CAPACITY TO CONTRACT

I, under the influence of liquor, executed a sale deed of a land in my friends favour. Though we agreed on a fair price, but the said land was my ancestral property and I would have never sold it on any price if I had not been drunk. What should I do as he is now not willing to return it even on refund of money with interest and on the other hand I am forced to listen all the abuses of my family members?

For making of a valid contract the basic essential is that the parties should be competent to contract. Competency to Contract disqualifies all persons like minors, insane, persons of unsound mind, lunatic, idiots, etc. who are not in a position to make a rational decision. If you can prove before the court that at the time when the sale deed was executed you were drunk till an extent that impaired all your capacity to make a rational decision, then the said contract may be declared null and void by the court of law.

DUTY TO SPEAK-NOT ALWAYS APPLICABLE

I had to purchase 30 computers at a time for upgradation of my office. The dealer finalized the contract, but next morning only I found that computer's price slashed by Rs. 2000/-. It is evident that the dealer certainly knew this. Moreover, as agreed, the delivery of machine was to be made in next 7 days. It has even put me in more uncomfortable situation to accept the delivery on a higher paid price when the existing price on the day of delivery

will be lesser. Can I claim the difference amount i.e. Rs.60,000/- in total?

A contract is concluded once the offer has been accepted and it is immaterial whether the same has to be performed on a future date. Hence, you both are legally bound to abide by the terms of the contract and the dealer has committed no wrong. However, if you at the time of contract had specifically asked about the change in prices and the dealer showed his ignorance of the same, and if you have proof which can establish that the dealer was very much aware of the reduction in prices, then the contract becomes voidable at your option, i.e. it is your wish whether you would go ahead with the contract or terminate the same. The law prescribes a duty to speak on part of the other party when he is asked to speak and any non-performance or false performance of such would amount to fraud or misrepresentation as the case may be. However, if there is no such case, and if the dealer fails to supply you the computer within the time stipulated, then in such a condition, you will be entitled to the full difference amount.

RESTRAINT OF LEGAL PROCEEDING

I am a businessman and operate from Delhi in various cities of India. My work is such that some or the other litigation takes place every day. I am therefore in a way forced to run from courts of one place to the other to deal with such legal problems.

Can anything be done in this regard?

As you mentioned that your work operates from Delhi and people dealing with you belong to various cities in India you might be forced to fight litigations in various courts in India. However, you can avoid this by restricting that a particular court will have jurisdiction over all litigations in respect of your trade. It is to be noted that such a condition has to be stipulated in the terms of the contract before the contract / deal is finalized. It will solve your problem till a great extent. If even though some one raises the matter in another court, it may not be entertained in general, but at last it all depends upon the discretion of that very court.

REIMBURSEMENT OF AMOUNT DUE BY OTHER PAID BY ANOTHER INTERESTED PARTY

I took a flat on rent for 11 months, but was shocked to see that several taxes / cess / bills were pending. I was served a notice that if those were not cleared then my water and electricity connection will be cut. I asked my landlord to pay the same but he took the plea that he has some financial constraint and will not be able to pay it. What can be done?

In this conditions we suggest you to pay the backdate bills and taxes from your side so that you can avail uninterrupted supply of water and electricity. You can then deduct the same from the rent payable and the landlord cannot escape from his liability. In other way you can compel him to reimburse the same in one time also, as the Indian Contract Act provides that a person who is interested in the payment of money which another is bound by law to pay and who therefore pays it is entitled to be reimbursed by the other.

AGENCY

In cases of agency, will I be bound by all the transactions carried out by my agent even though the same are not or even in cases contrary to my instructions?

Under the Law of Agency, as provided in the Indian Contract Act, a principal i.e. the person authorizing the agent, is liable for all deeds / acts done by the agent for which the agent has been duly and specifically authorized. However, if the agent performs an act for which he was not authorized to do, the same is not binding till the act is ratified / accepted by the principal and the agent is liable for the same personally. In cases where the agent acts beyond his authorization and if the authorized act can be separated from the unauthorized act, then the principal will be liable for the authorized act only. The principal can also claim damages from the agent for any loss so occasioned by the act of the agent done in his own sweet will.

Hence, if you can prove that the agent was acting beyond the authority, then you cannot be held liable for the same and the agent will be held liable. However, if you have suffered any loss / damage, you can claim damages from him. Further, such action on the part of the agent entitles you to terminate the contract of agency.

MINOR

I am a kid of 16 years. Can I enter into a contract?

No, for a valid contract you should be of the age of majority according to the law to which you are subject. This is 18 years in our country and if you are under a legal guardian i.e. under the care of some person other than your natural parents, the age of majority is 21 years. Therefore you are not competent to contract and if you enter into any agreement, the same will be void-ab-initio i.e. the contract is null and void from its very inception. You cannot even ratify the agreement made any during your minority on attaining the age of majority and thereby validate the same.

However, it is to be noted that if you have received some benefit, then the same is liable to be returned to the concerned person from whom you have derived benefit and if the same cannot be returned then an equivalent cost of the same is liable to be paid to him from your property.

INSANE

My father is sometimes sane and at times insane. Can he enter into a contract?

Yes. Your father can enter into a contract while he is of sane mind but cannot do so when he is not so. This condition is recognized as lunacy under the Indian Contract Act.

CONSENT

I received packed goods consisting of some journals and CDs via post along with a bill of Rs. 1200/-. The cover stated that if I did not wish to keep the same I should return it within one month or it will be a deemed acceptance. As I wasn't interested in it I decided to return the package but on enquiry I found that the same would cost Rupees 200/- via courier; hence I simply sent the package by ordinary post. After one and half months I received a demand notice. Am I bound to pay the said amount and was it really a contract?

This is the general form of deemed acceptance used in contract nowadays. However, legally speaking mere stating of a silence condition on the part of a party for a specified period cannot be deemed to amount to acceptance unless there has been some act showing acceptance of the terms. In this case, as you had already, by your act of sending the goods back, proved your intention of repudiating the contract, hence you cannot be held liable on this account.

However, the burden of proof lies upon you to prove that you had repudiated the contract.

DEEMED ACCEPTANCE

I received packed goods consisting of some journals and CDs via post along with a bill of Rs. 1200/-. The cover stated that if I did not wish to keep the same I should return it within 1 month or it will be a deemed acceptance. As I wasn't interested in it I decided to return the package but on enquiry I found that the same would cost Rupees 200/- via Courier, hence I simply sent the package by ordinary post. After one and half months I received a demand notice. Am I bound to pay the said amount and was it really a contract.

This is the general form of deemed acceptance used in contract nowadays. However, legally speaking mere stating of a silence condition on part of a party for a specified period cannot be deemed to amount to acceptance unless there has been some act showing acceptance of the terms. In this case, as you had already, by your act of sending the goods back, proved your intention of repudiating the contract, hence you cannot be held liable on this account.

However, the burden of proof lies upon you to prove that you had repudiated the contract.

RESTRAINT IN TRADE

We run a Call Center in Pune and for the same have employed professionals and provided them specialized training. However we feel insecure as some of them might leave our organization after obtaining the training/

experience and switch over to our competitors. Is there any way of stopping them?

The professionals may be prohibited from leaving the organization and working elsewhere. However there are certain restrictions for doing so. Generally speaking, a condition stipulating that the said professionals would not work in another organization after quitting, would amount to restraint in trade, which is barred by the Indian Contract Act.

However, prohibition in this regard for a limited period and in respect of working within a limited area would not be deemed so. You can also restrain the said employees from leaving the organization by asking them to sign a bond wherein it be mentioned that if they leave the organization within a specified period they will be liable to pay the amount incurred in their training in addition to damages suffered by your organization.

SPECIFIC PERFORMANCE

I entered into a contract with a renowned painter to paint my portrait and to this effect I also paid him some advance. However now the painter is not ready to do the same at the agreed price. Instead of having my money back I shall like my painting being made by him. Is there any provision in law, which can compel him to act in the agreed manner?

Under the Specific Relief Act, specific performance of contract can be claimed. The court generally grants specific performance–

a) Where there is no standard for ascertaining the actual damage caused by non-performance of the act agreed.
b) When compensation in terms of money for non-performance of the act would not be an adequate relief.

In your case as both these conditions are satisfied instituting a suit in the appropriate court can claim Specific Performance of Contract. Further compensation can also be claimed, which can be awarded by the court along with Specific Performance.

GOVERNMENT CONTRACT – STAMP DUTY

I am supposed to enter into a Government contract and would like to know as to who will pay the stamp duty.

No stamp duty would be leviable in cases of agreement executed between the government and a private party unlike in cases where stamp duty is required to be paid for agreements entered into between two or more private parties, as provided in the Indian Stamp Act.

SALE OF GOODS

I, in good faith, purchased a bike believing it to be of my friend. However later on I learnt that he was not the true owner and in fact the bike was a stolen one. Am I liable to return the bike or can I keep it as I have purchased it on payment of the desired consideration.

Under the law, a person can pass only the title, which he has, and no better. As your friend was not the true owner of the bike and the same was a stolen one, you are not entitled to possession/ownership of the same and the true owner can at any time claim the said bike. However, you can recover the amount paid to your friend and can also institute both civil and criminal proceedings against him.

LIABILTY OF SURETY FOR LOAN

I am a surety for the repayment of loan taken by one of my friends. If he ever fails to do so, can it be even recovered from my pocket?

By becoming the surety, you have accepted the responsibility of ensuring payment of the due amount. Hence, if your friend fails to pay the amount, the creditor, i.e. the person to whom the amount is owed, is entitled to have the same recovered from you.

However, once you have paid the amount, you step into the shoes of the creditor, i.e. you become entitled to recover the said amount from your friend, failing which you can have the same recovered through the process of law.

CHEQUE BOUNCING

I had sold goods to a trader who paid me by an account-payee cheque. However the same was dishonoured on the ground 'insufficiency of funds'. On approaching the trader he requested me to wait for some time and now after one month he is denying his liability. What is the fastest and

most effective mode of securing the payment due?

The legislature seeing the number of incidences of cheque bouncing (dishonouring) and its effect in trade made cheque bouncing / dishonouring a criminal offence wherein the drawer of the cheque would be liable for imprisonment of a term upto 2 years and / or fine upto twice the amount of the cheque under the Negotiable Instruments Act.

For this a complaint in a court of proper jurisdiction, being a court not inferior to that of a Metropolitan Magistrate or a Judicial Magistrate of the First Class, has to be instituted. The Act also specifies certain prerequisites for filing of a case, being, that a notice of demand has to be issued within 30 days of the intimation of the fact of dishonour from the bank wherein a period of 15 days is to be given to the drawer for payment and on his failure to pay, a complaint has to be filed within the next 30 days.

In your case, it does not appear as to whether a demand notice in writing was given to the trader. If it is given and the trader has not paid within the stipulated period of 15 days, you have to institute a case within the next period of 30 days. However, if there is any delay in instituting the case, the court is empowered to condone the delay if there is sufficient cause, which you will be liable to prove the same. However, if no notice has been given within the stipulated period, then the remedy under the Negotiable Instruments Act cannot be availed of.

It is to be noted that this Act is not meant for repayment of the amount but merely makes cheque bouncing a criminal case. But in practice the court generally grants the amount of fine equal to the cheque amount to the complainant. Also, a criminal case wherein imprisonment is a punishment deters persons from not repaying the dishonoured cheque amount.

Alternatively, you also have the option of approaching a civil court by filing a summary suit for recovery of dues with interest after giving notice. You can also avail both the remedies simultaneously.

PARTNERSHIP – MINOR
I wish to induct my son aged 16 years in our partnership

firm. What are the legal consequences of such induction?

No, you cannot make your son a partner in your partnership firm although he can be admitted to the benefits of a partnership. As per the Indian Contract Act every person who is of the age of majority and is of sound mind and is not disqualified from contracting by any law to which he is subject is competent to contract. Thus, a contract by a minor is void and unenforceable. Since the essential of a partnership is the contract entered into between the partners, and as a minor is not competent to contract, therefore, a minor cannot enter into a partnership.

However, it is to be noted that under the Partnership Act, though a minor cannot be made a partner in a firm, he may, with the consent of all the partners, be admitted to the benefits of partnership. Thus, a minor in such cases will have a right to a share in the property and to the profits in the firm and it will only be his share that will be liable and the minor in no circumstances will be personally liable for any act of the firm.

PARTNERSHIP - UNREGISTERED

I have entered into a contract with an unregistered partnership firm. The firm has now defaulted in payment. I am told that I cannot sue the firm. Is it true? How can I recover my money?

Under the law, unless a partnership firm is not registered, it has no legal existence and thereby neither it can sue in its name nor can it be sued in the name of the partnership firm. However, you can very well institute a suit against all the partners making them severally and jointly liable.

•••

CHAPTER-7
LAND AND PROPERTY

ADVERSE POSSESSION

My tenant is living in my house for a continuous period of 40 years for which I have duly received rent from time to time. Does a prolonged tenancy in anyway affect my title over the property as I have come to know that living in a place for more than twelve years entitles the person to claim ownership in the same by way of adverse possession?

No, a prolonged tenancy in no case can affect the right of ownership of the concerned person/owner.

For adverse possession, the essential ingredient is living openly, uninterrupted and for a continuous period of more that twelve years (and in case of government property for more than twenty years). Open means 'within the knowledge/in front of the eyes of the general public. Uninterrupted means without any obstruction from anyone claiming to be the real owner. As your tenant has been duly paying you the rent, it means he is recognizing your right of ownership and this amounts to interruption from your side.

Hence, there is nothing to fear that your tenant living for such prolonged period may become the owner. A tenant is always a tenant and nothing but a tenant.

TRANSFER OF PROPERTY - DESTRUCTION

I had leased out my shop on rent, which was washed away on account of massive flood. Now I am in no position to rebuild the same and would like to sell it. However, the tenant is ready to rebuild the same at his own expense provided he will deduct it from the rent. Am I bound to allow the tenant to do it? Can't I sell the property?

Subject to the relevant State laws and the terms of the contract, lease of a shop does not also mean leasing the land on which the shop has been constructed and hence, if the said shop is destroyed, the same amounts to destruction of the property in question and thereby termination of the contract as per the provisions of the Transfer of Property Act.

Hence, as the subject matter of the lease has terminated, the lease deed on its own comes to an end and you are not legally bound to allow the tenant to rebuild the shop and are very well competent to dispose of the same as per your wishes.

TRANSFER OF PROPERTY - SUB-LEASE

I am a tenant having rented a premise for office purpose. Now I wish to induct my son in the same premises who is determined to start another business. Can we continue both the businesses at the same premises? Would I be liable to pay any extra amount for the use by my son, though he is not contributing towards the rent or paying me any rent?

Subject to the relevant State Law and the terms of the contract and as per the Transfer of Property Act, a lessee may transfer or sub-lease his interest in the property. This means you can allow your son to use the office premises without being obliged to pay any extra charges.

However, it is to be noted that a lessee must not permit another to use the property for a purpose other than that for which it was leased. Hence, if the terms of the lease specify a business for which the premises can be leased then the premises can be used for that specific business purpose only and if it is used for any other purpose, then the owner has the right to demand additional rent or even in cases may ask for vacation of the premises.

TRANSFER OF PROPERTY – PART PERFORMANCE

An agreement to purchase a house was entered between the owner and myself and I have paid half of the

consideration amount and also obtained possession thereof. Now the said owner is not willing to execute the sale deed in my favour even though I have offered him the balance amount. On the other hand the owner has entered into an agreement to sell the house to another person. As there is no registered sale deed can I still compel the owner to sell me the house?

The legislature has provided for instances wherein the contract in respect of sale of immovable property may not be registered and has thereby given protection to the innocent purchasers.

Under the Doctrine of Part Performance as enumerated in the Transfer of Property Act, if there is a contract in writing entered between two persons, to transfer an immovable property and by virtue of the same, one party is in possession and has done some act in furtherance of the contract and the transferee is willing to perform his part of the contract, then he is entitled to protection. This is a defensive remedy and cannot be used to establish title over the said property but can only be used to defend one's title if claimed by another.

PURCHASE OF LAND – CLEAR TITLE

I wish to purchase a land in a new place, but I am afraid of being trapped in a legal battle over the land on account of defective title. Further, I have come across instances wherein the land sold to one is re-sold to another. Is there any way by which I can ascertain that the land in question has not been sold earlier and for preventing future unauthorized selling of such?

For getting a clear title over the said property, all the documents pertaining to the property in question ought to be verified and a title search should be conducted so as to ascertain the genuineness of the owner and to know as to whether he is the real owner capable of transferring the property.

Further, the search would also reveal as to whether the land has already been transferred to someone else or not and whether any sale deed or an agreement to sell has been executed. It is to be noted that an agreement to sell is also now compulsorily registrable and hence, if you intend to purchase the property, you should get the agreement to sell registered. Once such is done and you are in possession of the property, it will secure your right over the property and if at a later stage, if the owner refuses to sell you the land, you can claim specific performance of the contract, and if the owner has resold the same to someone else, you can defend your title over the same by taking help of the Doctrine of Part Performance.

TRANSFER OF PROPERTY – PART PERFORMANCE/ SPECIFIC PERFORMANCE

An agreement to sell has been registered for sale of a flat along with its furniture. I have paid Rs 10,00,000/- in pursuance to the contract. However the seller has gone oversees and there is no communication from his side as to the execution of the sale deed. What can be done? Can I break open the lock and shift in the said flat?

Generally speaking, the seller of an immovable property is bound to give the buyer possession of the property at the time when ownership transfers unless otherwise agreed. In your case there is a mere agreement to sell and the same has not given you any right over the said property except the right to claim specific performance and prevent transfer of the same to someone else. However, you are not entitled to enter the said premises forcefully.

The best mode is to institute a civil suit in an appropriate court of law claiming specific performance of the contract. However, the burden of proof lies upon you, to prove that the same had been sold to you. In case you break open the flat and take possession by yourself, this would be intentional intrusion in the property of another and you may be subject to liability for trespass and / or theft under the criminal law.

NON-REGISTRATION OF A LEASE DEED

Does non-registration of a lease deed of period exceeding 11 months render the lease deed void? Can the landlord evict me on this sole ground?

The lease deed for a period exceeding 11 months has to be

compulsorily registered under the Transfer of Property Act and the Registration Act. However, in case of failure to do so the owner of the property cannot evict the tenant on the ground of such non-registration. A lease is a transfer of a right to enjoy the property and such transfer can be made expressly or by implication.

It has been upheld by the Supreme Court that an unregistered instrument will not stand in the way to determine whether a lease otherwise exists than through such deed. It is to be noted that the landlord can seek eviction only on the grounds provided under the Transfer of Property Act and other State rent enactments. Also, if a registrable lease deed is not registered then the tenancy will be deemed to be a month-to-month tenancy and to terminate such, the landlord is required to fulfil the various requirements of law.

REGISTRATION OF SALE DEED

I wished to sell my ancestral land to my cousin for a token amount of Rs. 1000/- and applied for registration of the sale deed. However, the Registrar refused to do so stating that the consideration of the sale deed was much less than the market value of the property. No doubt the market value of the land is Rs. 2,00,000/- but can't I transfer the same at such price, which I think suitable.

The Registrar was partly justified in refusing to register the said document. Drastic amendments have been carried out during the turn of the century whereby the Government has prescribed a minimum value (commonly called Government valuation) for all lands. This minimum value is the least amount that will be the consideration amount in any sale-purchase of a land. Any sale of land at a consideration amount lower than the government valuation of the land empowers the government to purchase the land at such value. However, it is not necessary that the consideration amount should be the current market value of the property and any amount more than the minimum value so prescribed will suffice for the purpose of registration.

ACQUISITION OF PROPERTIES BY AN NRI

What is the mode of acquisition of properties in India

by NRIs?

The sale / purchase of property by NRIs/persons of Indian origin are governed by the Foreign Exchange Management (Acquisition and Transfer of Immovable Property in India) Regulations. Under this an NRI can acquire any property in India except that of agricultural, plantation or farmhouse. A person of Indian origin is also governed by the same but has to fulfil two more conditions pertaining to the funds out of which the property is purchased viz.–

1. The funds should be received in India by way of inward remittance from any place outside India,
2. The funds should be those maintained in any non-resident account in accordance with the provisions of the Foreign Exchange Management Act and the regulations made by the Reserve Bank of India.

It is to be noted that no specific permission is required for purchase of commercial property either on the part of the seller or the purchaser. However, if an NRI is using the property in connection with any business or professional activity, a prior permission from the RBI is necessary under the Foreign Exchange Management (Establishment in India of Branch or Office or Other Place of Business) Regulations.

IMPORT OF GOLD / SILVER BY AN NRI

I am an NRI, willing to bring gold / silver in India. What are the legal formalities, which I should comply with?

An NRI who has stayed abroad for a continuous period of six months is allowed to bring gold upto 10 kilograms and silver upto 100 kilograms as part of their baggage once in 6 months. Such gold may be brought in any form including ornaments but should not be studded with precious stones, diamonds or pearls. Also, the delivery of the metals can be taken from the custom bonded warehouses, operated by the State Bank of India and the Minerals and Metals Trading Corporation, and hence one need not carry the metals physically. Customs duty as prescribed has to be paid while bringing the same. It is to be noted that if the said imported metals are sold to ordinary residents, the same can be done by way of a crossed cheque in India and shall be credited to Ordinary Non-resident Rupee Account of the NRI.

SOCIETY REGISTRATION

I wish to form a society for promotion of fine arts. Please make me aware of the issues related to society formation.

The Societies Registration Act provides for registration of literary, scientific and charitable societies. The relevant provisions are as under–

a) A minimum of 7 persons should subscribe their names to the memorandum of association, which shall contain name and object of the society with the name, addresses and occupation of the members of governing body of such society who will be managing the affairs.

b) A copy of the rules and regulations of the society certified to be a correct copy by not less than 3 of the members of governing body shall be filed with it.

c) The registrar shall certify under this hand the society to be registered. A nominal fee of about Rs. 50/- is payable.

d) Once in every year, on or before the 14th day succeeding the day on which, according to the rules of the society, the annual general meeting of the society is held, or if the rules do not provide for annual general meeting, in the month of January, a list shall be filed with the Registrar of the Joint Stock Companies, of the names, addresses and occupations of the Governors, Council, Directors, Committee or other governing body entrusted with the management of the affairs of the society.

e) The property belonging to the society, whether movable or immovable, if not vested in trustees, shall be deemed to be vested for the time being in the governing body of such society, and in all civil / criminal proceedings, the same may be described as property of the governing body of such society for their proper title.

f) Society may sue or be sued in the name of President, Chairman, Principal Secretary or Trustees, as shall be determined by the rules and in default of determination, in the name of such person as shall be appointed by the governing body on that occasion.

g) The governing body may take decision at anytime to alter or extend the purpose within the meaning of the Act. Moreover it can also amalgamate wholly or partly with some other society.

h) Members not less than $3/5^{th}$ of the total may determine the dissolution of society and all necessary steps should be taken for the settlement of the property, claims and liabilities, according to the rules of the said society, and in absence of it as the governing body decides. If after the satisfaction of all the debts and liabilities, any property whatsoever, it shall not to be paid / distributed among members of the said society or any of them, but shall be given to some other society.

Thus you may take help of the above-mentioned provisions and register your own society.

SPECIFIC PERFORMANCE

I had purchased a land and paid an advance for the same. However there was no sale deed and merely an agreement to sell was registered. Later on I learnt that the same land has been sold to someone else and has been registered in his name. I have sent a notice demanding my money back. Can I still claim the land from the person?

By asking for refund of the advance money, you have lost your right to claim specific performance of the agreement to sell. However, on the basis of the agreement and subject to the conditions contained therein, you may file a civil suit for recovery of the advance made under the agreement along with interest and other damages before an appropriate court of law.

A criminal case for cheating can also be filed for which the punishment is imprisonment for a term extending to seven years and fine.

TRANSFER OF PROPERTY - STANDARD RENT & LEASE

During our grandfather's time, our land was leased for 99 years to a company, which still exists. The rent of Rs 10/- per month, which was fixed at that time and is still continuing. The lease tenure will expire in 5 years. During the meantime can't we have any increase in rent? Also, can we claim the ownership over the property once the lease tenure comes to an end?

Fixing and increase in rent is governed by the local State laws which differs from State to State. However, it is to be noted that in general and subject to the relevant State laws, an application for fixing the Standard Rent can be made and if the Court comes to the conclusion that the rent being paid is too low, it may fix a standard rent for the same.

In respect of your second query, it seems that you are quite worried of the fact that you might not be entitled to ownership as the lease deed is for a very long tenure. However, you need not worry, and as per the Transfer of Property Act, during the period of the lease, the tenant has the right to hold the property but on expiry of the same, the landlord is entitled to possession of the leased land and the tenant has to vacate the same. If the tenant does not do so, the landlord can file a suit for recovery of possession. A tenant has only a subordinate interest in the property, and he is not entitled to the absolute ownership of the leased property even after a very long lease period like 99 years. The rule that 'A tenant is always a tenant and nothing but a tenant' applies.

HOUSING LAWS – CHANGE IN PLAN

I have purchased a flat in an under-construction apartment whose plans have been duly approved by the civic authorities. The builder now wishes to make changes in the

plan. Can he do so at his own sweet will? What are the consequences if he does so?

Each State has enacted its own law for regulating the construction, sale, transfer, etc. of buildings and has duly framed regulations and bylaws for such. Generally an owner of a plot or the builder, who wishes to construct a building, is bound to erect the building in accordance with the law. For this he is required to obtain the sanction from the civic authorities.

The authority has been empowered to inspect any such building and give such directions as it deems fit at any time during the erection of the building or after its completion if it feels that the erection of any building is contrary or without the sanction and if such construction is carried on without approval or contrary to the sanction, the authority may order that such work be stopped and may further direct that the building may be demolished by the person at whose instance the work has been commenced or is completed within such time as it deems fit. However, before any order of demolition is made, the owner / builder shall be given sufficient opportunity to show cause as to why such should not be demolished. The builder always has the option to appeal to a court against the orders of the authority. In the event of failure to comply with the prescribed sanctions, the Act prescribes a penalty of simple imprisonment and also fine. Hence, carrying out any work contrary to the sanctioned plan is harmful and may result not only in demolition of the building but also imprisonment.

If you are an owner of a flat in the under-construction building which is being built not in accordance to the sanction, then you should immediately contact the builder and if he persists in going with his work, then you should withdraw your interest in the building and also inform the concerned authorities.

•••

CHAPTER-8
CONSUMER RIGHTS AND TORTIOUS LIABILITY

CONSUMER RIGHTS

I purchased a shoe. However the shopkeeper refused to provide any guarantee / warrantee over the same. The leather of the shoe cracked within 10 days of its use. The shopkeeper denied his liability. Is there any mode by which I can make the shopkeeper liable?

Consumer Courts are established to give the consumers right in speedy and less expensive manner and will be most suitable in such cases where there is deficiency in service or defect in goods or the manufacturer / seller resorts to unfair trade practices. Such cases, which can be filed before the consumer fora, are those involving defect in goods, deficiency in services and unfair trade practices adopted by the seller. A District Consumer Forum is entitled to accept complaints to the tune of Rs 20 lakhs. Complaints involving amounts more than 20 lakhs but less than 1 crore can be made to the State Commission and any complaint above such value can only be made to the National Commission.

On the unwillingness of the seller as in this case a complaint by way of an application may be made to the consumer forum. On making such complaint the forum will serve a copy thereof to the other party and call upon it to present its case and hear the parties. In such instances proof of purchase of the good from the relevant shop (like cash memo, receipt, credit card bill etc) is essential unless the shopkeeper admits of the purchase. The forum may issue an order on the allegations being proved based on the evidence given by the parties. Such order may contain a direction to remove the defects in the goods or deficiency in the service in question or may even direct to replace the goods in total or may order for refund of price with or without compensation/costs. However the order so passed will be in conformity with the relief claimed and hence it is important that the reliefs are clearly and precisely mentioned. Even appointment of an advocate is not essential and the consumer may pursue the case himself.

Consumer fora are an alternative to the time taking, costly civil courts which are burdened with high technicalities and filing of a complaint petition is very easy and cost effective.

MEDICAL NEGLIGENCE

I was treated by a doctor in a government hospital free of cost but due to his negligence my legs had to be amputated. Can I do anything?

For claiming damages one has two remedies - he can approach the civil court or the consumer forum. However for approaching the consumer forum one must satisfy certain conditions apart from jurisdiction, that is–

1. The doctor does not work under a contract of personal service, or
2. The hospital, be it government or non-governmental, does not render free treatment without any exception.

Thus, even if there is a single paid bed in the hospital, irrespective of the fact whether one has paid any fee or not or the hospital is a government one, then in case of deficiency in service, one is entitled to claim damages.

However, where the hospital renders free treatment to all and does not charge anything, even though there might be deficiency in service, one can not approach the consumer forum, but a complaint can be lodged with the Medical Council of India and moreover the civil court too can be approached to make the hospital compensate / pay damages / penalty / fine for the loss suffered. The court while calculating the compensation takes various factors into consideration in respect to the patients like injuries suffered, social status, number of dependants, age of deceased, pecuniary loss suffered, etc.

It is to be noted that for damages, the consumer forum is the most suitable option and to establish criminal liability such as rash and negligent act, the regular Session Court is to be approached. Moreover there is no bar in approaching both courts simultaneously.

TORTS

I parked my vehicle in a pay-n-park stand. A tree, which was growing in the area so used for parking vehicles, fell on my car thereby heavily damaging it. Can I recover the expenses incurred in repair, and if so, from whom?

If there is no municipal law which grants or authorizes you to compensation, then such type of cases fall within the category of civil wrong under the Law of Torts. According to Law of Torts, a person who has any dangerous material over his land is liable to take all reasonable care to prevent the same from injuring others. Failure on part to take steps to prevent such occurrence of the injury warrants liability on part of the owner / possessor of the premises. Thus in these type of cases, the owner / possessor of the pay and park premises may be sued for the damages incurred, if it may be proved that there was likelihood of the tree falling on account of weak roots, or loose soil or otherwise and that the owner / possessor of the premises had not taken reasonable care to prevent its fall and that the fall was not an outcome of the external forces beyond the control of the owner / possessor like heavy wind, storm, flood, etc.

In case of a branch falling down and causing damage, if the tree belonged to the municipality and if it can be shown that the fall was a result of the municipality not performing its duties like identifying the dangerous branches and regularly trimming them or cutting them then the municipality can be made liable to pay damages.

For this you will have to approach the civil court which may grant such amount of compensation depending upon various factors like injuries suffered, damages caused, if death, then social status, number of dependants, age of deceased, pecuniary loss suffered, etc. are also taken into consideration.

•••

CHAPTER-9
INTELLECTUAL PROPERTY RIGHTS

PATENT, DESIGN, TRADEMARK

I am engaged in the field of developing a Perfume and would like to know about the Intellectual Property Rights which I can avail of, including those associated with its packing too.

To clarify your concept we take an example of Perfume itself–

The perfume may be packed in a certain unique 'U' shaped bottle, which is its design. Thus design is the features of shape, configuration, pattern, or ornament or composition of lines or colours or combination thereof applied to the article, whether 2 dimensional or 3 dimensional or in both forms, by any industrial process or means, whether manual, mechanical or chemical, separate or combined, which is in the finished article, appeal to and are judged solely by eye, but does not include any mode or principle or construction or anything which is in substance a mere device, and does not include any Trade Mark as defined in the Trade Mark Act.

The perfume or the scented liquid has been made by some specified process and it has specific composition of compounds which when mixed gives a unique odor. The composition and the odor are patent protected. Thus Patent is a monopoly right granted to a person who has invented a new and useful article or an improvement of an existing article or a new process of making an article. It consists of an exclusive right to manufacture the new article invented or manufacture an article according to the invented process for a limited period.

The Bottle has on its label printed a mark 'X', which is its Trade Mark. Thus Trade Mark may be any mark, symbol, letter, brand, devices, numerals or any combination thereof, used or proposed to be used by manufacturers of goods to identify and to distinguish their goods from goods manufactured and sold by others.

Intellectual Property Rights grant protection of rights in form of Patents, Designs, Trade Marks, Copyrights, etc.

Patent is the protection given to the inventor over his rights in the new invention.

Designs are the protection of the special outward appearance of the good that makes it identifiable and distinguishable from other similar goods.

Trade Marks are the protection given for the use of the marks, be it in form of symbol, logo, punch line etc. that helps in the easy identification of the source of the goods.

Patents are granted in case of invention of a new product. However, in case of medicines / drugs, full product patent is not granted and only process patent in respect of exclusive marketing right is granted. The patent can be obtained by making an application in the said format detailing about the product along with the relevant specification i.e. details of manufacturing. Patent once granted gives the patentee the exclusive right to use the said product for a term of 20 years, which is counted from the date of filing of the application for patent. A patent is kept alive only by paying the renewal fee from time to time. However, no patent is granted in case of inventions relating to atomic energy.

It is to be noted that as you are still in the process of inventing the Anti-AIDS vaccine, you can apply for patent of the same by submitting a provisional specification, and the complete specification of the invention has to be filed within a period of 12 months thereafter failing so your application will be deemed to have been abandoned. This provisional specification will entitle you to claim priority of patent over your product.

In the case of designs, the right granted is the exclusive right to apply the design registered under the Design Act for a period of 10 years, in relation to the class of goods for which it is registered, renewable for a further period of 5 years. Thus, the copyright on design is for a maximum period of 15 years.

Trademarks also similarly grants the exclusive right over the use of such distinguishable marks, logo, punch lines, etc. granted for a period of 10 yrs. that can be renewed from time to time for period of 10 years on payment of the prescribed fees.

It is to be noted that these rights can be licensed for use by third parties or assigned to any person. Also, on the expiry of the term of the intellectual property right, anybody can use the same.

The purpose of having such intellectual property right is for protection from unauthorized use of the said product or from copying its outward appearance and making it resemble a good, and thereby selling the same as that, which it is not. Such rights therefore grant exclusive right to use the product and also the right to license the same.

COPYRIGHT

I wish to publish a work of a renowned writer, presently dead. The work was previously published in a newspaper around 10 yrs ago and I wish to include the same in my book. Would I be violating any law?

A written or literally work once published, the author is granted protection against any publication of the same without permission. Such right by which the author is protected is known as copyright. Copyright is granted for literary, artistic, musical, cinematographic films, dramas, computer programs and the likes and this right commences from the date of publication of the work and continues throughout the life of the author and 60years after his death. This 60-year period starts from the year after the year of death of the author. In cases of joint authorship, the said tenure of 60 years is to be calculated after the year of death of the last surviving author and in case where the author is unknown or non-traceable like as in anonymous writings, the copyright over the said work remains till a period of 60 years commencing from the year after the year of publication.

No person can use the said work during the said period without the permission of the author. Hence, as only 10 yrs have expired, you cannot publish the work without the consent of the author, and if there is no author, without the consent of the newspaper. Permission can be so granted on payment of a charge or even without so, depending upon the discretion of the person.

COMPARITIVE ANALYSIS OF PATENT, COPYRIGHT AND TRADEMARK

	PATENT	COPYRIGHT	TRADEMARK	Design
Right Protected	Right conferred in respect of manufacture and sale of a product of new invention but in case of medicines only patent of exclusive marketing rights is granted.	Right conferred in respect of original, literary, dramatic, musical, artistic works, cinematograph film and records, software programmes	Right conferred to use a particular mark, which may be a symbol, word, device applied to articles of commerce to indicate the distinctiveness of goods.	Right conferred to use a special outward appearance of the goods making it identifiable and distinguishable from other similar goods.
Who Can Register	Actual inventor or an assignee of the right to make an application or legal representative of either.	The author or publisher of, or owner of or other person interested in the copyright in any work.	Proprietor of the trademark and application may be made in the name of an individual, partners of a Firm, Corporation, Government department or Trust.	Any person claiming to be the proprietor of any new and original design not previously published in any country may apply for the registration of design.
Remedy for infringement	Injunction, Damages, Accounts of profits.	Civil, Criminal, Administrative.	Injunction, Damages, Accounts of profits	Interlocutory injunction, damages or compensation

Objection Your Honour

Time required for the grant of Intellectual Property Rights in India.

IPR's	Time taken for the Grant	Validity Period	Renewal Period
Patent	3-5 Yrs	20 Yrs	Annual
Trademark	1-2 Yrs	7 Yrs	First renewal period 6 Yrs from lodgment date. To further renewal 5 Yrs.
Design	6-8 Months	10 Yrs	5 Yrs
Copyright	1-12 Months	Lifetime plus 60 years for literary, dramatic, musical and artistic works. 60 years from year of publication for records.	Not applicable

CHAPTER-10
INFORMATION TECHNOLOGY

HACKING

I often access Internet to check e- mails and visit different sites, at the same time I have my own website. One day I forgot to log off my e-mail and after a few days when I was accessing my site I found certain information, image display and links of my site has been changed and unwarranted matters have been put up. Moreover my computer security system has been broken certain document present in the computer system has been altered. What should I do now?

The incident that has taken place on your site is called hacking and the person who has done it, is termed as hacker. Under The Information Technology Act-2000, hacking is a gravest offence and the remedies available are punitive as well as compensatory in nature.

Hacking is a process, generally committed on internet, through which a person tries to enter into any other computer system and likely to cause wrongful loss or damage to the public or any person destroys or deletes or alters any information present in a computer resource or diminishes its value or utility or affects it injuriously by any means such as computer program or any other software.

The person who commits hacking (hacker) shall be punished with imprisonment up to three years, or with fine, which may extend up to two lakh rupees, or with both.

To enforce this remedy the grieved person must file a suit in the court of Judicial Magistrate First Class. [JMFC]

There are various other modes of hacking such as
1. Unauthorized Access
2. Viruses
3. Worms
4. Trojan horses
5. Logic bomb
6. Data diddling:
7. Tempest Attack
8. Password cracking

1. Unauthorized Access: - This activity is commonly referred to as hacking. The Indian Law has however given a different connotation to the term hacking. It can be motivated by a computer hacker's curiosity or by a desire to sabotage the computer system.

2 Viruses - A virus is a program that may or may not attach itself to a file and replicate itself. It can attack any area from corrupting the data of the file that it invades using the computer's processing resource in an attempt to crash the machine.

3. Worms: Worms may invade a computer and steal its resources to replicate itself. They use the network to spread themselves. "Love Bug" is one of them.

4. Trojan Horses: Trojan Horses are dicey and appear to do one thing but does something else. The system may accept it as one thing and upon execution it may release a virus, worm or logic bomb.

5. Logic Bombs: Is an attachment trigged by an event like a computer clock reaching a certain date. Chernobyl and Melissa are the other recent examples.

6. Data Diddling: This kind of an attack involves altering the raw data just before a computer processes it and then changing it back after the processing is completed.

7. Tempest Attack – This is one of the most recently developed mode through which hacking is easily possible and in present it is popular only in highly developed countries like U.S.A and Russia.

Tempest is the ability to monitor electromagnetic emissions from computers in order to reconstruct the data. This allows remote monitoring of network cables or remotely viewing monitors. The word **TEMPEST** is usually understood to stand for "**Transient Electromagnetic Pulse Emanation Standard**". There are some fonts that remove the high-frequency information, and thus severely reduce the ability to remotely view text on the screen. PGP also provides this option of using tempest resistant fonts.

For an example: - An appropriately equipped computer / laptop can be taken near the target computer or the target premises and from there it can remotely catch all the keystrokes and messages displayed on the computer video screen of the target system. This even includes passwords; messages, images and others displayed items. Such attack can be thwarted by properly shielding computer equipment and network cabling so that they do not emit these signals.

PORNOGRAPHY

I am a young lady and I often use e-mail to send my photograph to my relatives who reside abroad. One day when I visited a cyber café, I was shocked to see my nude photo on the net, which was displayed by an unknown site. What should I do to prevent this and to whom should I approach?

Pornography under the information technology act is considered as one of the most serious offences. It is explicit representation of sexual activity in literature; film etc intended to stimulate erotic rather then aesthetic or emotional feelings. Publishing of information, which is obscene in electronic form, is an offence under the Act.

The Information technology Act 2000 has clearly laid that any person who publishes or transmits or causes to be published in the electronic form, any material which is lascivious or appeals to the prurient interest or if its effect is such as to tend to corrupt persons who are likely, having regard to all relevant circumstances, to read, see or hear the matter contained or embodied in it commits an offence under the Act.

The person committing such an offence shall be punished on first conviction with imprisonment of either description for a term which may extend to five years and with fine which may extend to one lakh rupees and in the event of a second or subsequent Conviction, with imprisonment of either description for a term which may extend to ten years and also with fine which may extend to two lakh rupees.

To avail the remedy, the aggrieved person must file a suit under section 67 of the Act in the Court of Judicial Magistrate First Class. Moreover an F.I.R. must be lodged in the nearest Police Station. Some states like Maharashtra, Karnataka & Goa has formed a Special Cyber Crime Police Station. The Police can take assistance of a cyber-expert to deal with such cases.

DIGITAL SIGNATURE

I have to send documents through e-mail on regular basis. Is there any provision of signature, which can authenticate the documents? Please help.

The Information Technology Act 2000 has provided a magnificent provision regarding digital signature. Digital signature basically provides authentication to the documents, which are send through Internet. For example in case of e-mail, there is button which provides digital signature if a person press that button the system ask for a password which may be any word, sentence, numeral or combination of all these. Once the user gives the password, it is considered as his digital signature. And later on when the user mails any document through e-mail, his password will be also accompanied with the document. The only important thing is that the receiver must have knowledge of the digital signature of the sender of the document in form of password, to ascertain it.

ELECTRONIC CONTRACT

I am a businessman and my business has expanded a lot and now I am preparing to carry it even through 'E-Contract'. Please guide me on the issue in detail.

The provision of E-Contract has been elaborately dealt in the Information Technology Act 2000. Electronic Contract is such a transaction, which is mainly carried out by means of electronic data interchange, or by other means of electronic communication, which is generally called "Electronic Commerce". This involves the use of other modes rather than paper-based methods of communication and storage of information.

In case of 'E-Contract' the parties are called 'originator and addressee' instead of 'Proposer' and 'accepter' as in case of general contract.

In case of E-contract, Originator is a person who offers any contract through Internet and addressee is the person to whom the offer is made.

In case of general contracts, delivery is considered to be an important factor. Delivery, makes both the parties aware, of the physically transfer of the document. However, this is not the same with E-contract. The knowledge, that whether the other party has received the document or not is difficult to obtain. Therefore acknowledgement of such that it has been received in correct form, plays an important part.

Moreover in case of E-Contract, the place and time of Contract are immaterial since the transmission of data defeats both time and geographical barriers.

Similar as to general contract even in E-Contract the essentials are offer, acceptance and consideration. Moreover such E-Contract should not be one opposing the public interest, like committing any crime or publishing obscene images etc.

The terms and condition of such Contract should be in clear words. Performance should be made within thirty days of order unless the contrary is expressly agreed.

Moreover there are various techniques / methods to protect the consumers against unknown sellers and sellers against unknown buyers.

The payment of such transaction too is generally done on-line or through Credit Cards etc.

If any of the party does not acts according to the agreed conditions like not supplying the pre-determined quality or quantity of goods or service or non-payment of the amount due, makes the party liable for Breach of Contract. The party becomes liable as an according to the Indian Contract Act too.

CYBER CRIME

I frequently access Internet and talk to unknown people. Due to the same I have lots of chat-friends. On a friendly talk with one of such chat-friends, I told him that my entire secret documents, credit card numbers, passwords etc. are stored in my computer and did challenge him to break my security system. I was shocked to note that he not only did break into my system, but also literally changed the ingredients therein and is also now threatening me of either fulfilling his demands or else he would create havoc in my life. He has also threatened me of transmitting a nude photo of mine across the net. Can I stop him from doing so?

Under the Information Technology Act, any person who tampers or hacks a computer system with the intention of causing wrongful loss or damage or destroys or deletes or alters any information residing in a computer resource or diminishes its value or utility or affects it injuriously by any means is said to commit the offence of hacking and is liable for imprisonment upto three years and/or with fine which may extend upto two lakh rupees. Also, publishing or transmitting any obscene material shall be punished on first conviction with imprisonment of either description for a term which may extend to 5 years and with fine which may extend to one lakh rupees and in the event of 2nd or subsequent conviction with imprisonment of either description for a term which may extend to 10 years and also with fine which may extend to Rs. 2,00,000/-.

However, it is to be noted that ascertaining a person on the Internet is a tough task, though not impossible. A complaint can be lodged under the Information Technology Act with the special authorities so appointed therein or can also be lodged with the police. The whereabouts of the said person can be traced by using the specialized and highly technical software and the accused is liable to be convicted under the said Act and also under the Indian Penal Code. Thus, the only remedy available in such situations is to contact the authorities concerned and render them all possible help, which would lead to the arrest and conviction of the accused.

•••

CHAPTER-11
BUSINESS ACTIVITIES

COMMENCING BUSINESS

I wish to start a business along with my friends. I have been told that registering a 'Company' is a tedious task whereas 'Partnership' limits the scope of extension. I am totally confused; please suggest?

A business can be started in 2 ways: - by forming a Company or by entering into a Partnership. The technicalities involved in registering a partnership is much simpler than that required for registration of a company. The basic principle of Partnership is sharing the profits of business. The maximum number of members, which can form a partnership, is 20 (10 in case of banking business) and it requires least formalities for commencing a business. However, it has a major disadvantage that the liability of the member is unlimited i.e. the members can be made liable for the whole of the debts / losses so occasioned. The requisites of a partnership is entering into a partnership deed and thereby eventually determining the rights, duties and liabilities of the partners. A partnership firm is to be registered with the Registrar of Firms in the prescribed format containing details of the firm and its members. It may be noted that the registration of a partnership firm is not essential, however, registration has an added advantage that the partners may sue and be sued only in the name of the firm.

In case of a Company the liability of the members can be limited but formation of a Company requires a lot of formalities, as it is a legal entity thereby having the capacity to sue and be

Objection Your Honour

sued. A Company's name is required to be approved by the Registrar of the Companies. Before doing so, the name and logo of the Company is required to be verified as to whether any similar name / logo is existing or not. Thereafter, Memorandum of Association and Articles of Association is to be finalized and attached along with the registration form. This is to be followed by a statutory declaration by an authorized person, a notice of the place of business, details of the Directors and other minute requisites are to be submitted within a period of 6 months from the date of approval of the Company's name by the Registrar.

In case of Partnership, if any of the partners dies, retires or becomes insolvent a new contract of partnership is required whereas in case of a company it has perpetual succession. Moreover in partnership, a partner is not entitled to transfer his interest without the consent of the other partners whereas in Company every member has a right to transfer his share. In partnership, all persons are regarded as joint-owner, whereas a Company being a separate person has its own property. Partnership has a major advantage in sense that each partner is entitled to participate in the management, whereas in Company members seldom have right to share in the management. Other advantage in a partnership is that, the share capital and the terms of the contract may vary by mutual consent, whereas in Company, it cannot be altered except under certain conditions. Moreover a Company's account is required to be audited every year whereas in Partnership, it is not necessary but mere desirable.

Thus both the entities have its merits and demerits. In small scale i.e. where the number of members is quite less and the stakes in terms of money involved are not quite large, a partnership firm is more advisable. However, in the long run a Company is more beneficial as it gives the flexibility of increasing the capital in the business through public investment by way of shares, debentures and likes. Further in a Company the liability of the members are limited to the amount of their respective shares wherein in a partnership the members are personally liable for the entire liability of the partnership firm. It is to be noted here that a partnership firm can be converted into a Company as and when required.

INCORPORATION

I wish to start my own company. What are the legal formalities necessary to do so?

Incorporation (or in other terms registration) of a company involves satisfaction of the various legal formalities enunciated under the Companies Act, which are as under:

1. Submission of an application for getting approval in respect of the name of the company, to the Registrar of the Companies through Form-1A and thereby furnishing details as to the company's activities, authorized capital, list of Directors and Promoters, etc. along with the prescribed fees. It should be noted that a minimum of 2 Directors and a Minimum Paid-Up Capital of Rs 1 Lakh is required for setting up of a Company.

2. After receiving the aforesaid approval, the following additional requisites are to be fulfilled within a period of 6 months, viz:

   a) A Statutory declaration by an authorized person is required to be executed in the prescribed manner,

   b) Copy of letter of Registrar indicating approval of name,

   c) Notice of address of registered office of the Company,

   d) Particulars of the Directors like their name, address, etc.

   e) Power of Attorney from the subscribers authorizing any one person to act on their behalf at the Registrar's office.

   f) The Memorandum and Articles of Association is to be signed by at least two subscribers and witnessed by one person.

After scrutiny of the documents the Registrar, if satisfied, may issue a Certificate of Incorporation.

MEMORANDUM OF ASSOCIATION

I am going to start a company. I wish to know the importance of Memorandum of Association in a Company.

Memorandum of Association is a document which sets out the constitution of a Company and as such it is really the foundation on which the structure of the company is based. Thus it defines relation of the company with the outside world, its scope and activities.

The main objects of the MOA are–

i. The intending Corporator, contemplating the investment of the capital comes to know within that field it is to be put at risk.

ii. Anyone dealing with the Company comes to know without reasonable doubt, whether the Contractual relation into which he contemplates entry with the Company is one relating to the matter within its corporate object.

As the MOA is a public document so every person dealing with the Company is presumed to have the knowledge of its contents. Whoever dealing with the company may ask from it a copy of its MOA and the company is bound to supply the same on a payment of a fee of Rs. 1. At Registrar's Office too it is kept open for public inspection.

MOA contains clauses relating with Name, Situation, Object, Territory, Liability, Capital, Association etc.

ARTICLE OF ASSOCIATION

I know about Memorandum of Association, but what is Article of Association?

Like Memorandum of Association, even Article of Association is a document of a Company containing rules and regulations, necessary for the administration of the company. Thus this is called Article of Association or internal rules of a company by which it is governed.

Article of Association regulates the rights of the members of a company among themselves and the manner in which the business of the company shall be conducted.

Company limited by guarantee, Company limited by shares and unlimited company must register the Article of Association along with the Memorandum of Association.

It is not absolutely necessary for a Public Company limited by shares.

The Article of Association deals with definition of important terms and phrases, exclusion, total or partial of Table (a), adoption or execution of preliminary contracts, procedure of making calls and forfeiture of shares, share capital and rights attached to different clauses of shares, appointment of Managerial personnel e.g. Directors, Managing Directors, their rights-duties and powers, rules regarding transfer and transmission of shares, issue of shares, meetings, general meeting, dividends, alteration of share capital, remuneration to directors etc, accounts and audit, lien on member's shares and winding up the company.

The Article of Association should not be in contradiction to Memorandum of Association.

COMPANY SHARES

There are various offers in the newspaper of the Companies inviting people to buy their shares. I would like to know more about the same esp. as to what is a share and whether after buying I can re-sell the same at a profit.

Companies who are public limited i.e. are registered as Public Companies with the Registrar of Companies often call for investments in the Company from the public by issuing shares / debentures. Shares is a mode of investment made by an individual and is not a sum of money but represents an interest measured by a sum of money and made up of diverse rights contained in the contract and guided by the Articles of association of a company. Once a person subscribes to a share in a company, he is making an investment in the company and can be said to become a member of the company. He is entitled to profits by way of dividends or bonuses and is also liable for loss up to the amount he has invested in the company. The share may be issued at a premium i.e. more than its nominal value or at a discount, i.e. less than its market value.

An application for share is an offer and may be a conditional one and lapses if not accepted within a reasonable time. Generally an allotment is made once minimum subscription is received. The company is entitled to fix such amount as application money, which shall not be less than 5% of the nominal amount. If the minimum subscription is not received within 120 days from the first issue of prospectus, the company is bound to return the same before the 130th day, failure to do will make the director's liable to pay the amount with interest @ 6% per annum.

There are basically two types of Share Capitals:
1. Preference share capital
2. Equity share capitals.

1. Preference share capital means that part of the share capital, which fulfills the following requirements, viz., -
a) during the continuance of the company it will carry preferential right in respect of dividends, and
b) in the event of winding up of the company, it will have a preferential right as to the repayment of the paid-up capital.

It is to be noted that Preference share capitals holders have right to vote on only those resolutions which directly affects the rights attached to the preference shares. Preference shares may be of 3 types–

i) Participating and non-participating preference shares- those preferential share holders who have the additional right to participate in the surplus dividends or the surplus capital along with the equity shareholders are participating preference shares and those who are not entitled to share the surplus after paying them the fixed rate of dividend are called non-participating preference shares.

ii) Cumulative and non-cumulative preference shares-in case of cumulative preference shares, if there are no sufficient profits to pay the dividends to the preference shares in a particular year, the deficiency is carried forward and paid from the profits of the subsequent year while in cases where the dividends cannot be carried forward and it lapses, the same is known as non- cumulative preference shares.

iii) Redeemable and irredeemable preference shares-those which can be paid back are known as redeemable preference shares and those which cant are irredeemable preference shares (irredeemable preference shares and redeemable preference shares redeemable after 20years are prohibited from being issued).

2. All other share capitals are known as Equity share capitals. It may with -

a) Voting rights, i.e. right to vote in respect of such capital on any resolution placed before the company, which will be in proportion to his share of the paid-up equity capital of the company.

b) Differential rights as to dividend, voting or otherwise.

There's yet another category of shares, viz., Sweat Equity shares, i.e. shares issued by the company to employees or directors at a discount or for consideration other than cash like for providing know-how or making available rights etc.

Once a person has purchased shares of a company, a certificate under the seal of the company (Share Certificate) specifying the number of shares held by the member and this would be prima facie proof of his being a member of the company. The said certificate has to be issued within 3 months of the allotment of any share or within 2 months after the application for registration of the transfer of any such share is received. Failure to do so makes every officer so liable for fine extending to Rs. 5000/-.

Shares once bought are transferable, as it is a movable property. However the same is subject to the terms specified in the Articles of the company. The Board of directors may prohibit transfer only in the interest of the company. While transferring shares an application for registration of the transfer may be made either by the transferor or the transferee along with the production of the instrument of transfer in the prescribed form duly stamped, executed by both the parties along with the share certificates. However, if the Board refuses to register the transfer, it has to give a notice of refusal within two months from the date of receipt of instrument of transfer. An appeal against the said notice can be made to the Company Law Board within 2 months of the receipt of notice or within 4 months from the date of delivery of instrument to transfer in absence of any communication within 2 months of the date of delivery of instrument.

It is to be noted that now, all companies whose initial public offer is more than Rs 10 crore are issuing the same in electronic (dematerialized) form thereby making purchase and selling of shares very easy and quick.

DEBENTURES

I had invested in debentures of a company. More than one and a half year has elapsed and the company has not commenced business. I am quite worried about my investments. Please advise.

Investment in nature of debenture is a quite secured investment and this can be equated to a loan given to the company. A debenture holder is the creditor of the Company and not the member and whatever be the fate of the company the debenture holder has always the 1st right to be repaid. Hence there is not much need to worry and you may even apply for redemption of the debentures.

OPPRESSION BY MAJORITY

I am a minority shareholder in a Company. The majority shareholders are conducting the day to day functioning of the Company in a manner detrimental to my interest. Is there any way of protecting my interest?

The Company Law emphasizes upon functioning of the company for the benefit of the Public and especially it's members. If any member is being oppressed or the acts of the Company is detrimental to the public interest then the concerned member or any one can make an application to the Company Law Board which in turn may make such order as it deems fit including the order of winding up. The Company Law Board is also competent to bring about any material change in the management or control of the company in case of mismanagement. However in cases of oppression and mismanagement, only a member or members holding not less than $1/10^{th}$ of the issued share capital of the company (in case of a company having a share capital and having not less than 100 members) while in cases where the company is not having share capital, a minimum of $1/5^{th}$ of the total number of members can apply to Company Law Board to seek relief against oppression and mis management.

MERGER

I am an employee of a company and also have purchased

some of its shares. However, I have heard that it is merging with another company. I am quite afraid about my rights. Please do state the complete aspect of merger as well as its effect on the rights of the shareholders and the workers.

Merger of a Company is occasioned by formulation of a scheme-an agreement wherein all the assets, liabilities and rights of one company are taken over by another company. This is to be occasioned by a scheme, which is required to have sanction of the Court. However, it is to be noted that while granting such sanction, the Court would look into the interests of the affected people especially the workmen and may enforce conditions in respect of their absorption where possible or otherwise payment of appropriate sum including all legal dues, which is generally paid by the company so merging.

FRAUD

I had applied for shares of a particular company after seeing its prospectus, which stated that it had acquired some oil wells. However, later on I learnt that the said statement was false. Though no loss has been suffered by me, but I would like to make the director liable for such false statements. Can I do so?

According to the Companies Act, where a prospectus contains some untrue statements, any person who acts on the basis of such is entitled to claim compensation for loss or damage sustained by him due such statements in the prospectus. Such compensation is liable to be claimed from–

a) Director of the company;
b) Every person who has himself authorized to be named in the prospectus;
c) Promoter;
d) Every person who is authorized to issue the prospectus.

It is to be noted that such persons are competent to defend themselves by pleading ignorance of the fact in the prospectus. However, they will have to prove such and also that as soon as they came to know of the fact of the untrue statement, a public notice to the effect that the said statement was issued without their knowledge was required to be immediately given and in case one had consented to the prospectus, the consent was to be immediately withdrawn and a notice to such effect was immediately given but before the issuance of shares.

Hence, in this case, you could have sued for compensation if any loss / damage, would have occasioned, but as this is not the case, no compensation can be claimed from the Directors. However, you can make all such persons involved in the issuance of the prospectus criminally liable for such misstatements and the punishment provided to such person is imprisonment upto 2 years and or fine upto Rs. 50,000/-. Still in such cases, the concerned persons can escape punishment by proving that the statement was immaterial, or he had reasonable ground to believe the statement to be true.

It is to be noted here, that if the company had literally come near being the owner of the oil wells and if it was merely some procedural delays which prohibited them from being such, they would not be liable for deceit as there was no intention of doing such.

WINDING UP OF COMPANY

Please guide me about the procedure, circumstances and consequences of winding-up of a Company?

Winding up of a company is the process whereby its life comes to an end and its property is administered for the benefit of its creditors and members.

The modes of winding up of a company are as following–
1. Winding up by the Tribunal; and
2. Voluntary winding up.

1. Winding up by Tribunal.

A Company may be wound up at an order of the Court. This is called Compulsory winding up, which can take place in following circumstances.

i. Special Resolution

A Court may pass an order of winding up of a Company, if

the Company has, by special resolution, resolved that it would be wound up by the Court.

ii. Default in holding Statutory Meeting

If a Company has made a default in delivering the statutory report to the Registrar or in holding the Statutory meeting, it may be ordered to be wound up.

iii. Failure to commence business

If a Company does not commence business within a year from its incorporation or has suspended business for a whole year, it may be ordered to wound up.

iv. Reduction in membership

If the number of members is reduced in the case of a public company, below seven, and in the case of a private company, below two, the company may be ordered to wound up.

v. Inability to pay debts

A Company may be awarded to be wound up if it is unable to pay its debts.

vi. Just and equitable reason

Another ground on which a Tribunal may order the winding up of company is when it is of the opinion that it is just and equitable that the company should be wound up. This gives the Court a very wide discretionary power to order winding up whenever it appears to be desirable, keeping the interest of the company, its employee, creditors, shareholders and public interest in mind.

vii. Default in filing documents

The Tribunal may pass an order of winding up if the company has made a default in filing with the Registrar its balance sheet and profit and loss account or annual return for any five consecutive financial years.

2. Voluntary Winding up

The law provides for winding up by the Tribunal, where a company is being wound up voluntary.

According to that provision:

i. Where a company is being wound up voluntarily a petition for winding up by the Tribunal may be presented by any of

the following persons:
- a. any person authorized to do so, i.e.
  - i) a company;
  - ii) any creditor or creditors;
  - iii) any contributory or contributories;
  - iv) all or any of the above parties separately or jointly
  - v) the Registrar;
  - vi) the Central Government
  - vii) the Central or State Government
- **b. The Official Liquidator**

(2) The Tribunal shall not make an order on a winding up petition, unless it is satisfied that the voluntary winding up cannot be continued with due regard to the interests of the creditors or contributories or both.

Commencement of Winding up takes place in the following way–

i. Where before the presentation of a petition for the winding up of a company by the tribunal, a resolution has been passed by the company for voluntary winding up of the company shall be deemed to have commenced at the time of the passing of resolution.

ii. In any other case, the winding up of a company by the Tribunal shall be deemed to commence at the time of the presentation of the petition for the winding up.

Consequences of winding up order–

The following are the consequences of winding up order:

i. Firstly, the Court shall intimate the winding up order to be sent to the liquidator and the Registrar. It is also the duty of the petitioner of the Company to file with the Registrar, within 30 days, a certified copy of the order.

ii. Secondly, winding up order is deemed to be a notice of discharge to the Officers and employees of the company, except when the business of the Company is continued.

iii. Thirdly, the order operates in favour of all the creditors and all the contributories of the company.

Fourthly, on a winding up order being made in respect of a company, the official liquidator, by virtue of his office, becomes the liquidator of the company.

FOREIGN INVESTMENT

I wish to start a business with foreign collaboration and the said foreigners are ready to invest money in such joint venture. What are the legal formalities involved in such foreign investments?

For foreign investment it is necessary that the money be used for investing in the shares of the Indian Company. Under, the Foreign Exchange Management (Transfer of Security by a Person Resident outside India) Regulation issued by the Reserve Bank of India (RBI), under Foreign Exchange Management Act (FEMA), foreign investment in India is allowed through two routes: the Automatic Route and by Government Approval.

Automatic route is that where no approval from the Foreign Investment Promotion Board / RBI is required for making the investment. Under this foreign investments upto 100% is permitted in certain sectors, while in others there is a ceiling for such investment.

Government approval is necessary for – all proposals that require an Industrial License, which includes–

(i) Items requiring an Industrial License under the Industries (Development and Regulation) Act, 1951;

(ii) Foreign investment if it is more than 24% in the equity capital of units of manufacturing items reserved for small scale industries;

(iii) All items which require an Industrial License in terms of the Location Policy notified by Government under the New Industrial Policy of 1991;

(iv) All proposals in which the foreign collaborator has a previous venture / tie-up in India in same or allied field (this, however, shall not apply to investment made in the Information Technology Sector);

(v) All proposals relating to acquisition of shares in an existing Indian company in favour of a foreign investor; and

(vi) All proposals falling outside notified sectoral policy/caps or under sectors in which Foreign Direct Investment is not permitted.

TRUST FORMALITIES

I wish to donate some of my property to a trust for the benefit of the public. What are the legal formalities for doing so? Can I impose a condition that some part of the property would be used for the benefit of my family members?

While donating the property to a trust the only requisite is that you should be the owner of that property and the transfer should be occasioned by a valid deed of transfer. The trust property can be donated to any established trust and you can also form a trust with the permission of the principal Civil Court.

Imposing a condition is not possible in case of bequeathing the property to a public trust; however, you can create a separate private trust in favour of your family members. The essential conditions for creating a trust is that it should be for a lawful and a charitable purpose and can be created by every person competent to contract, such trust may be either private or public trust.

DELEGATION OF POWER OF A TRUSTEE

I am a co-trustee and wish to delegate my powers to a third person. Can this be done?

A co-trustee is entitled to delegate his powers to another person in very limited circumstances, i.e. where the–

a. Instrument of trust provides so
b. Delegation is in the regular course of business
c. Delegation is essential
d. Beneficiary, being competent to contract consents to the delegation

Hence, though delegation can be made but one shall do it in the limited sphere as allowed.

TRUST – DEFENDING THE SUIT

A suit has been instituted against the trust property. I am a trustee of the same and wish to defend the suit. Can I do so? Who will be liable for the expenses incurred by me?

For the protection and benefit of the trust property a suit can be instituted by any one whether a beneficiary or a trustee. The expenses so incurred including the execution thereof as well as any act so done in the interest of the property, can be reimbursed. Even in situation of loosing the case, if one is honest in respect of the deeds performed and have taken leave of the court to sue or defend, all such expenses are entitled to be reimbursed. In a situation where no leave is applied for, the cost of litigation will be reimbursed only if the action was defended or brought in the interest of the Trust.

SETTLEMENT THROUGH ARBITRATOR

I entered into a contract with a person. However, disputes have arisen between us and we now wish to have the same settled through arbitration. Can we do so even though there was no arbitration agreement in the original contract? What is the mode of doing so?

Arbitration is the alternate remedy to the lengthy, expensive judicial mode of settlement of dispute. It is an adjudication over the disputes between the parties other than by means of a Court, by a person who has been agreed upon by the parties, to be the judge, and decide the matter and while doing so, the technicalities of Law are set aside and the principles of Natural Justice is much adhered to.

For arbitration the most essential element is the existence of an Arbitration Agreement or an Arbitration Clause in the Original Agreement. The agreement may be for all future disputes so arising between the parties and can also be for all existing disputes. An arbitration agreement may be in form of an arbitration clause or a separate agreement.

However, it is required to be in writing and the fact of arbitration can also be inferred from the documents of communications between the parties. The provision regarding the number of arbitrators can also be prescribed, however, such shall not be even. In case of no prescribed number, it will be deemed to be a Sole Arbitrator. The parties can prescribe the procedure for selection of the arbitrator and in case a party does not go ahead with the selection of the same, the Chief Justice of the High Court can be approached for selection who will do so keeping in view the procedure prescribed.

However, not all matters are arbitral and matters for which 'Special Courts' have been created or matters pertaining to Family disputes, Crime as provided in Indian Penal Code, and those not arising from Contracts are not triable in arbitral proceedings.

The judgment given in Arbitration is known as 'Award' and is equally binding as that made by a Civil Court. No court is competent to interfere in the arbitral proceedings till its disposal. The parties are free to prescribe the procedure to be followed by the arbitrator and the Arbitral Tribunal is competent to ask for court assistance in taking evidence as well as seeking Expert Opinions.

However, in certain instances the Award can be challenged and set aside, viz–

a. The party was under some incapacity;
b. Arbitration agreement is not valid under the law;
c. Party was not given adequate notice of the appointment of arbitrator, commencement of proceedings or was not able to present his case correctly;
d. Composition of arbitral tribunal not in accordance to the procedure prescribed;
e. Arbitral Award is beyond the point of reference;
f. Arbitral Award in conflict with the public policy of India;
g. Dispute not arbitral.

However, such setting aside application is required to be made within 3 months from the receipt of the Arbitral Award, and the court can still entertain the same on sufficient grounds within a further period of 30 days.

Thus, even if there is no arbitration clause in the original agreement, the parties may, if they wish, amend the same or make another agreement expressly stating their intention to go for arbitration in case of any dispute.

•••

CHAPTER-12
TAXATION

INCOME TAX

I wish to start a business. I know that I will be liable to pay Income Tax. However, I hardly know anything about it. I would like to know the general concept about tax. Please advice.

Tax is a mode of income (earning) of the government. There are two types of taxes-

a) Direct Tax- it can be understood as the tax which is directly demanded from the person / individual or in other words, a tax taken directly from income or property.

b) Indirect Tax- the tax demanded from one person in the expectation and intention that he will indemnify himself at the expense of another. E.g. Excise or Custom tax.

Income tax is a form of Direct tax, which an individual is liable to pay from his earnings.

There are some major terms which are required to be understood for the purpose of Income Tax, viz–

a) Previous Year also known as Accounting Year- it is the year preceding the year of Assessment.

b) Assessment Year- it is the period of 12 months starting with April 1st of the year and ending on March 31st of the next year.

c) Person means an individual, Hindu Undivided Family (HUF), Company, Firm, Association of Persons (AOP) or body of individuals (BOI), local authority, and artificial juridical person.

An income earned in a previous year is taxable immediately in the following assessment year. In case a business is set up or a profession is started, the previous year is counted from the date of setting up of the business and ending on the immediate following March 31st.

For e.g.- If a business is started on 5th Dec 2004. The Previous Year for the same is 5th Dec 2004 to 31st March 2005 and the assessment year is 2005-06.

Every income how so small is taxable. However, in cases of income of an individual, the individual is not liable to pay any tax for income upto Rs. 50,000/-

Income is the gain (profit) which is the proceeds (result / outcome) from labor, business or property of any kind. However, the Income Tax Act does exempts certain income for the purpose of calculation of Income Tax. The Income Tax Act exempts more than 36 types of incomes from being classified as Income for the purpose of income tax. The important ones are as follows:

a) Agricultural Income
b) Share of Profit from a Partnership firm.
c) Gratuity
d) Provident Fund, Leave, Travel Allowance
e) House rent to the extent which is the minimum of the following three is exempted-
  i) Original House Rent Allowance received.
   ii) 50% of salary (Basic salary + Dearness Allowance) in metros and in other areas, 40% of the salary (Basic salary + Dearness Allowance).
   iii) Actual rent paid –(minus) 10% of the salary (Basic salary + Dearness Allowance)
f) Interest from notified bonds, securities etc like RBIs relief bonds.
g) Dividend from company(s)
h) Minor's income upto Rs. 1.500/- per year
i) Capital gains arising out of transfer of listed / recognized shares

j) Scholarships granted to meet the cost of education Etc.

Income under the Income Tax Act is classified under 5 heads-

I. Salary
II. Income from House property.
III. Income from business or profession
IV. Income from capital gains
V. Income from other sources.

I. **Salary**- it is the remuneration paid by one person to another for services rendered by that another in the person's business or profession. Hence the very essential for an income to be a salary is that there has to be an employer- employee relationship. It includes wages, annuity, pension, gratuity, bonus, fees, commissions, profits, payment for earned leave, additions in Provident fund accounts, etc. Allowances and perquisites are also added while computing salary.

There are certain salaries that are exempted. The general ones are–

1. Leave salary received at the time of retirement-
    i) government employees- 100% exemption
    ii) for other employees- the taxable amount is amount received as leave salary less the minimum of following-
    a. Earned leave not availed during service (subject to maximum of 30 days for every completed year of service) * average salary.
    b. average salary * 10
    c. Rs. 3,00,000/-
    d. Amount actually received.
2. Salary to partner is not taxable as salary income but taxable under the head "Profits and gains of business or profession"
3. Gratuity received by-
    i) central / state government or local authority employee- 100% exempted
    ii) employee covered by the payment of gratuity Act-the

taxable amount is amount received as gratuity less the minimum of following-
   a. 15 days (in case of seasonal employment- 7 days) salary * salary last drawn for every completed year of service;
   b. Rs. 3,50,000/-
   c. Gratuity actually received.
   iii) other employees- the taxable amount is amount received as gratuity less the minimum of following-
   a. (completed years of service * average salary)/2
   b. Rs. 3,50,000/-
   c. Gratuity actually received
4. Pension received-
   i) from United Nations Organization- fully exempted
   ii) commuted pension received –
   a) government employee- fully exempted
   b) other employees- amount taxable is amount less one half of the pension which he is normally entitled to receive if employee does not receive gratuity else it is less one third of the pension which he is normally entitled to receive.

Etc.

Allowances include

a) Dearness Allowance- fully taxable
b) house rent allowance is taxable on the amount minus least of the following-
   i. Original House Rent Allowance received.
   ii. 50% of salary (Basic salary + Dearness Allowance) in metros and in other areas, 40% of the salary (Basic salary + Dearness Allowance).
   iii. Actual rent paid –(minus) 10% of the salary (Basic salary + Dearness Allowance)
c) Entertainment allowance is taxable on the amount minus least of the following-

  i. Rs 5,000/-
  ii. 20% of Basic salary
  iii. actual amount received.
 d) Fixed medical allowance-fully taxable.
 e) Servant allowance- fully taxable.
 Etc.

 Perquisites are rent free home, medical facilities, amenities, etc.

II. House Property. For incomes from house property there are three essentials, viz.-
 a) there should be land and a building.
 b) The assessee should not occupy it
 c) The assessee should be the owner of the same.

III. Business or profession.

 For business, the taxable income is profits, while for profession it is income.

Tax is to be paid after deducting the admissible deductions, expenses and depreciations. In case of partnership, salary of partners is exempted from tax and so is interest to partners upto 12%. Loss, if any accrued can be set off against other incomes and the unsettled loss can be adjusted in subsequent assessment years subject to a maximum of 8 years.

IV. Capital Gains.

 Any profit or gains arising from the transfer of capital asset is taxable. For this there has to be a capital asset sold during the previous year. Capital asset is that made for purpose of investment / earning like shares, etc. and may be Short term or Long term.

 Short term- All the capital assets that are sold off within a limited period, viz.- for immovable assets- within 3 yrs and for movable assets- within 12 months.

 Long term- All the other capital assets are long term assets.

 It is to be noted that capital loss, if any can only be adjusted against capital gains.

V. Income from other sources.

Any income which cannot be categorized into the above heads is classified in this head and includes generally interests like- bank interests (savings interest, fixed deposit interests etc.), debenture interests, interest on securities, Post office interest, etc.

All incomes from the aforesaid 5 heads are to be added together to obtain the Gross Total Income.

In computing the taxable income, the Act allows certain deductions, which are to be subtracted from his gross total income. Deductions can be of two types-

a) Deductions in respect of certain payments.
b) Deductions included in the gross total income.

The applicable deductions and the extent of deductions are as under:-

1. Amount contributed towards pension fund-

a) of LIC or any other insurer for receiving pension from the fund. Deduction permitted is to the amount deposited or Rs. 10,000/- whichever is less.

b) Of Central Government- Deduction permitted is to the amount paid by the assessee and the Central Government to the notified pension scheme is deductible. However no deduction in excess of 10% of employees salary is permitted from the employer or employee's contribution.

2. Amount contributed towards Medical Insurance Premium (Mediclaim). Deduction permitted is to the amount deposited or Rs. 10,000/- whichever is less. Where premium is paid on account of insurance on the health of a senior citizen (who is of more than 65 yrs of age on any day of the previous year), the deduction permitted is to the amount deposited or Rs. 15,000/- whichever is less.

3. Amount spent towards maintenance or medical treatment of dependant who is disabled. Deduction permitted is to the fixed deduction of Rs. 50,000/- and where disability is more than 80% Rs. 75,000/-.

4. Amount spent towards medical treatment of specified

diseases like Cancer, AIDS, Hemophilia, etc. Deduction permitted is to the amount spent or Rs. 40,000/- whichever is less. However in case of treatment of senior citizen, the deduction permitted is to the amount spent or Rs. 60,000/- whichever is less.

5. Amount spent on repayment of loan or interest thereon taken for an individual for higher education. Deduction permitted is to the amount paid towards repayment or Rs. 40,000/- whichever is less. However, this deduction is permitted for a period of 8 yrs or till the principal amount with interest is liquidated.

6. Amount spent on payment of rent for the purpose of his own residence and he is not in receipt of any House Rent Allowance, or his spouse or minor child or the HUF of which he is a member does not own any residence in the same place. Deduction permitted is the least of the following:-

a) Rs 2000/- per month; or
b) 25% of the adjusted total income (total income after excluding long-term capital gains and specified income u/s 115 A or 115D)
c) the excess of actual rent paid over 10% of the adjusted total income.

7. Amount given as donation to certain institutions for scientific research or rural development by assessee whose gross total income does not include income taxable under the head "Profits and gains of business or profession". Deduction permitted is the amount given. However it is to be noted that if deduction under this provision is allowed, no other deduction will be allowed.

8. Amount made as contribution to any political party by an assess other than local authority and every artificial juridical person (except an Indian Company) wholly or partly funded by the government. Deduction permitted is the amount given.

9. Amount given as donation to certain funds, charitable institutions etc. Deduction permitted is:-

a) In case of contribution to the National Defence Fund set up by the Central government or the PM's National Relief fund / Armenia Earthquake relief fund, fund set up by the State Government for the medical relief to the poor, CM's relief fund, etc- the entire amount given is deductible.

b) In case of contribution to the Jawahar Lal Nehru Memorial Fund, PM's Drought Relief Fund, National Children's Fund, Indira Gandhi Memorial Trust, Rajiv Gandhi Foundation, 50% of the amount given is deductible.

c) In case of contribution to government or approved local authority, institution or organization to be used for promoting family planning or sponsorship of sports and games in India, 100% of the amount given is deductible subject to the condition that it does not exceed 10% of adjusted gross total income.

d) In case of contribution to any other fund or institution, which satisfies conditions so specified and does not fall in the aforesaid head, 50% of the amount given is deductible subject to the condition that it does not exceed 10% of adjusted gross total income.

The Total Income of an assessee is the Gross Total Income less the deductions and Tax is payable on the Total Income.

The rate at which tax is payable is as follows:-

FOR income of Individuals, HUFs, AOPs, BOIs, and artificial juridical persons-

Net income range	Rate of Income- Tax
Up to Rs 50,000/-	Nil
Rs. 50,000/- to Rs. 60,000/-	10% of the amount by which the total income exceeds Rs. 50,000/-
Rs. 50,000/- to Rs. 1,50,000/-	Rs. 1000/- plus 20% of the amount by which the total income exceeds Rs. 60,000/-
Rs. 1,50,000/- and above-	Rs. 19,000/- plus 30% of the amount by which the total income exceeds Rs. 1,50,000/-

Surcharge is also leviable @ 10% of Income tax if net income exceeds Rs 8,50,000/-

Education cess @ 2% on – a) Income tax after providing rebate and, b) surcharge of Income tax is leviable.

For Income of a Firm, a domestic company is taxable @ 35% and surcharge @ 2.50% and education cess @ 2%on - a) Income tax after providing rebate and, b) surcharge of Income tax; is leviable.

For income of a co-operative society-

Net income range	Rate of Income Tax (per cent)
Up to Rs. 10,000/-	10
Rs 10,000/- to Rs 20,000/-	20
Rs 20,000/- and above	30

The tax is payable on the above rates. However the Income Tax Act does provide for rebates which can be availed of from the tax liability.

The tax rebates so admissible are:-

1. Rebate from tax liability in respect of LIC premium, contribution to Provident Fund, etc.

This rebate is only available to an individual and a Hindu Undivided Family. The rates thereof are:-

a) 30% rebate is admissible in cases where income chargeable under the head 'Salaries' before giving deductions does not exceed Rs. 1,00,000/- or where income chargeable under the head 'Salaries' is not less than 90% of gross total income.

b) 20% rebate is admissible in cases where gross total income does not exceed Rs. 1,50,000/-

c) 15% rebate is admissible if gross total income exceeds Rs. 1,50,000/- but does not exceed Rs. 5,00,000/-

d) No rebate is admissible if gross total income exceeds Rs. 5,00,000/-

This percentage of rebate is admissible on the total investment so made subject to the terms of the Act, viz.:-

a) Amount paid in the following investments by an individual or HUF will qualify for rebate, however, for the same the aggregate cannot exceed Rs. 70,000/-

Objection Your Honour

i) Payment of LIC premium subject to 20% of actual capital sum assured.
ii) Contribution towards Provident Fund Account PPF subject to a maximum of Rs 70,000/-
iii) Amount deposited for 10/15-year account under Post Office Savings Bank (CTD) Rules.
iv) Subscription to National Savings Bank Scheme, 1992.(It is to be noted that the scheme is discontinued from 1st November, 2002)
v) Subscription to National Savings Certificate, VI, VII or VIII (VI and VII are discontinued)
vi) Contribution to Unit Linked Insurance Plan (ULIP) of UTI or LIC Mutual Fund (Dhanraksha plan).
vii) Payment of notified annuity plan of LIC.
viii) Subscription towards notified units of Mutual Fund of UTI subject to a maximum of Rs. 10,000/-
ix) Amount paid as subscription to Home Loan Account Scheme or contribution to any notified fund of the National Housing Bank
x) Payment towards cost of purchase of or construction of a residential house including repayment of loan taken from the Government bank, co-operative bank, National Housing Bank or assessee's employer if employer is a public company or a public sector undertaking, university, co-operative society subject to maximum of Rs. 20,000/-
xi) Contribution by an individual towards superannuation fund.
xii) Amount paid as tuition fees by an individual for full time education to any institution or university subject to a maximum of Rs. 12,000/- per child for 2 children.
xiii) Contribution by an individual towards Statutory or Recognized Provident Fund.

b) Amount paid in the following investments by an individual or HUF will qualify for rebate, however, for the same the aggregate cannot exceed Rs. 1,00,000/-

i) Subscription to equity shares or debentures forming part of any eligible issue of capital.
ii) Subscription to any units of any mutual fund referred in the

Act and approved by the Board.

However it is to be noted that for rebate the maximum permissible rebate is either the aggregate of investments or deposits referred to in sub-para a) & b) above or Rs 1,00,000/- whichever is less.

2. An assessee who is of the age of 65 years or more (Senior Citizens) at any time of the previous year is allowed a rebate equal to the amount of Income tax payable without rebate or Rs. 20,000/- whichever is less.
3. An assessee who is a woman resident of India and below 65 years is allowed a rebate equal to the amount of Income tax payable without rebate or Rs. 5,000/- whichever is less.
4. An individual whose taxable income (gross total income-deduction) is Rs 1,00,000/- or less is allowed a rebate equal to 100% of the income tax he is liable to pay. However, if the income is more than Rs. 1,00,000/-, then the rebate so admissible is to be calculated as follows:-
    i) Calculate the tax payable on total income (without the rebate).
    ii) Calculate the total income exceeding Rs. 1,00,000/-.
    iii) The amount of rebate admissible is (i) – (minus) (ii)

The amount so arrived after deducting the rebate is the tax liability of an assessee and Education cess @ 2% is payable thereon. The net amount is the amount payable as tax.

SERVICE TAX

We are a group of professionals catering to various needs of the society. We have learnt that we are liable to pay service tax to the Government. Is it so? Could you tell us as to what services are taxable.

Under the Law, various services are taxable. Basically, service tax is chargeable on the gross amount received / charged from the client and a uniform rate of 10% is applicable as service tax. Literally every profession except that of an advocate and doctor is within the purview of Service Tax. The various services, which are taxable and the amount on which, the same are taxable are as follows–

Service rendered by	Taxable on
1. Advertising Agencies-	Gross amount charged by the Agency from the client.
2. Air/Rail travel Booking agencies	Gross amount charged on booking and the commission received from the airline excluding airfare.
3. Architect	Gross amount charged from the client
4. Banking and other financial institutions.	-do-
5. Beauty treatment clinics	-do-
6. Broadcasting Agency providing broadcasting services including selling of time slots or obtaining sponsorships.	-do-
7. Business auxiliary services like– a) promotion or marketing or sale of goods, services	-do-
b) any customer care services,	-do-
c) support services for billing, collection or recovery of cheque, accounts or remittances, evaluation services etc.	-do-
8. Cable operators	-do-
9. Agency providing Cargo handling services excluding export cargo or passenger booking except actual transportation of goods.	-do-
10. Charted Accountant	
11. Agency providing clearing and forwarding services of any manner	-do-
12. Commissioning or installation services	-do-
13. Charted Secretary	-do-
14. Agency providing services in relation to holding of conventions	

	or the like.	-do-
15.	Cost Accountant	-do-
16.	Courier Agency	-do-
16.	Credit Rating Agencies	-do-
17.	Customs House Agent providing customs clearing services.	-do-
18.	Dry Cleaning Agency	-do-
19.	Consulting Engineer rendering advice consultancy or technical assistant.	-do-
20.	Event management service.	-do-
21.	Agency/Authority providing similar services as that provided by telegraph authority in relation to communication to a subscriber	Gross amount charged from the client minus initial deposit received from the customer, which is taxable if adjusted.
22.	Fashion designing Agency/Designer.	Gross amount charged from the client
23.	Franchiser providing franchise services	-do-
24.	Agency providing Health & Fitness services	-do-
25.	Insurance Companies including insurance services provided by intermediary, Agent, Company etc.	Amount of premium received from policy holder
27.	Insurance Agent/intermediary providing insurance services	Amount of commission received from the insurer.
26.	Interior Decorator	Gross amount charged from the client
27.	Interned Café or where interned accessing facility is provided.	-do-
28.	Telegraph authority providing leased circuit service.	Gross amount charged from the client minus initial deposit received from the customer, which is taxable if adjusted.
29.	Agency providing maintenance and repair services.	Gross amount charged from the client.

30.	Management Consultant	-do-
31.	Mandap keepers providing mandap services including catering etc.	-do-
32.	Market Research Agency	-do-
33.	Service and repair station or center authorized by manufacture.	Gross amount charged from the client minus the cost of spare parts or accessories sold during repair excluding the reimbursements received by it.
34.	Maintenance and repair service provider.	Gross amount charged from the client
35.	Agency providing online information and database access or retrieval services.	-do-
36.	Pager services or telegraph/telex services provider.	Gross amount charged from the client excluding deposits if made but chargeable when adjusted.
38.	Photographic services including sound recording or video tape production service provider	Gross amount charged from the client minus the cost of unexposed film or tape etc. sold to the client during the course of service.
39.	Agency providing placement services	Gross amount charged from the client
40.	Port services provided by a port under the Major port Act or any other person authorized by the port.	-do-
41.	Real Estate Agent.	-do-
42.	Renting a Cab service-providing Agency.	-do-
43.	Scientist of technocrat or an institution or organization rendering Scientific or technical consultancy.	-do-
44.	Security Agency including those	

	providing investigation, detection, verification etc.	-do-
45.	Share Broker dealing with securities, recognized stock exchange.	Aggregate of commission/ brokerage received from client.
46.	Agency providing steamer agent's services to Shipping Line including booking, advertising or canvassing of cargo including container feeder services.	Gross amount charged from the client
47.	Storage & Warehouse keeper.	-do-
48.	Agency providing Technical inspection, certification excluding inspection and certification of pollution levels.	-do-
49.	Agency providing technical testing and analysis services in relation to physical, chemical, biological or any other scientific testing or analysis service provided in relation to human beings or animals.	-do-
50.	Tour Service operators.	Gross amount charged from the client including charges for accommodation, food etc.
51.	Training and Coaching service providers.	Gross amount charged from the client
52.	Underwriter service providing agency.	Gross amount charged from the client

All the above-mentioned service providers are required to be registered. Registration can be done at all Commissionerates of Central Excise which have a Service Tax Cell (which is headed by Assistant / Deputy Commissioner) and where no service tax division constituted, the Assistant / Deputy Commissioner can be approached for such. A form is required to be filled within a period of 30 days since the date the said service is being provided or when the service has been declared as taxable. The competent authority is required to issue registration certificate within a period of 7 days and if not granted then the same is deemed granted. Such providers who provide services at different places but have only one centralized billing office then only one registration is needed but in case where the branches do their own billing, then individual registration of the same is required. If the business is transferred, the transferee has to obtain fresh license and if the business ceases, the license is required to be surrendered. Non-registration is punishable with a fine upto Rs. 500/- only.

Tax is payable by a challan in specified banks and only specified accessies who have 15 digit Service Tax Payer can file returns online. If no service rendered, then also the Nil Return has to be duly filed. Failure to pay tax warrants penal interest @ 15% per annum. No PAN is necessary for paying service tax.

If the service tax is charged from the client then the same is to be clearly indicated.

Further, education tax is also leviable over the said 10% of the Service Tax, thereby making the entire amount leviable as Tax to 10.2%.

•••

CHAPTER- 13
WORK AND LAW

FACTORIES ACT

SETTING UP A FACTORY

I recently opened a small-scale industry. What kind of working environment am I liable to maintain in the factory, in respect of the workers?

The Factories Act lays down elaborate provisions in respect of working environment to be maintained in the factory premises. Every owner is entitled to ensure the following:

i) A reasonable degree of health, safety and welfare of all workers.

ii) Prohibition of young persons from working on dangerous machines.

iii) Prohibition of women and children to be employed as cotton openers in any part of the factory in which a cotton opener is at work.

iv) Providing suitable goggles where the workers' eyes can otherwise be at risk due to any particle or light.

v) Separate washing facility for male and females and space for drying them.

vi) Suitable arrangement for sitting.

vii) A First Aid Box in an accessible place to be kept.

viii) Canteen for certain factories.

ix) Shelters, restrooms and lunch rooms where the workers are more than 150.

x) Where the workers' number is more than 30 there should be a separate room for children under the age of six years of such women.

xi) Weekly holidays, one day in a week and in addition compulsory holidays on certain notified days.

xii) Time limit of work should not exceed nine hours in a day, except with the approval of Chief Inspector.

xiii) There should be interval of minimum of half an hour and at any stretch no worker should be made to work for more than 5 hours in continuity.

xiv) Spread over of working hours a day shall not be more than ten and a half hours including the interval period of at least half an hour for adult workman.

xv) Working period in night shift is regulated as follows: -

1. Where a worker in a factory works on a shift, which extends beyond midnight-

   a) A weekly holiday and compulsory holiday, a holiday for a whole day shall mean in his case a period of twenty-four consecutive hours beginning when his shift ends;

   b) And the following day for him shall be deemed to be the period of twenty-four hours beginning when such shift ends and the hours he has worked after midnight shall be counted in previous day.

2. Overlapping of shifts is prohibited in relays of workmen that work shall not be carried on in any factory by means of a system of shifts so arranged that more than one relay of workers engaged in work of the same kind at the same time.

3. Workers to be paid extra for overtime

xvi) Employment of children under the age of 14 years is prohibited.

xvii) Children shall not be made to work for more than four and a half hours in a day.

xviii) Annual leave with wages shall be given to all the workers who have worked for a period of 240 days or more in a factory during a calendar year; during subsequent calendar year for a number of days calculated at the rate of –
   a) In case of an adult, one day for every twenty days of work performed by him during the previous calendar year;
   b) In case of a child, one day for every fifteen days of work performed by him during the previous calendar year.
xix) Payment in advance for leave with wages in specified conditions.
xx) Protection under the Industrial Disputes Act in respect of the right of workman who is laid off, to receive compensation, safeguards against retrenchment, compensation to workmen in case of transfer of undertakings, right to get sixty days notice in case of closing down an undertaking, right to re-employment of retrenched workmen.
xxi) Protection under the Workmen's Compensation Act.

TIME FRAME OF WORK — GENERAL

What is the maximum limit of working hours in a factory?

A factory is basically an establishment employing 10 persons (20 in case of work carried without power) wherein manufacturing process is carried on.

The employee i.e. the workman–

a. Cannot be employed for more than 48 hours in a week;
b. Is to be given a holiday in a week or a compensatory holiday, if deprived of such;
c. Cannot be employed for more than 9 hours in a day;
d. After every 5 hours of work, to be given a rest interval of at least half an hour.
e. A worker cannot be made to work for more than 10 ½ hours in a day including the rest intervals.

f. If works for more than 9 hours a day or 48 hours in a week, he shall be paid overtime, twice the rate of ordinary wages.

However the State Government may by rules exempt such limitation but in such a case the total hours of consecutive work shall not exceed 10 hours daily or 60 hours weekly (including overtime). Moreover, the total hours including rest interval period shall not exceed 12 hours in a day and the total number of overtime hours shall not exceed 50 in any one quarter.

TIME FRAME OF WORK—WOMEN AND CHILDREN

What are the limitations on the employer in respect of working hours of women and children?

Under the Factories Act, 1948–

a. A woman cannot be employed except between 6 am and 7 pm.

b. A child below 14 years cannot be employed.

c. A child who is of more than 14 years but less than 15 years can be employed but only for a maximum period of 4½ hours.

d. A child cannot be employed in night i.e. 10 pm to 6 am.

e. Child worker employed must have a certificate of fitness.

If any such provision is contravened the employer is liable for punishment for imprisonment upto 2 years or fine upto 1 lakh or both and in case of subsequent contravention, for imprisonment upto 3 years and fine not less than Rs 10,000/- and not more than 2 lakh rupees.

INDUSTRIAL DISPUTES ACT

CLOSING INDUSTRY—LEGAL REQUISITES

Due to some personal reason I wish to close down my industry. What am I supposed to do?

If there are more than 50 workman working on an average per day in the preceding 12 months, a 60 days prior notice is to be given to the appropriate government seeking permission for such by stating clearly the reasons for closure. Moreover, such notice is to be served upon the representatives of the workmen in the prescribed manner. If no order, either granting or refusing permission, is given within a period of 60 days from the date of application, such will be treated as deemed granted. It is to be noted that such order will remain in force for one year; however, the same may be reviewed at any stage.

On closure, every workman who has worked for more than one year is entitled for compensation equivalent to average pay of 15 days for every completed year of service or any part thereof in excess of 6 months. However, in case of closure on account of unavoidable circumstances, the compensation shall not exceed average pay of 3 months.

If the permission for closure is not obtained, the employer is liable for imprisonment upto 6 months and /or fine upto Rs. 5000/-. In respect of closure in contravention of the order refusing permission to close down, the employer shall be liable for imprisonment upto one year and /or fine upto Rs. 5000/- and in case of continued contravention with a further fine of Rs. 2000/- per day during which the contravention continues.

TERMINATION—WAGES DURING SUSPENSION

The Labour Court set aside the order of termination of my employment. However the employers preferred an appeal and also meanwhile stopped paying me the wages. What can I do?

If there is no stay granted by the appellate court, you can ask for enforcement of the award from the tribunal itself. Irrespective of the same you are entitled to full wages last drawn by you, which would also include the maintenance allowance if any payable to you during pendency of the proceedings as per the Industrial Disputes Act.

For the same you should apply to the appellate court with an affidavit stating that you are not employed elsewhere. The appellate court will grant an order directing payment of wages to you. However, if you were employed elsewhere the appellate court may refrain from granting such order.

TERMINATION — REMEDY

I work in an industry; the employer has terminated my service without any cause. What can I do?

If you are a workman and have been terminated from services and hence as the matter relates to the employment / non-employment, an industrial dispute can be raised subject to the condition that a substantial number of workmen or a recognized trade union supports the cause.

For this, the demand of reinstatement should be raised by the union before the management and if it is rejected an industrial dispute can be raised. On raising an industrial dispute the Government may refer it for conciliation or for adjudication to the Labour Court. It may also be referred to arbitration if not referred to the Labour Court.

STRIKE

We are a group of workers, in a factory and are forced to work under unhealthy conditions. In spite of several requests to the employer, no changes have been brought in. Can we go on strike to get our rights enforced, and what will be the effect on our salary? What if the management declares that any person not working will be deemed to have vacated their jobs? Also specify can the employer terminate our job if we do so?

Strike is recognized under the Industrial Disputes Act and is considered as a weapon in the hands of workers to pressurize the management to agree to their demands, look into safeguarding their culture and fulfilling their basic economic needs. This is basically a collective stoppage of work by the workmen. Industrialization has no doubt led to progress but also has seen employer – employee disputes known as industrial disputes.

Industrial disputes can be raised in relation to all workers irrespective whether skilled, unskilled, manual, clerical, technical or supervisory work for hire or reward are covered. However, those who are employed in a managerial capacity or those employed in supervisory capacity and getting salary above Rs.1600 a month are not covered under such.

The essential condition for calling a strike is that:

i) No conciliation proceedings should be pending or seven days have expired after the conclusion of such.

ii) No arbitration proceedings should be pending or 2 months have expired after the conclusion of such.

iii) No settlement or award is in operation in respect of any of the matters covered by the settlement of the award.

iv) In public utility services, a notice of minimum of 14 days is to be given to the employer and such strike has to be called within 6 weeks from the date of giving of notice.

v) Strike should not be called before the date of strike specified in the notice.

Any strike violating any of these essential conditions is illegal and for the same the workman is liable for imprisonment upto one month and / or with fine upto Rs 50/-

When the workmen go on strike, they cannot be deemed to have abandoned their employment. In case of illegal strike the employer may take disciplinary actions against the concerned workmen. But he cannot declare that those workmen who did not join the work by a particular date would be treated as having left their services. In respect of salary during the strike period the same will have to be negotiated upon during the negotiation proceedings or should be a part of the demand in the strike.

RETRENCHMENT

I am working in a factory and now the management has imported certain machines due to which there is excess of labour force. The management is now retrenching the excess staff. Can we have any legal recourse wherein we can protect our rights?

Retrenchment is one of the forms of termination of services of the employee by the employer. An employer has the right to re-organize his business and while doing so if the management opines that for the purpose of economy or the like, some employees are required to be terminated it can do so, provided that such termination should be with a bona fide intention and not in any way to harass the employee. The necessity of retrenchment is entirely an internal management decision and the Industrial Tribunal will generally not interfere.

However, the employer while doing so has to follow certain guidelines—

i) One month's notice in writing has to be given to the workman indicating the reasons for retrenchment or in lieu of such one-month's wage is required to be paid to the workman.

ii) He has to follow the rule of 'last-come first-go' in respect of choosing the workmen to be retrenched.

iii) At the time of retrenchment the workman is required to be paid compensation equivalent to 15 days average pay for every completed year of continuous service or any part in excess of six months.

iv) A notice of retrenchment has to be given to the appropriate government by the employer

It is to be noted that only those workmen who have been in continuous service for not less than one year are governed by the procedure.

Therefore, unless you can prove that the services have been terminated for mala fide reasons or to harass you or the prescribed procedure has not been followed, you cannot challenge the retrenchment.

LAY-OFF

My employer prohibited me from work on the ground that the products that are being manufactured are not being sold and hence there is excess products lying in the stock. He is also not ready to let me work elsewhere, as he says

that I will be needed after a day or two. Am I entitled to claim any wage for the same?

Such situation where an employer is incapable of providing employment to a worker who is in the muster roll is known as layoff. A worker who is so laid off is entitled to 50% of the basic wage along with Dearness Allowance. However, the worker is not entitled for such if he refuses to accept an alternative employment or does not present himself for work at the appointed time during working hour's at least once a day. It is to be noted that lay-off can be done with the prior permission of the Government.

WORKMEN'S COMPENSATION ACT

COMPENSATION

My right arm was amputated from my shoulder as a result of injury suffered by me in course of employment. My employer removed me from the work, as I became incapable of performing my duties. How just is it?

Under the Workmen's Compensation Act, a worker is entitled to claim compensation for personal injury by accident arising during the course of employment from his employer. The employer shall be liable to pay compensation in accordance with the provisions of the Act.

However, the employer will not be liable in the following cases–

a) In respect of any injury which does not result in total or partial disablement of workman for a period exceeding three days;

b) In respect of any injury, not resulting in death, caused by an accident which is directly attributable to-

   i) The workman having been at the time of the accident under the influence of drink or drugs, or

   ii) The wilful disobedience of the workman to an order expressly given, or to a rule expressly framed, for the purpose of securing the safety of workman; or

iii) The wilful removal or disregard by the workman of any safety guard or other device, which he knew to have been provided for the purpose of securing the safety of workmen.

The worker is liable for compensation at the rate of:

a) In case of death: An amount equal to 50% of the monthly wages of the deceased worker multiplied with the relevant factor (as provided for in Schedule IV of the Act) subject to a minimum of Rs. 50,000/-

b) In case of permanent total disablement: An amount equal to 60% of the monthly wages of the deceased worker multiplied with the relevant factor (as provided for in the second column of Schedule IV) subject to a minimum of Rs. 60,000/-

c) In case of permanent partial disablement: Such percentage (equal to the percentage of disablement) of the 'amount' payable as compensation. The 'amount' being equal to 60% of the monthly wages of the deceased worker multiplied with the relevant factor (as provided for in the second column of Schedule IV) subject to a minimum of Rs. 60,000/-

d) In case of temporary disablement (total or partial): Recurring half-monthly payment of the sum equivalent to 25% of monthly wages of workman.

Monthly wage means any wages due to a workman in a month irrespective of the fact that wages are paid on day-to-day wages. The monthly wages is to be calculated as:

a) Where workman employed for more that 12 months— $1/12^{th}$ of the sum of the total wage of the workman during the last proceeding 12 months.

b) Where workman employed for less than 1 month— average monthly amount, which during the 12 months preceding the accident a worker performing same work was getting.

c) In other cases or where no information regarding wage can be derived— 30 times the total wages earned in respect of the last continuous period of service (uninterrupted period of service exceeding 14 days) immediately preceding the accident divided by the number of days comprising the period.

Hence, in your case you are liable to receive compensation accordingly. Also, the employer cannot merely terminate your services, but if you are fit for some other service and you are ready to work, he will have to provide you such.

LIMITATION FOR FILING CLAIM

My husband was injured while working in a factory. The employer got him admitted in a hospital. During the entire course of treatment he was paid 50% of his salary as subsistence allowance. However he died during the course of treatment, which ran for more than 6 months. I was not aware of any right, hence did not send any application to claim the amount. Now it's more than 3 years and I have come to know that the employee was liable to pay the compensation. Can I make a claim application now?

Under the Workman's Compensation Act a claim for compensation will be entertained by the Commissioner only if the notice of the said accident has been given to him within two years of the occurrence of the incident or within two years of the death. Hence your claim is time barred and the Commissioner is empowered to refuse compensation in respect of death of your husband. However you are entitled to claim service / death benefits of your husband.

MATERNITY BENEFIT ACT

MATERNITY BENEFIT

I am opening a poultry farm. There are quite a number of females willing to work in it. I have heard that according to Maternity Benefit Act, I am liable to pay them wages without work during pregnancy, delivery and postdelivery period. I don't want to do so, as it will unnecessarily burden me financially. Can I make them sign an agreement, which will absolve me from such responsibility?

The conditions given under the Maternity Benefit Act are compulsory upon the employer and the employer cannot do away

Objection Your Honour

with the same by entering into a contract. The Act applies to all factories, mines and other similar establishments and not only protects the mother but the unborn child in the womb too.

Under the Act, the employer is prohibited from making the pregnant lady, who is in an advanced stage of pregnancy, to do tough jobs or to do any work, which requires her standing for a long period or anyway causes trouble in the normal growth of child in womb. Further, the woman is not to work 6 weeks after delivery or miscarriage. The employer is also required to pay the pregnant working women wages for 6 weeks before and 6 weeks after delivery. Thus, altogether the female worker is to be given the benefit for a period of 12 weeks during her pregnancy. However, no payment is to be made, if the worker has worked with the employer for less than 160 days in the preceding 12 months.

Maternity Benefit Act also provides in certain cases for payment in case of death, medical bonus, leave for miscarriage, leave with wages for tubectomy operation. It is to be noted that if there are terms in the contract, which are violative of the Act, such will be struck down and the employer is liable to make the payments. Hence, you will be liable to make payment on the basis of Maternity Benefit Act and cannot escape from it.

EQUAL REMUNERATION ACT

PROHIBITION OF DISCRIMINATION (MEN & WOMEN)

Can the employer restrict or discriminate between men and women for the purpose of recruitment or payment of salary?

No, under the Equal Remuneration Act, the employer cannot discriminate between men and women while making recruitment except where the employment of woman in such work is prohibited or restricted by or under any law for the time being in force.

Moreover, the employees have a duty to pay equal remuneration to men and women workers for the same work or work of similar nature. If he contravenes the same, will be liable for punishment of fine upto Rs 5000/-

LEAVE WITH PAY

I have been working in a factory for more than 10 years. I intend to go to my maternal house for some personal purposes. I have heard that a worker is entitled to leave with wages. I would like to know as to how many days one can avail leave with wages?

An employee is entitled for one day of leave with wage for every 20 days (in case of a child 15 days) of work performed by him during the previous calendar year. Such leave cannot exceed 30 days (40 in case of child) in a year and shall be exclusive of all holidays either during or at either end of leave period and wages in respect of the same is to be paid before leave begins.

In case a worker is no longer in employment, he or in case of his death his nominees are entitled to be paid wages in lieu of annual leave not encashed.

EMPLOYEE'S PROVIDENT FUNDS AND MISCELLANEOUS PROVISIONS ACT (EPFMP)

This Act is applicable to establishments employing 20 or more persons.

CONTRIBUTION BY EMPLOYER

Is my employer liable to contribute to my Provident Fund, Family Pension etc? If so to what extent?

Every employer of an establishment employing 20 or more persons is liable to contribute to the Provident Fund of the employee who draws wages not exceeding 5000/- per month (Here Wage = Basic pay + Dearness Allowance + Retaining Allowance). The employer is liable to contribute @ $8^{1/3}$ (and in case persons employed is more than 50 then 10 %) of employee's pay to Provident Fund Account. The employee is also liable to contribute equally to his Provident Fund Account. He may also contribute more subject to a maximum limit of 10% (and in case persons employed is more than 50 then 12%).

WITHDRAWAL OF PROVIDENT FUND

When can I avail of advances / withdrawals from my

Objection Your Honour

Provident Fund Account?

An employee can avail of his non-refundable withdrawals / advances from his Provident Fund Account for construction of houses, sickness, education, marriage. On super-annuation, the member is entitled for full Provident Fund balance at member's credit with interest or lump sum withdrawal benefit under Family Pension Scheme depending upon the salary and years of service.

PENSION

Can my family get pension on my death during service tenure?

A minimum of 10 years contributory service is required for an employee / his dependants to be entitled for pension. The pension scheme provides for payment of monthly pension in the following cases–

a) On superannuation;

b) Retirement;

c) Permanent total disablement;

d) Death during service;

e) Death after retirement / superannuation / permanent total disablement;

f) Children pension;

g) Orphan pension;

$$\text{Member's Pension} = \frac{\text{Pensionable Salary} \times (\text{Pensionable Service} + 2)}{70}$$

A widow is entitled to pension of a minimum of Rs. 450/- per month, which may go upto Rs. 2500/- per month if member worked for more than 33 years.

In addition to above, children pension is also admissible @ 25% of widow pension subject to a minimum of Rs. 115/- per month per child upto 2 children and till they attain the age of 25 years. If no parents are alive, the scheme envisages payment @ 75% of widow pension subject to a minimum of Rs. 170/- per month per orphan.

Also, the legal heir / nominee is entitled for a lump-sum payment of Rs. 5000/- as life insurance benefit under the Employees Family Pension Scheme and also to an amount equal to the advance balance in the Provident Fund Account of the deceased during the preceding one year subject to a maximum of 25,000/- under the Employees Deposit Limited Insurance Scheme.

APPLICABILITY—SALARY LIMIT

I receive salary of more than Rs 5000/-. Is there any way for me to still claim the benefit of EPFMP Act?

In general the Act is not applicable to employees drawing salary more than Rs. 5000/-. So clearly if the salary is more than rupees 5000/- provisions of EPFMP Act would not be applicable.

However, if in the term of contract of employment, the employee agrees that a particular sum should be excluded, it cannot be treated as the basic wages and as such the salary if it is within the limitations, the provision of the EPFMP Act can apply.

REFUND OF P.F. ON LEAVING

If I leave the job, whether I would be entitled to full share of Employers Provident Fund?

Yes, the employees will be entitled to the full payment of employer's contribution along

with the interest in addition to their own share even if he leaves the job, provided that he completes specified period of service.

APPLICABILITY—CONTRACTOR'S EMPLOYEES

I am employed by a contractor; can I take the benefits of the EPFMP Act?

Yes, the contractor's employees have also become eligible for the provident fund benefits with effect from 31/11/63. The workers employed through the contractor are employees under EPFMP Act and as such entitled to the benefits. . .

Objection Your Honour

CONTRIBUTION IF NOT PAID

What if my employer does not deposit the contribution in the Provident Fund?

The employer, if the EPFMP Act is applicable, will be liable to pay the contributions with the Provident Fund authorities every month before 21st of the following month and if he fails, the Central Provident Commissioner is entitled to recover the same by way of penalty and the employer is also entitled for a sentence of not less than 3 months. The employer is restrained from taking the plea of financial difficulties as a reason for the default.

CHECKING CONTRIBUTION PAID OR NOT

How can I know whether my employer has paid the contribution or not?

The contribution of both the employee and the employer is to be entered by the employer in contribution card opened in the name of each member and kept with him and any member can inspect the same or have it inspected within 72 hours of making request for such, provided such request is not made more than once in 2 months.

EMPLOYEE'S STATE INSURANCE ACT

LEAVING SERVICE-PAYMENT OF COMPULSORY DEDUCTIONS

I voluntarily left my previous job after working for 10 years as I got a better one. How should I claim the compulsory deductions made by the employer from my salary?

Under the relevant rules governing the service law, an employer is required to make contributions towards provident fund, gratuity, employees state insurance fund, pension etc. Some of these are strictly to be contributed by the employer while in others contributions is to be made only when the organization is an industry or other similar clauses. If the employer on his own behalf or by way of deductions has made any contribution, the same is liable to be paid to the employee at the time of leaving the job.

In order to claim such contributions the employee has to demand the same from the employer, in the prescribed form, if available. However if the employer fails to pay the same within a reasonable time then the employee can approach the appropriate Court for the said relief. In case of Government employees and employees in Public Sector Undertakings, the appropriate Court is the Central Administrative Tribunal / Hon'ble High Court while in others the appropriate forum is the normal Civil Court though the Hon'ble High Court can also be approached.

CONTRIBUTION

My employer has been deducting some part of my salary stating it to be contribution to the Employees State Insurance Fund. Am I liable to make any contribution to such?

Contributions to the Employees State Insurance Fund are payable both by the employer and the employee. The employer's contribution is a sum equal to 4.75% of wages payable to employee and employee's contribution is a sum equal to 1.75% of the wages payable to the employee.

It is to be noted that if the employer deducts any amount payable by him from the employees' wages the same amounts to an offence and the employer will be liable for imprisonment for a term, which may extend to one year, or with a maximum fine of Rs 400/- or both. And if the employer again commits the same offence, he is liable for imprisonment upto 2 years or fine upto Rs. 5000/-.

BENEFITS

What are the benefits available under Employee's State Insurance Act?

The Employees State Insurance Act provides for various benefits, which are as follows–

A. Sickness Benefit— Insured persons are entitled to receive sickness cash benefits at the standard benefit rate for a period of 91 days in any 2 consecutive benefits periods, which is nearly 50% of the wages.

B. Extended Sickness Benefit— If the member is entitled to such, he will receive extended sickness benefit at a rate for a period of 124/309 days and which comes down to approximately 70% of wages.

C. Maternity Benefits— Insured woman is entitled to maternity benefit at double the standard benefit rate, which is equal to full wage. She is entitled to such for a total period of 12 weeks; 6 weeks pre-delivery and 6 weeks post-delivery, provided that a maximum of 6 weeks shall precede the expected date of delivery. Additional benefit for a period of 4 weeks can be granted on medical advice.

D. Disablement Benefit—Insured person is entitled to disablement benefit in cash for the period the disablement continues i.e. for temporary disablement till disablement continues and for permanent disablement till the whole life. For temporary disablement, the insured person is paid at approximate 70% of the wages subject to disablement lasting for minimum of 3 days excluding the day of accident and in case of permanent disablement, the insured person will be given life pension subject to a maximum of 70% of wages.

E. Dependant's Benefit— The dependants of the Insured person i.e. the widow till her life or remarriage, parents for life and legitimate dependant children below 18 years, are entitled to dependants benefit at the rate of 70% of the wages at a specified proportionate rate to individual dependents.

F. Funeral Benefit—An amount not exceeding Rs. 1500/- is payable as funeral benefit to the eldest surviving member of the family of the decease insured person which has to be claimed within 3 months from the death of the insured person.

G. Medical Benefit— This benefit is not payable in cash but free medical attendance and treatment of insured person and their families is provided therein. It may be–

  i. Restricted Medical Care—Outpatient medical care at dispensaries or panel clinics.

  ii. Expanded Medical Care—Consultation with specialists and supply of such medicines and drugs as may be prescribed by them.

iii. Full Medical Care—Hospitalization facilities, services of specialists and such drugs and diet as required.

EMPLOYEES EXCHANGE (COMPULSORY NOTIFICATION OF VACANCIES) ACT

EMPLOYMENT / VACANCY

I have contacted the Employment Exchange for employment. I would like to know as to whether all vacancies so arising are enlisted in the exchange or only some vacancies are enlisted?

Under the Employees Exchange Act, every vacancy in a public sector is required to be notified to the Central and the local Employment Exchange. In case of private sector vacancies, the Government may by notification require any such vacancy arising to be notified to the Central or local Employment Exchange. If the employer of such undertaking fails to do so, he can be liable for a fine upto Rs. 500/- for the 1st offence and Rs. 1000/- for every subsequent offence.

THE PAYMENT OF BONUS ACT

BONUS

I am an employee working in a private firm. The employer dismissed me from work on 25/10/04 on account of my violent behaviour after holding an inquiry. I was asked to collect all the entitled dues. However I learnt that on 30/10/04 the employer declared bonus of Rs. 2000/- to every employee. On claiming for the same, the employer refused it by stating that I was not entitled for such. Is such refusal legal? Shouldn't I be entitled to the bonus as even I have worked during the aforesaid period for which the bonus was being awarded?

The law makes paying bonus mandatory in every establishment where 20 or more workmen are employed on any day during an accounting year. Every employee receiving a salary / wages upto

Rs. 3,500/- per month is entitled to bonus for every accounting year if he has worked for at least 30 working days in that year. However employees of universities, educational institutions, hospitals, chamber of commerce, social welfare institutions, LIC, RBI, IFCI and UTI are not entitled to bonus under the Payment of Bonus Act.

An employer is required to pay bonus even if he suffers losses during the accounting year or there is no allocable surplus. The minimum bonus so payable is 8.33 % of the salary or wages during the accounting year, or Rs. 100/- in case of employees who have worked for more than 15 years and Rs 60/- in case of employees whose tenure of work is less than 15 years, calculated at the beginning of the accounting year, whichever is higher. The Act also fixes the maximum bonus payable to be 20% of salary or wages.

The bonus should be paid in cash within 8 months from the closure of the accounting year. However if there is sufficient cause, the employer may seek extension for payment of the same. It is to be noted that in case of an employee receiving salary or wages above Rs. 2,500/- the bonus payable is to be calculated as if the salary or wages were Rs. 2,500/- per month only. Hence, if an employer refuses to pay bonus without any just cause, he will be liable for imprisonment upto 6 months, or fine up to Rs.1000/- or both.

The Act however exempts employees for payment of bonus if, the employer is dismissed from service for fraud or riotous or violent behaviour while in the premises of the establishment or theft, misappropriation or sabotage of any property of the establishment.

In your case as the dismissal was on one of the above-enlisted grounds, hence the employer is justified in refusing payment of bonus to you.

SERVICE MATTER

COMPASSIONATE GROUND

I am a resident of Dhanbad. My husband died 7 years ago while in service of B.C.C.L. I have been told that in lieu

of death of my husband, I am entitled for compassionate appointment. I applied for it recently. However the management has denied giving me compassionate appointment. Please advise.

Compassionate appointment is given to the dependant of the deceased in order to help him / her to face the financial problems which the family encounters on account of the sudden death of the earning member. Compassionate appointment is hence not a right but any one dependant is entitled to such, provided there is an agreement or rule, which prescribes so. In respect of colliery companies there is a National Coal Wage Agreement entered by the management and the workers, which prescribes compassionate appointment to a dependant of the deceased. However the said appointment can be availed of within a specified duration, which at present is one year as per the judgment of the Hon'ble High Court of Jharkhand. As you have not made the application within the said duration, the management was justified in rejecting your claim.

SUSPENSION

I have been suspended from my service on account of false allegations. I know that the allegations can never be proved but I am afraid that the said inquiry would take quite a long time and I would be forced to starve. Am I entitled to the salary for the period, during which the inquiry continues, as I cannot even take any alternate employment as the management has directed me to be present during the entire proceeding?

In case of an employee being suspended, he is not entitled to draw his full salary. However, he is to be paid subsistence allowance during the period for which the suspension continues. The competent authority (management) is liable to pay the same and such shall in any case not be less than $1/4^{th}$ of the salary and shall not exceed 1/2 of the salary. Hence, you are entitled to receive the same during the period of suspension.

•••

CHAPTER - 14

SAFETY ON ROADS

MOTOR VEHICLES ACT, 1988
CENTRAL MOTOR VEHICLES RULES, 1989

OFFENCES AND PUNISHMENT TABLE

Description of Offence	Max Punishment (Imprisonment/Fine)
Driving without holding an effective driving licence	3 months or Rs. 500 or both
Driving by an under-aged person (Minor driving vehicle)	3 months or Rs. 500 or both
Owner or person in-charge of a vehicle permitting an unlicensed or an under-aged person to drive it. (Parents / guardians /friends permitting minor to drive vehicle)	3 months or Rs. 1000 or both
Holder of a driving licence permitting some other person to use the said licence.	Rs. 100 for the first offence Rs. 300 for the subsequent offence
Driving a vehicle at an excessive speed	Rs. 400 for first offence Rs. 1000 for subsequent offence
Driving dangerously / its abetment	6 months or Rs.1000 or both for first offence 2 years or Rs. 2000 or both for subsequent offence committed within 3 years of previous commission.

Driving when mentally or physically unfit to drive / its abetment	Rs 200 for first offence Rs. 500 for subsequent offence
Driving by a drunken person or by a person under influence of drugs / its abetment	6 months or Rs. 2000 or both on first offence 2 years or Rs. 3000 or both for subsequent offence committed within 3 years of previous commission
Driving an uninsured vehicle	3 months or Rs. 1000 or both.
Driver's failure to obey traffic signs (red light jumping, violation of yellow line, changing lane without indication, etc.)	Rs. 100 for the first offence Rs. 300 for the subsequent offence.
Driver of a two-wheeler / motor cycle carrying more than one person in addition to himself (triple riding)	Rs. 100 for the first offence Rs. 300 for the subsequent offence
Driver and pillion rider failing to wear protective head gear (helmet)	Rs. 100 for the first offence Rs. 300 for the subsequent offence
Using mobile phone while driving a vehicle	Rs. 100 for the first offence Rs. 300 for the subsequent offence
Demanding excess fare by auto rickshaw / taxi	Rs. 100 for the first offence Rs. 300 for the subsequent offence
Driving motor vehicles without number plates (not displaying number plates)	Rs. 100 for the first offence Rs. 300 for the subsequent offence
Driver in a public place and failing to produce licence on demand to any police officer in uniform.	Rs. 100 for the first offence Rs. 300 for the subsequent offence
When any person is injured or any property of a third party is damaged in a motor vehicles accident, the driver or person in charge of the vehicle: (a) not providing medical aid to the victim of the accident. (b) not giving information regarding the accident, etc., on demand by the police officer or the nearest police station. (c) not giving information regarding the accident, to the insurer	3 months or Rs 500 or both for the first offence and 6 months or Rs. 1000 or both for subsequent offence

Objection Your Honour

Plying a vehicle with registration mark of other state for more than 12 months.	Rs. 100 for the first offence Rs. 300 for the subsequent offence
Racings and trials of speed	One month or Rs 500 or both Rs 1000 for first offence 6 months or Rs 2000 or both for subsequent offence

SALE-PURCHASE OF VEHICLE / TRANSFER / REGISTRATION

I recently bought a bike from my friend and paid him the full consideration and thereby obtained possession of the same. Are there any other legal formalities essential to complete my ownership over the said bike?

No doubt, for ownership to pass over a movable property, mere transfer of the same to the purchaser is enough. However, after affecting the said transfer, other formalities as prescribed by the law need to be fulfilled.

Under the Motor Vehicles Act, all vehicles are to be registered by the owner of the vehicle and the registered owner is deemed to be liable for the traffic offences committed with that vehicle. Further, in case a registered motor vehicle is sold, the transferee is required to have the vehicle registered in his name. The transferor is also duty bound to inform the registering authority of the sale and send a copy of the same to the purchaser.

Hence, no doubt your ownership is complete, but as the vehicle is still in the name of the previous owner, under the law he is deemed to be the owner of the same and the said previous owner is competent to do anything with it (like resell it, etc.) which might land you in trouble and then you will have to prove that you are the true owner by producing proofs pertaining to payment receipts and delivery. To avoid the same it is advisable to have the same transferred in your name.

COMPENSATION IN CASE OF ACCIDENT

I was injured in a motor vehicle accident and thereby became permanently disabled. The owner of the said vehicle offered me an amount of Rs. 5000/- saying that I would not be able to get anything more than this. Is it so? What is the method of computation of compensation?

Under the Motor Vehicles Act, any person injured in a motor vehicle is liable to receive compensation that is to be 'just'. There is no exact or uniform rule or precise mathematical calculation for measuring the value, either of human life or limb and thereby assessing the amount of damages payable. Under the Act, the injured is liable to receive an amount of Rs. 60,000/- in case of permanent disablement, which will be interim compensation so payable to the injured immediately after filing of the claim petition.

Further, the amount of compensation so receivable can be calculated with reference to the Second Schedule of the said Act, which takes into account two relevant factors, viz—

a) The annual income of the injured,

b) The age of the injured.

As per the age of the injured, the Second Schedule specifies the appropriate multiplier, which is to be multiplied with the annual income of the deceased and the amount so arrived at is the maximum amount, which the injured is liable to receive. However, the precise amount is to be determined by the court after taking into consideration other relevant considerations. It is to be noted that the final amount so arrived will be payable after deducting the amount received as interim compensation.

Hence, the statement of the owner that you will not be entitled to receive anything more than Rs. 5000/- is untrue and you will atleast be liable to receive a minimum compensation of Rs. 60000/- if your injury has resulted in permanent disablement.

JURISDICTION OF MOTOR VEHICLE TRIBUNAL

I have recently been hit by a car and suffered several physical injuries. I wish to file a claim for compensation. Is it true that such a complaint is not to be filed in an ordinary court?

The legislature has enacted a special enactment dealing with motor vehicle accident cases viz, The Motor Vehicles Act and thereby has created a 'Special Court'/Tribunal to deal with such cases. By the creation of the Motor Vehicle Accident Claims Tribunal the ordinary courts are debarred from exercising jurisdiction over cases pertaining to claim for injury/death in motor vehicle accident cases. The jurisdiction of the Claims Tribunal is determined with respect to the place where the accident has occurred. Also, claim cases can be filed at the place where the defendant resides (and if there are more than one defendants, where one of them resides).

TRANSFER OF VEHICLE TO OTHER STATE

I have to take my bike for a 3-year graduation course from Jharkhand to Maharashtra and then again bring it back to the native state. Do I have to get a No-Objection Certificate and then get it registered in the other state?

Under the provisions of the Motor Vehicles Act, whenever the motor vehicle is to be transferred to another state for a period of more than 12 months, a No-Objection Certificate is to be obtained from the Registering Authority. The No-Objection Certificate basically signifies that the registering authority has no objection in respect of the transfer of the motor vehicle, which is generally given when no case is pending / complaint lodged in respect of the motor vehicle and no Government dues like road tax, insurance, etc. is pending. An application has to be made to obtain the same and if the application is not rejected within 30 days, it is deemed granted.

RECOVERY FROM INSURANCE COMPANY

Accidentally I hit an old man by my car. I took him to the hospital and incurred a huge sum of Rs. 75,000/-. Can I recover the said amount from the insurance company?

Under the Motor Vehicles Act, all motor vehicles have to be compulsorily insured in respect of 3rd party risks and failure to do so calls for punishment of imprisonment extending to 3 months and / or with fine extending to Rs. 1000/-. As your vehicle is insured, you are entitled to recover the amount, which you paid for medical expenses.

However, it is not necessary that the insurance company will pay you the whole amount but can reimburse only that part of the same, which it thinks to be reasonable. If the insurance company fails in doing so, you can approach the consumer forum on the ground for deficiency in part of services of the said company. Basically, an insurance company indemnifies only such amount, which are awarded by the court / tribunal.

HIT & RUN

I have been hit by a speedy car, which left me lying on the road and fled away. I could not even note down the number of the vehicle. I have incurred huge expenses towards medical treatment. Isn't there any provision in law which can at least take care of my medical expenditures?

The Motor Vehicles Act contemplates such situations and provides for adequate relief therein. These cases of accident arising out of motor vehicles, which cannot be traced, are designated as 'Hit and Run Motor Accidents'.

Under the law, in respect of death of any person arising out of hit and run accident, a fixed sum of Rs. 50,000/- is payable and in cases of grievous hurt, a fixed sum of Rs. 25,000/- is payable.

An application for making a claim for such amount is to be made before the appropriate authority so appointed by the Central

Government and where there is no such authority, the Motor Vehicles Accident Claims Tribunal having jurisdiction over the place of accident may grant the amount to be paid from the insurance company, which has taken upon itself to do so in cases of accident arising within its zone. It is to be noted here that under an agreement, India has been divided into 4 zones and each insurance company has taken the responsibility for payment of compensation for under this case for any accident occurring within its zone. The zones and the companies liable to pay compensation are:-

The Eastern Zone—National Insurance Co. Ltd.

The Western Zone—New India Assurance Co. Ltd.

The Northern Zone—Oriental Insurance Co. Ltd.

The Southern Zone— United India Insurance Co.

The 4 National Insurance companies have the responsibility to pay compensation for any damages in cases of hit and run accidents, which occur, within its zone. The main principle behind this is that, by virtue of the agreement, an insurance company of a particular zone is deemed to be the insurer of the unascertained vehicle and hence liable to pay compensation. But such compensation is fixed to the amount stated above.

DRIVING LICENCE— TERMS

My son is 16 yrs old and wishes to drive a bike. Will he get a driving licence?

Under the Motor Vehicles Act, no person under the age of 18 years shall drive a motor vehicle in any public place. However, motorcycles with engine capacity not exceeding 50 cc may be driven in a public place by a person after attaining the age of 16 years. Hence, your son is entitled to drive a motorcycle without gear and for the same he will receive a learner's licence.

•••

CHAPTER - 15
RAILWAYS

TRANSFER OF TICKET TO OTHERS

I am a Karnataka Government employee and have to represent my department in a meeting in New Delhi. For the same, I duly booked a railway ticket and was lucky to get a reserved berth. However, due to some other engagements on the said day, I will not be able to go and it has been decided that a fellow lady officer will now represent the department in the said meeting. On trying to get a reservation for her it was found that there was no availability of any berth on the said date. Can she travel on my ticket?

Though traveling on other person's ticket is a crime under the Railways, however, there are provisions wherein a reserved ticket may be transferred to specified persons in certain circumstances. The Chief Reservation Supervisor of important stations is authorized by the railway administration to permit the change of name of a passenger having a seat or berth reserved in his name in certain circumstances, viz:

1. Where the passenger is a government servant, proceeding on duty and the appropriate authority makes a request in writing 24 hours before the scheduled departure of the train for the change of name;

2. Where the passenger makes a request in writing 24 hours before the scheduled departure of the train that the reservation

made in his name may be transferred to another member of his family which includes his father, mother, brother, sister, son, daughter, husband and wife;

3. Where the passengers are students of a recognized educational institution and the head of the institution makes a request in writing 48 hours before the scheduled departure of the train, that the reservation made in the name of any student be transferred to any other student of the same institute;
4. Where the passengers are members of a marriage party and any person deemed to be head of such party makes a request in writing 48 hours before the scheduled departure of the train that the reservation made in the name of any member of the marriage party be transferred to any other person;
5. Where the passengers are a group of cadets of National Cadet Corps and any officer, who is the head of the group, makes a request in writing at least 24 hours before the departure of the train that the reservation made in the name of any cadet be transferred to any other cadet.

However, it is to be noted that such request will only be granted once and in respect of students, marriage party members, NCC cadets, a request for change in excess of 10 % of the total strength of group will not be granted.

CIRCULAR JOURNEY TICKETS

We are retired couple, willing to go on a pilgrimage tour covering 6 to 7 major holy places, but it seems quite tough planning for so many tickets. It is also becoming a costly affair. Is there any provision, which can help us in such situations?

Under the Railways, senior citizens (citizens above the age of 60 years) have been given concession for travelling which is 30 % of the normal fare. However, in case of travelling which includes pilgrimage, sight seeing etc. where the originating and terminating point of the journey are the same, a facility of booking Circular Journey Tickets is available. Circular Journey Tickets can be purchased for all classes of travel. A maximum of eight break journeys will be admissible on these tickets. Zonal Railways for the convenience of tourists also offer standard Circular Journey Tickets covering popular destinations. The details of the routes, fares etc., for these tickets can be obtained from nominated stations in each Zonal Railway. These tickets can be purchased on basis of convenience or in the alternative one can also inform the Zonal Railways about the detailed route and accordingly Circular Journey Tickets can be drawn up to suit the specific requirements. These tickets give you the benefit of telescopic rates, which are considerably economic than the regular point-to-point fare rates. Also, with these tickets, one not only saves time but also the inconvenience of booking tickets at each leg of the journey.

After finalizing the precise schedule, one can approach the Divisional Commercial Manager of the Division of certain major stations to which the journey commencing station belongs. The Divisional Commercial Manager or the station authorities will then calculate the cost of the tickets based on the schedule. He shall also inform the Station Manager of the same in a prescribed format. The Circular Journey Tickets can thereafter be purchased on presenting the said form at the Booking Office of the station where one wishes to start the journey. After purchasing the Circular Journey Ticket, the Reservation Office is required to be approached to reserve the accommodation for various laps of your journey. A reserved journey tickct will accordingly be issued for the journey.

A Circular Journey Ticket is charged for as two single journeys, the length of each single journey being taken as half of the total distance and a senior citizen is entitled to 30% concession on the cost of the Circular Journey Tickets when travelling a minimum distance of 1000 kms.

It is also worthwhile to mention here that senior citizens are required to carry some documentary proof showing their age or date of birth, issued by any government institution / agency / local body like identity card, driving licence, passport, educational certificate, certificate from local bodies like panchayat /

corporation / municipality, or any other authentic and recognized document. This documentary proof of age should be produced when demanded by the Railway officials during the journey. However, in case such documentary proofs are not carried or cannot be produced on demand then such persons are liable to pay, the difference of the regular fare payable and the concessional fare paid and the provisions of penalty will not apply.

BOOKING LUGGAGE

I intend to go to my hometown to attend a marriage and have to carry quite a number of gifts along with me. I don't want to book them in the luggage van, as I fear loss / damage to the goods. I have also heard that there is restriction as to the weight of the luggage that can be carried in the railway compartment. Can I reserve another berth with me so that I can keep the same on that?

Railway berths / seats are reserved for passengers and not for luggage. Hence, if you wish to book a ticket in someone else's name and intend to carry luggage on that berth, it cannot be done. Also, that berth is liable to be allotted to RAC or WL passengers.

Under the railways, each passenger is entitled to carry a limited quantity of luggage with him. The table given below elaborates the same.

Class	Free allowance	Marginal allowance	Maximum quantity permitted in the comp-rtment. (Including free allowance)
AC (First Class)	70 Kgs.	15 Kgs.	150 Kgs.
AC 2-Tier (Sleeper/First class)	50 Kgs.	10 Kgs.	100 Kgs.
AC 3-tier (Sleeper/ AC chair car)	40 Kgs.	10 Kgs.	40 Kgs.
Sleeper class	40 Kgs.	10 Kgs.	80 Kgs.
Second class	35 Kgs.	10 Kgs.	70 Kgs.

Free allowance is the weight that a passenger is authorized to carry along with him in the railway compartment. If your luggage marginally exceeds the free allowance, you will be charged at the normal luggage rates applicable to your class of travel. In case the passenger is a child aged above 5 years and below 12 years, free allowance subject to maximum of 50 Kgs is allowed to be carried by them.

The excess luggage is to be booked in the luggage office on payment of the prescribed charges and the tickets are to be endorsed by cross-referencing the luggage ticket details, before commencing the journey.

It is to be noted that the free allowance is not admissible for articles such as scooters, cycles etc. Also, the charges for books, milk and eatable oils are less than the normal charges whereas in case of newspapers, the luggage charge is $1/3^{rd}$ the normal charge.

Hence, you have to pay the booking charges and in case of loss / damage to the booked luggage—

1. If value of the goods booked has not been declared by the consignor and percentage charges is not paid, the monetary liability of the railways is limited to Rs. 100/- per kg,
2. If the consignor has declared the value of the consignment and also paid the percentage charges, he will be entitled to get the claimed amount, which will not exceed the value of the luggage so declared.

Thus, it is advisable to book the luggage and declare the value of the goods and keep away the worries about damage / loss to the goods.

However, if you contravene the limits of luggage, then you are liable to pay penalty to the extent of 6 times the regular charge on the excess luggage.

TICKET LOSS—ISSUANCE OF DUPLICATE

I have misplaced the ticket in my home. Can I get a

duplicate one?

Duplicate ticket can be issued in cases of lost/torn/mutilated tickets that are either confirmed or are RAC.

A duplicate ticket can be issued against the original ticket lost / torn / mutilated on reporting the said fact to the railway authorities. The passenger is allowed to travel on the accommodation reserved by him, on getting a duplicate ticket after payment of the prescribed fare viz: -

A) When duplicate ticket is asked for before the chart has been prepared.

Conditions		Distance	Fare to be paid
a)	For trains other than Rajdhani / Shatabdi	1) Up-to 500 Kms 2) More than 500 Kms	1) 25% of the total fare 2) 10% of the total fare subject to min. of 25% of the fare for 500 Kms
b)	For Rajdhani /S Shatabdi point to point fixed	All distances	3) 25% of the total fare

B) When duplicate ticket is asked for after the chart has been prepared.

Conditions		Distance	Fare to be paid
c)	Confirm lost tickets	All distances	50% of the total fare
d)	Confirm torn/ mutilated tickets	1) Up-to 500 Kms 2) More than 500 Kms	25% of the total fare 10% of the total fare subject to min. of 25% of the fare for 500 Kms
e)	RAC/torn/ mutilated tickets	All distances	25% of the total fare

It is to be noted that no duplicate ticket is issued against lost RAC ticket after the chart is prepared and against Wait List lost / torn / mutilated tickets.

However, in case where the lost ticket is found, then a refund of the amount paid for the duplicate ticket is possible on presenting the original ticket along with the duplicate ticket before the departure of the train. The charges for the duplicate ticket so paid is liable to be refunded after deduction of 5% of the charges paid, subject to a minimum of Rs. 20/-. Thereafter, original ticket becomes valid for travel as well as for refund.

LATE RUNNING OF TRAIN

In various instances trains arrive quite late. However, we are forced to board the same only for the sole reason that if the ticket is cancelled, we will get a very meager amount as refund. Isn't the railway morally responsible to refund the entire amount on such cancellation, as the delay is occasioned not by our fault?

The railway permits full refund of the fare in case of cancellation of tickets due to late running of trains for more than three hours. However, for such, tickets are required to be cancelled before the actual departure of the train.

DEFICIENCY IN SERVICE

I was travelling in AC 2 tier; however, due to some technical problems the AC failed working. Can I make the railway liable for the inconvenience caused to me?

Under the relevant provisions regulating the railways, when the air-conditioning has not worked for a portion of the journey, refund for such portion of the journey is granted at the destination of the train on production of a certificate of the conductor / guard to this effect. For the same the ticket is required to be produced within twenty hours of the arrival of the train. The refund so admissible is as follows:

1) In case of AC first class, the difference between the AC first class fare and first class mail fare.

2) In case of AC 2 tier sleeper / AC 3 tier sleeper class, the difference between the AC 2 tier / AC 3 tier fare and the sleeper class mail /express fare.

3) In case of AC chair car class the difference between the AC chair car class and second-class mail / express fare.

4) In case of executive class ticket of Shatabdi trains, the difference between the notified executive class fare for the concerned section and first class mail / express fare for the concerned distance of that section.

You can also sue the railways for deficiency in services in the consumer forum.

MISSING ONWARD TRAIN —REFUND

I booked ticket from Pune to Ranchi. As there is no direct train, a ticket from Pune to Ranchi via Jamshedpur was issued which had reservation in two different trains and the boarding point of the connecting train was Jamshedpur. However, the train arrived at Jamshedpur quite, late due to which I missed my connecting train from Jamshedpur to Ranchi. On claiming for refund the Station Master told me that the amount, which I will be getting, would be quite meager. How much refund am I entitled to get?

Since you have availed a part of the journey and non-travelling was not a result of your fault, you are entitled to claim refund for the journey that has not been availed of and not for the entire journey. For this a ticket deposit receipt issued by the station master is to be collected and then the ticket holder may apply for refund to the Chief Commercial Manager (Refunds) of the concerned railway. However, the said amount would be quite less than the amount you will have to spend for booking another ticket from the said station to your destination station. Thus, if you wish to avail refund, the refund amount payable to you will be the amount you had paid minus the fare from Pune to Jamshedpur. This amount will definitely be less than the fare between Jamshedpur to Ranchi. It is advisable that in such circumstances, one should approach the Station Master and request for permission for traveling in some other train. The Station Master on being satisfied will grant such by making an endorsement on the back of the ticket to this effect and then you are permitted to travel in any train of the same status upto the destination station. It is to be noted that though you are entitled to travel in such trains, you cannot claim reservation unless the seats / berths therein are vacant.

BOARDING AT OTHER STATION

I have a reservation from Howrah to Pune. However, due to some engagement I am required to be in Tatanagar on the date of boarding the train from Howrah. As Tatanagar station is enroute Howrah to Pune I intend to board the train from there itself. Can I do so or will my berth be allotted to some other passenger if I don't board it from Howrah?

If one does not board the train within the specified period, his reservation is liable to be forfeited and transferred to some other RAC / WL passenger. You can avoid such by making a specific request in writing to the effect that your Boarding Station should be changed to Tatanagar. Such request is to be made at any computerized reservation centre at least 24 hours before the scheduled departure of the train from the starting station.

The railway administration has the right to use such accommodation from the originating station up to the station at which the passenger is due to board and no refund will be permissible for the portion of journey not availed by the passenger.

RAIL ACCIDENT — INSURANCE

My father, while travelling in the railway, died in an accident, which took place due to inadvertence of the railway staffs. He was the only earning member in our family. It has become quite difficult to lead our life since then. Can I claim monetary damages from the railway?

The Indian Railway insures not only passengers on board but the platform ticket holders, passengers in waiting room / reservation / booking office or any other place within the premises of railway station against death or injury in case of any accident or even untoward incident caused due to any terrorist act, violent attack, robbery, dacoity, rioting, shootout or arson.

The amount of compensation so payable is as follows:

In case of death or permanent disability:	Rs. 4 lacks.
In case of injuries:	A minimum of Rs. 32,000/- & a maximum of Rs. 3,60,000/- (Depending upon the gravity of injury).

Ex-gratia amount for injury varies depending on the circumstances.

In case of death to dependant:	Rs. 15000/-
In case of grievous injury:	Rs. 5000/-
In case of simple injury:	Rs. 500/-

It is to be noted that all the claims are to be settled by the Railway Claims Tribunals so constituted under the Railways Act.

SPEEDY DISPOSAL—RAILWAY CLAIM

My son died in a railway accident. Is there any mode of obtaining speedy compensation from the Railways?

First of all a notice demanding the compensation from the Railways has to be made to the appropriate authority specifying the details of the accident. If there is no response from the department within a reasonable time, compensation can be claimed from the railway by approaching the Railway Claims Tribunals. However if no tribunal has been constituted having jurisdiction over the place of occurrence, the High Court can be approached.

•••

APPENDIX–I

- **CRIME AND SOCIETY**

FIR [Sec 154, 155 CRIMINAL PROCEDURE CODE]

DELAY IN LODGING FIR [Sec 154, 155 CRIMINAL PROCEDURE CODE]

BAIL [Sec 436, 437, 439 CRIMINAL PROCEDURE CODE]

BAIL AS A MATTER OF RIGHT [Sec 436, 437 CRIMINAL PROCEDURE CODE]

ANTICIPATORY BAIL [Sec 438 CRIMINAL PROCEDURE CODE]

ARREST WITHOUT WARRANT [Sec 43 CRIMINAL PROCEDURE CODE]

RIGHTS OF AN ARRESTED PERSON [Sec 50,54,55,56,57,75,76, 303 of CRIMINAL PROCEDURE CODE and Art. 20(1) of the CONSTITUTION OF INDIA]

CONFESSION [Sec 24-29 INDIAN EVIDENCE ACT]

SELF - INCRIMINATION [ref: Art. 20(3) of the CONSTITUTION OF INDIA & State of U.P. v. Boota Singh. AIR 1978 SC 1770]

SEARCH WITHOUT WARRANT [Sec 103, 153, 165, 166 of CRIMINAL PROCEDURE CODE]

TIME LIMIT FOR TAKING COGNIZANCE [SEC 467 to 473 of the CRIMINAL PROCEDURE CODE]

ABETMENT [Sec 107-111 INDIAN PENAL CODE]

RIGHT OF PRIVATE DEFENCE [Sec 96-106 INDIAN PENAL CODE]

CULPABLE HOMICIDE / MURDER [Sec 299, 300, 302, 306, 307, 308 INDIAN PENAL CODE]

INDECENT REPRESENTATION OF WOMAN [Sec 6/3, 6/4, 4 INDECENT REPRESENTATION OF WOMAN (PROHIBITION) ACT 1986]

RAPE – AGE FACTOR [Sec 375, 376, 376-A, 376-B, 376-D INDIAN PENAL CODE]

RAPE – CONSENT [Sec 375,376,376-A, 376-B, 376-D INDIAN PENAL CODE]

RAPE – NON COMPOUNDABLE [Sec 375,376,376-A, 376-B, 376-D INDIAN PENAL CODE]

KIDNAPPING [Sec 359,360,361,363,363-A, 364 INDIAN PENAL CODE]

DOWRY DEATH [Sec 304-B, 498-A INDIAN PENAL CODE, Sec 2,3,4 DOWRY PROHIBITION ACT 1961 & 13-b INDIAN EVIDENCE ACT]

EUTHANASIA [Sec 299, 300, 302, 306, 309 INDIAN PENAL CODE]

PRESUMPTION AS TO SUICIDE [Sec 306, 307, 308, 498-a INDIAN PENAL CODE & Sec 113-a INDIAN EVIDENCE ACT]

SATI [Sec 202 INDIAN PENAL CODE & Sec 2(1)(b), 2(c), 3, 4, 5 COMMISSION OF SATI PREVENTION ACT 1987]

PATERNITY OF CHILD CRIMINAL PROCEDURE CODE [Sec 112 of the INDIAN EVIDENCE ACT]

CAUSING MISCARRIAGE [Sec 312 INDIAN PENAL CODE]

DEATH DUE TO NEGLIGENCE [Sec 304-A INDIAN PENAL CODE]

RASH AND NEGLIGENT DRIVING [Sec 279 INDIAN PENAL CODE]

RAGGING

OBSCENE MATERIAL [Sec 292, 293 INDIAN PENAL CODE]

DEFAMATION [Sec 499,500,501,502,504 INDIAN PENAL CODE]

MEDICAL NEGLIGENCE (CRIMINAL) *[DR. SURESH GUPTA V/S GOVT OF NCT OF DELHI & ANR (2004) 6 SCC 422]*

JUVENILE JUSTICE [Sec. 2, 4, 8, 9, 11, 12, 14, 15, 16, 17, 29, 40 of THE JUVENILE JUSTICE ACT, 2000]

PROBATION OF OFFENDERS [SEC. 3 TO 6, 9, 11 AND 13 OF THE PROBATION OF OFFENDERS ACT, 1958]

PRODUCING FALSE COMPLAINT [SEC. 211 OF THE INDIAN PENAL CODE AND SEC 195 OF THE CODE OF CRIMINAL PROCEDURE]

FALSE DOCUMENT IN COURT [SEC. 194 AND 195 OF THE INDIAN PENAL CODE AND SEC. 195 OF THE CODE OF CRIMINAL PROCEDURE]

DISHONEST MISAPPROPRIATION OF PROPERTY [SEC. 403 TO 409 AND 415 TO 420 OF THE INDIAN PENAL CODE]

SUPERDARI [SEC 451 OF THE CODE OF CRIMINAL PROCEDURE]

DYING DECLARATION [SEC 30(1) INDIAN EVIDENCE ACT]

TAPE RECORDER AS EVIDENCE [SEC 3, 7, 64 INDIAN EVIDENCE ACT]

HOSTILE WITNESS [SEC 191,192,193,194,195 INDIAN EVIDENCE ACT]

EXPERT OPINION [SEC 45, 46, 47 INDIAN EVIDENCE ACT]

ESTOPPEL [SEC 115,116,117 INDIAN EVIDENCE ACT]

ORGAN TRANSPLANT TRANSPLANTATION OF THE HUMAN ORGANS ACT

ARMS KEEPING [SEC 1-32 ARMS ACT 1955]

PROSTITUTION [Sec 366-b, 372 and SEC 2 to 7 of the IMMORAL TRAFFIC (PREVENTION) ACT, 1956]

• **FAMILY**

SUCCESSION [SEC 6, 9-16 HINDU SUCCESSION ACT 1956]

WILL-LEGAL FORMALITIES [SEC 30 HINDU SUCCESSION ACT]

WILL- REQUISITES [Sec 30 HINDU SUCCESSION ACT & 2 (h), 59, 60, 61, 62, 69-74 INDIAN SUCCESSION ACT 1925]

WILL-EXECUTOR-RECEIVING BENEFIT [SEC 30 HINDU SUCCESSION ACT & Sec 2 (h), 59, 60, 61, 62, 69-74 INDIAN SUCCESSION ACT 1925]

GIFT [SEC 122 TO 129 OF THE TRANSFER OF PROPERTY ACT, 1882]

ADOPTION [SEC 7,8,9,10,11 HINDU ADOPTION & MAINTENANCE ACT 1956]

CUSTODY-HINDU [SEC 26 HINDU MARRIAGE ACT, 1955]

CUSTODY-MUSLIM

REMARRYING WIFE-MUSLIM LAW

MUTA MARIAGE

TALAQ

TALAQ-MUSLIM FEMALE

MAHR

SHUFFA

HIBA

WAKF

MARRYING MINOR [SEC 5 HINDU MARRIAGE ACT AND SEC 3 TO 7 OF THE CHILD MARRIAGE RESTRAINT ACT, 1929]

CEREMONIES OF MARRIAGE [SEC 7 HINDU MARRIAGE ACT]

PROHIBITED DEGREES IN MARRIAGE [SEC 5 HINDU MARRIAGE ACT]

INTER-RELIGION MARRIAGE [SEC 4, 5, 8, 11 SPECIAL MARRIAGE ACT]

RESTITUTION OF CONJUGAL RIGHTS [SEC 9 HINDU MARRIAGE ACT & 36 SPECIAL MARRIAGE ACT & 32, 33 INDIAN DIVORCE ACT & 36, 37, 38 PARSI MARRIAGE & DIVORCE ACT]

JUDICIAL SEPARATION [SEC 10, 13, 25 HINDU MARRIAGE ACT & SEC 125 CRIMINAL PROCEDURE CODE & SEC 22,23,24,25,26,27,28 INDIAN DIVORCE ACT & SEC 34 PARSI MARRIAGE DIVORCE ACT]

DIVORCE -HINDU [Sec 13, 13(1), 13(1-a), 13-a, 13-B, 14, 15 HINDU MARRIAGE ACT]

DIVORCE -HINDU [Sec 13, 13(1), 13(1-a), 13-a, 13-B, 14, 15 HINDU MARRIAGE ACT]

DIVORCE-CHRISTIAN [Sec 10,11,13,14,16,17 INDIAN DIVORCE ACT]

STRIDHAN

RECOVERY OF DOWRY [SEC 1, 2, 3, 4 DOWRY PROHIBITION ACT]

MARRIAGE OUTSIDE INDIA [FOREIGN MARRIAGE ACT]

MAINTENANCE [SEC 24, 25 HINDU MARRIAGE ACT & 125 CRIMINAL PROCEDURE CODE]

MAINTENANCE-MUSLIM [Sec 125 CRIMINAL PROCEDURE CODE & Mohd Ahmed Khan V/s Shahbano Begum AIR 1985 SC 945]

LEGITIMACY OF A CHILD [SEC 16 OF THE HINDU MARRIAGE ACT]

HOMOSEXUALITY [SEC 377 OF THE INDIAN PENAL CODE]

MARRIAGE CERTIFICATE [SEC 8 OF THE HINDU MARRIAGE ACT]

PROOF OF MARRIAGE [SEC 7 OF THE HINDU MARRIAGE ACT]

COURT MARRIAGE [SEC 2 TO 18 OF THE SPECIAL MARRIAGE ACT, 1954]

SEX DETERMINATION [PRE-NATAL DIAGNOSTIC TECHNIQUES ACT]

- **THE PROCEDURE OF COURTS**

INSTITUTING SUIT [SEC 9, 15, 16,17,18,26,109,113,114,115 CODE OF CIVIL PROCEDURE]

SUIT BY MINOR [O32R (1), O32R (2)1, O32R4, O32R (13)1 CODE OF CIVIL PROCEDURE]

INDIGENT PERSON [O33R1, O33R9A CODE OF CIVIL PROCEDURE]

NOTICE TO GOVERNMENT [SEC 79, 80 CODE OF CIVIL PROCEDURE]

AMENDMENT [SEC 152, 153-A CODE OF CIVIL PROCEDURE]

SUMMON

INTERIM ORDER [SEC 151 & O39R1, O39R2, O41R5 CODE OF CIVIL PROCEDURE]

EX-PARTE [Or 9 R 13, Or 47 R 1, Sec 96(2) of CODE OF CIVIL PROCEDURE & Pandurang v/s Shanti Bai AIR 1989 SC 2240]

CAVEAT [SEC 148 CODE OF CIVIL PROCEDURE]

EXEMPTION FROM ATTACHMENT [SEC 60 – 64 & RULES 41 – 57 OF OR 21]

INTERPLEADER SUIT [SEC 88(1) CODE OF CIVIL PROCEDURE]

RES JUDICATA [SEC 11 CODE OF CIVIL PROCEDURE]

RES SUBJUDICE [SEC 10 CODE OF CIVIL PROCEDURE]

DELAY IN SUIT DISPOSAL [AMENDMENTS OF 1976, 1999 & 2002]

ALTERNATIVE FORUM

TRANSFER OF CASE [SEC 24, 25 CODE OF CIVIL PROCEDURE]

MESNE PROFITS [SEC 2(12) CODE OF CIVIL PROCEDURE]

BENAMI TRANSACTION

• RIGHTS AND LAW

CITIZENSHIP [ART 5,6,7,8,9,10,11 CONSTITUTION]

BIRTH CERTIFICATE [SEC 23 AND 28 OF THE BIRTHS, DEATHS AND MARRIAGES REGISTRATION ACT, 1886]

PUBLIC INTEREST LITIGATION [ART 32, 226 CONSTITUTION]

UNIFORM CIVIL CODE [ART 44 CONSTITUTION]

RIGHT TO EQUALITY [ART 14,15,16,17,18 CONSTITUTION]

RIGHT TO EQUALITY [ART 14,15,16,17,18 CONSTITUTION]

RIGHT TO PROPERTY [ART 19(F), 300-A CONSTITUTION]

DOUBLE JEOPARDY [ART 20 CONSTITUTION]

NATIONAL FLAG [PREVENTION OF INSULTS TO NATIONAL HONOR ACT]

PROTECTION OF LIFE & LIBERTY [ART 21 CONSTITUTION]

TELEPHONE TAPPING [ART 19 CONSTITUTION & PUCL V/S UNION OF INDIA, 1996]

BONDED LABOUR [ART 23 CONSTITUTION & BONDED LABOUR SYSTEM (ABOLITION) ACT 1976]

CONTEMPT OF COURT [CONTEMPT OF COURTS ACT]

ATTORNEY GENERAL [ART. 76 OF THE CONSTITUTION OF INDIA]

ADVOCATE/BARRISTER/ATTORNEY/SOLICITOR

UNTOUCHABILITY [3, 4, 5, 6, 7-A, 10-A, 11 PROTECTION OF CIVIL RIGHTS ACT 1955 & 3 THE SCHEDULED CASTES AND SCHEDULED TRIBES (PREVENTION OF ATTROCITIES ACT) 1989 & ARTICLE 15 CONSTITUTION]

ADVOCATE LOSING CASE WILLINGLY [Sec 35 to 36B, 42 and 49(1)(c) of the ADVOCATES ACT, 1961.

ELECTION IRREGULARITIES - VOTER CARD

CHANGE IN NAME

WRITS [ART 32,226 CONSTITUTION]

HABEAS CORPUS [ART 32,226 CONSTITUTION]

MANDAMUS [ART 32,226 CONSTITUTION]

QUO-WARRANTO [ART 32,226 CONSTITUTION]

PROHIBITION [ART 32,226 CONSTITUTION]

CERTIORARI [ART 32,226 CONSTITUTION]

RIGHTS OF AN HIV INFECTED PERSON [ART 21 CONSTITUTION]

DISABILITY – [PERSONS WITH DISABILITIES (EQUAL OPPORTUNITIES, PROTECTION OF RIGHTS AND FULL PARTICIPATION) ACT; NATIONAL TRUST FOR WELFARE OF PERSONS WITH AUTISM, CEREBRAL PALSY, MENTAL RETARDATION AND MULTIPLE DISABILITIES ACT; REHABILITATION COUNCIL OF INDIA ACT]

• **OUR ENVIRONMENT**

NOISE POLLUTION [THE NOISE POLLUTION (REGULATION & CONTROL) RULES]

WATER & AIR POLLUTION [SEC 3, 4, 16 to 18, 20 to 26 of the WATER (PREVENTION AND CONTROL OF POLLUTION) ACT, 1974; AIR WATER (PREVENTION AND CONTROL OF POLLUTION) ACT, 1981 & 277, 278 INDIAN PENAL CODE]

WILDLIFE [WILDLIFE PROTECTION ACT 1972 & 289 INDIAN PENAL CODE & CONVENTION ON INTERNATIONAL TRADE OF ENDANGERED SPECIES & PREVENTION OF CRUELTY TOWARDS ANIMALS ACT, 1960]

SMOKING [K. RAMAKRISHNAN V/S STATE OF KERELA AIR 1999 KER 385, MURLI. S. DEORA V/S UNION OF INDIA, CIGRETTES & OTHER TOBACCO PRODUCTS (PROHIBITION OF ADVANCEMENT & REGULATION OF TRADE & COMMERCE, PRODUCTION SUPPLY & DISTRIBUTION) ACT 2003

• **CONTRACTUAL ASPECT**

INVITATION TO AN OFFER [Sec 2(a), 2(b) INDIAN CONTRACT ACT]

OFFER- COMMUNICATION NECESSARY [Sec 2(a), 2(b), 2(d), 2(e), 2(h) INDIAN CONTRACT ACT]

CROSS-OFFER [Sec 2(a), 2(b), 2(e), 2(h) INDIAN CONTRACT ACT]

REVOCATION OF AN OFFER [Sec 4, 5, 6 INDIAN CONTRACT ACT]

OPPORTUNITY TO REVIEW TERMS OF CONTRACT [Sec 2(a), 2(b), 2(d), 2(e), 2(h) INDIAN CONTRACT ACT]

DEEMED ACCEPTANCE [Sec 2(b) INDIAN CONTRACT ACT]

CAPACITY TO CONTRACT [Sec 10,11 INDIAN CONTRACT ACT]

MINOR [10,11 INDIAN CONTRACT ACT]

INSANE [10,11 INDIAN CONTRACT ACT]

DUTY TO SPEAK-NOT ALWAYS APPLICABLE [17 INDIAN CONTRACT ACT]

RESTRAINT IN TRADE [27 INDIAN CONTRACT ACT]

RESTRAIN OF LEGAL PROCEEDING [28 INDIAN CONTRACT ACT]

REIMBURSEMENT OF AMOUNT DUE BY OTHER PAID BY INTERESTED PARTY [SEC 69 INDIAN CONTRACT ACT, 1872]

AGENCY [SEC 182 TO 238 OF THE INDIAN CONTRACT ACT, 1872]

PARTNERSHIP-MINOR [SEC 30 OF THE INDIAN PARTNERSHIP ACT, 1932, 10,11 INDIAN CONTRACT ACT]

PARTNERSHIP-UNREGISTERED [SEC 56 TO 69 OF THE INDIAN PARTNERSHIP ACT, 1932]

SPECIFIC PERFORMANCE [SEC 10,14,15, 21 OF THE SPECIFIC RELIEF ACT, 1963]

SPECIFIC PERFORMANCE- LOST RIGHT [SEC 73 OF THE INDIAN CONTRACT ACT, 1872]

SALE OF GOODS [SEC 27 OF THE SALE OF GOODS ACT, 1930 AND SEC 72 OF THE INDIAN CONTRACT ACT, 1872]

GOVERNMENT CONTRACT—STAMP DUTY [SEC 3 OF THE INDIAN STAMP ACT]

LIABILTY OF SURETY FOR LOAN [SEC 128 AND 140 OF THE INDIAN CONTRACT ACT, 1872]

CHEQUE BOUNCING [SEC 138 TO 142 OF THE NEGOTIABLE INSTRUMENT ACT]

- **LAND & PROPERTY**

TRANSFER OF PROPERTY- DESTRUCTION [SEC 108 OF THE TRANSFER OF PROPERTY ACT]

TRANSFER OF PROPERTY -SUB-LEASE [SEC 108 OF THE TRANSFER OF PROPERTY ACT]

TRANSFER OF PROPERTY -PART PERFORMANCE [SEC 53-A OF THE TRANSFER OF PROPERTY ACT]

TRANSFER OF PROPERTY - PART PERFORMANCE / SPECIFIC PERFORMANCE [SEC 53-A OF THE TRANSFER OF PROPERTY ACT AND SEC 10,14,15, 21 OF THE SPECIFIC RELIEF ACT, 1963]

PURCHASE OF LAND - CLEAR TITLE

NON-REGISTRATION OF A LEASE DEED [SEC 107 OF THE TRANSFER OF PROPERTY ACT]

REGISTRATION OF SALE DEED [SEC 71 AND 78 OF THE TRANSFER OF PROPERTY ACT]

ADVERSE POSSESSION [SEC. 65 OF THE LIMITATION ACT]

SOCIETY REGISTRATION [SEC 1 TO 7 OF THE SOCIETIES REGISTRATION ACT, 1860]

HOUSING LAWS -CHANGE IN PLAN

ACQUISITION OF PROPERTIES BY NRI [FOREIGN EXCHANGE MANAGEMENT (ACQUISITION AND TRANSFER OF IMMOVABLE PROPERTY IN INDIA) REGULATIONS]

IMPORT OF GOLD & SILVER BY NRI

• CONSUMER RIGHTS & TORTIOUS LIABILITY

CONSUMER PROTECTION [Sec 2(1)(d), 10 – 27 CONSUMER PROTECTION ACT]

MEDICAL NEGLIGENCE [I.M.A. v/s V.P. Shantha & Ors 14 (SC) MNCR]

TORTS [SEC 2(1) OCCUPIERS LIABILITY ACT 1957]

• INTELLECTUAL PROPERTY RIGHTS

PATENT, DESIGN, TRADEMARK [Sec 2(m), 2(1)(j), 3 –11, 48, 70, 104, 122 of PATENTS ACT 1970 & PATENT (AMENDMENT) ACT 2002]

[Sec 2(1)(m), 2(1)(zb), 2(1)(z), 6 –11, 28, 30 TRADE MARK ACT 1999]

[2(j), 5, 11, 22 DESIGN ACT 2000]

COPYRIGHT [Sec 2, 11 - 14, 22 – 29, 33 – 38, 51, 52,, 74, Rule 16 of CHAPTER VI COPYRIGHT RULES 1958]

• **INFORMATION TECHNOLOGY**

HACKING [SEC 66 INFORMATION TECHNOLOGY ACT 2000]

DIGITAL SIGNATURE [SEC 35 INFORMATION TECHNOLOGY ACT 2000]

PORNOGRAPHY [SEC 67 INFORMATION TECHNOLOGY ACT 2000]

E-CONTRACT [SEC 11, 12, 13 INFORMATION TECHNOLOGY ACT 2000]

• **BUSINESS ACTIVITIES**

COMMENCING BUSINESS [SALOMAN v/s SALOMAN & Sec 3(1)(i) INDIAN COMPANIES ACT 1956 & Sec 4 of INDIAN PARTNERSHIP ACT]

INCORPORATION [Sec 2(36), 20, 21, 26, 30, 31, 33,34, 70, 149 INDIAN COMPANIES ACT]

MEMORANDUM OF ASSOCIATION [2(28), 16, 36 INDIAN COMPANIES ACT 1956 & Ashbury v/s Riche 1875 L.R.7,HL 653]

ARTICLE OF ASSOCIATION [Sec 2(2), 31, 36 INDIAN COMPANIES ACT 1956 & Ashbury v/s Riche 1875 L.R.7,HL 653]

SHARES [Sec 2(46), 69 – 73, 82, 86, 108 –117 INDIAN COMPANIES ACT 1956]

DEBENTURES [Sec 2(12), 117, 118, 119, 152 INDIAN COMPANIES ACT 1956]

OPPRESSION BY MAJORITY [Sec 397 – 409 OF INDIAN COMPANIES ACT 1956 & FOSS V/S HARBOTTLE]

MERGER [SEC 395 INDIAN COMPANIES ACT 1956]

FRAUD [Sec 2(36), 56, 59, 62, 63, 65, 68 INDIAN COMPANIES ACT]

WINDING UP OF A COMPANY [Relevant Sec 425 – 585 INDIAN COMPANIES ACT 1956]

FOREIGN INVESTMENTS [FOREIGN EXCHANGE MANAGEMENT (TRANSFER OF SECURITY BY A PERSON RESIDENT OUTSIDE INDIA) REGULATION UNDER FOREIGN EXCHANGE MANAGEMENT ACT (FEMA)]

TRUST - FORMALITIES [SEC 4 TO 10 OF THE INDIAN TRUST ACT, 1882]

DELEGATION OF POWER OF A TRUSTEE [SEC 47 OF THE INDIAN TRUST ACT, 1882]

TRUST - DEFENDING THE SUIT [SEC 55 TO 69 OF THE INDIAN TRUST ACT, 1882]

SETTLEMENT THROUGH ARBITRATOR [SEC 7 TO 36 OF THE ARBITRATION AND CONCILIATION ACT, 1996]

- **INCOME TAX AND SERVICE TAX**

INCOME TAX [REF: SEC 2, 10, 22, 80, 88]

SERVICE TAX

- **WORK AND LAW**

FACTORIES ACT

SETTING UP A FACTORY [ART 39(e) CONSTITUTION, Sec 6, 7, 11-91]

TIME FRAME OF WORK- GENERAL [Sec 51-66]

TIME FRAME OF WORK- WOMEN AND CHILDREN [Sec. 51 to 58, 66, 22, 23, 27, 87(b)]

LEAVE WITH PAY [SEC 78 AND 79 OF THE FACTORIES ACT]

INDUSTRIAL DISPUTES ACT

CLOSING INDUSTRY-LEGAL REQUISITES [SEC 25-FFA, 25-FFF, 25-R, 30-A of THE INDUSTRIAL DISPUTES ACT, 1947]

TERMINATION-WAGES DURING SUSPENSION [Sec 17B of the INDUSTRIAL DISPUTES ACT, 1947]

TERMINATION-REMEDY [Sec 2 (k)of THE INDUSTRIAL DISPUTES ACT, 1947]

STRIKE [22-28]

RETRENCHMENT [Sec 2(oo), 25-F to 25S]

LAY-OFF [S 2 (kkk), 25-A to 25E]

WORKMEN'S COMPENSATION ACT

COMPENSATION [SEC 3 - 18A]

LIMITATION FOR FILING CLAIM [10]

MATERNITY BENEFIT ACT

MATERNITY BENEFIT [5(1), 5(2), 5-b, 7, 8, 9, 9-a, 10, 11]

EMPLOYEE'S STATE INSURANCE ACT, 1978

LEAVING SERVICE-PAYMENT OF COMPULSORY DEDUCTIONS [SEC 74 AND 75 OF THE ESI ACT AND ART. 226 OF THE CONSTITUTION OF INDIA]

EQUAL REMUNERATION ACT, 1976

PROHIBITION OF DISCRIMINATION (MEN & WOMEN) [4 - 18]

EMPLOYEES' PROVIDENT FUNDS AND MISCELLANEOUS PROVISIONS ACT, 1952 (EPFMP).

CONTRIBUTION BY EMPLOYER [SEC 6]

WITHDRAWAL OF PROVIDENT FUND [Sec 51(b) and Schedule II of the EPFMP Act]

PENSION [EMPLOYEES PENSION SCHEME FRAMED UNDER THE ACT]

APPLICABILITY-SALARY LIMIT [SEC 1 OF THE EPFMP ACT]

REFUND OF P.F. ON LEAVING [SEC 17-A OF THE EPFMP ACT AND SEC 74 AND 75 OF THE ESI ACT AND ART. 226 OF THE CONSTITUTION OF INDIA]

APPLICABILITY- CONTRACTOR'S EMPLOYEES [1, 2, 2-A]

CONTRIBUTION IF NOT PAID [SEC 7-A TO 7- Q, 8, 8A, 14 TO 14B]

CHECKING CONTRIBUTION PAID OR NOT

EMPLOYEE'S STATE INSURANCE ACT

CONTRIBUTION [38 - 45-I]

BENEFITS [46 - 73]

EMPLOYEES EXCHANGE (COMPULSORY NOTIFICATION OF VACANCIES) ACT 1959

EMPLOYMENT / VACANCY [Sec 2 - 8]

THE PAYMENT OF BONUS ACT, 1965

BONUS [8, 9]

SERVICE MATTER
COMPASSIONATE GROUND [NATIONAL COAL WAGE AGREEMENT]
SUSPENSION [SEC 17B OF THE INDUSTRIAL DISPUTES ACT, 1947]

• ***SAFETY ON ROAD***
MOTOR VEHICLES ACT 1988
SALE-PURCHASE OF VEHICLE / TRANSFER / REGISTRATION [SEC 39 - 65]
COMPENSATION IN CASE OF ACCIDENT [Sec. 140, 166]
JURISDICTION OF MOTOR VEHICLE TRIBUNAL [Sec. 165-175]
TRANSFER OF VEHICLE TO OTHER STATE [Sec. 60]
RECOVERY FROM INSURANCE COMPANY
HIT & RUN [Sec. 163]
DRIVING LICENSE- TERMS [Sec. 3 - 28]

• **RAILWAYS**
TRANSFER OF TICKET TO OTHERS
CIRCULAR JOURNEY TICKETS
BOOKING LUGGAGE
TICKET LOSS-ISSUANCE OF DUPLICATE
LATE RUNNING OF TRAIN
DEFICIENCY IN SERVICE
MISSING ONWARD TRAIN - REFUND
BOARDING AT OTHER STATION
RAIL ACCIDENT - INSURANCE
SPEEDY DISPOSAL-RAILWAY CLAIM

APPENDIX–II

(THE ACT AND THE YEAR OF THE VARIOUS LAWS REFERRED TO BE INSERTED WITH APPENDIX)

CRIMINAL PROCEDURE CODE, 1973

CODE OF CIVIL PROCEDURE, 1908

BENAMI TRANSACTION (PROHIBITION) ACT, 1988

INDIAN PENAL CODE, 1860

CONSTITUTION OF INDIA, 1950

INDECENT REPRESENTATION OF WOMAN (PROHIBITION) ACT 1986

INDIAN EVIDENCE ACT, 1872

COMMISSION OF SATI PREVENTION ACT 1987

JUVENILE JUSTICE ACT, 2000

PROBATION OF OFFENDERS ACT, 1958

TRANSPLANTATION OF THE HUMAN ORGANS ACT, 1994

ARMS ACT, 1959

IMMORAL TRAFFIC (PREVENTION) ACT, 1956

HINDU SUCCESSION ACT, 1956

INDIAN SUCCESSION ACT 1925

THE TRANSFER OF PROPERTY ACT, 1882

HINDU ADOPTION & MAINTENANCE ACT, 1956

HINDU MARRIAGE ACT, 1955

THE CHILD MARRIAGE RESTRAINT ACT, 1929

SPECIAL MARRIAGE ACT, 1956

INDIAN DIVORCE ACT, 1869

PARSI MARRIAGE & DIVORCE ACT, 1936

DOWRY PROHIBITION ACT, 1961

FOREIGN MARRIAGE ACT, 1969

PRE-NATAL DIAGNOSTIC TECHNIQUES (REGULATION AND PREVENTION OF MISUSE) ACT, 1994

BIRTHS, DEATHS AND MARRIAGES REGISTERATION ACT, 1886

PREVENTION OF INSULTS TO NATIONAL HONOR ACT, 1971

BONDED LABOUR SYSTEM (ABOLITION) ACT, 1976

CONTEMPT OF COURTS ACT, 1971

PROTECTION OF CIVIL RIGHTS ACT, 1955

THE SCHEDULED CASTES AND SCHEDULED TRIBES (PREVENTION OF ATTROCITIES ACT), 1989

ADVOCATES ACT, 1961

PERSONS WITH DISABILITIES (EQUAL OPPORTUNITIES, PROTECTION OF RIGHTS AND FULL PARTICIPATION) ACT, 1995

REHABILITATION COUNCIL OF INDIA ACT, 1992

WATER (PREVENTION AND CONTROL OF POLLUTION) ACT, 1974

AIR WATER (PREVENTION AND CONTROL OF POLLUTION) ACT, 1981

WILDLIFE PROTECTION ACT 1972

CIGARETTES & OTHER TOBACCO PRODUCTS (PROHIBITION OF ADVANCEMENT & REGULATION OF TRADE & COMMERCE, PRODUCTION SUPPLY & DISTRIBUTION) ACT, 2003

FOREIGN EXCHANGE MANAGEMENT ACT, 1999

INDIAN CONTRACT ACT, 1872

INDIAN PARTNERSHIP ACT, 1932

SALE OF GOODS ACT, 1930

THE INDIAN STAMP ACT, 1899

THE SPECIFIC RELIEF ACT, 1963

NEGOTIABLE INSTRUMENT ACT, 1881

THE TRANSFER OF PROPERTY ACT, 1882

LIMITATION ACT, 1963

SOCIETIES REGISTRATION ACT, 1860

CONSUMER PROTECTION ACT, 1986

OCCUPIERS LIABILITY ACT 1957

PATENTS ACT 1970

TRADE MARK ACT 1999

DESIGN ACT 2000

COPYRIGHT ACT, 1957

INFORMATION TECHNOLOGY ACT 2000

INDIAN COMPANIES ACT 1956

THE INDIAN TRUST ACT, 1882

THE ARBITRATION AND CONCILIATION ACT, 1996

INCOME TAX ACT, 1961

FACTORIES ACT, 1948

INDUSTRIAL DISPUTES ACT, 1947

WORKMEN'S COMPENSATION ACT, 1923

MATERNITY BENEFIT ACT, 1961

EMPLOYEE'S STATE INSURANCE ACT, 1978

EQUAL REMUNERATION ACT, 1976

EMPLOYEES' PROVIDENT FUNDS AND MISCELLANEOUS PROVISIONS ACT, 1952

EMPLOYEE'S STATE INSURANCE ACT, 1948

EMPLOYEES EXCHANGE (COMPULSORY NOTIFICATION OF VACANCIES) ACT 1959

THE PAYMENT OF BONUS ACT, 1965

MOTOR VEHICLES ACT, 1988

WAKF ACT, 1954

MUSALMAN WAKF ACT, 1923

MUSALMAN WAKIF VALIDITY ACT, 1930

ABOUT THE AUTHORS

Nishant Kashyap is a Graduate in Socio-Legal Sciences from Pune University and persuing Law (Final Year) from Symbiosis. He is the Co-editor of the book 'Medical Negligence Case Reporter' which was published during the course of his graduation. More than 50 articles of his have been published in various newspapers.

He successfully worked for the Human Rights related issues of the prisoners of Yerwada Central Prison, Maharashtra. Taking cognizance of his complaint, the former Chief Justice of India and the National Human Rights Commission Chairperson Justice A. S. Anand visited the jail and issued several directions to the State Government, which resulted into tremendous changes. He is working with the 'People for Animals', Jharkhand to rescue birds and animals from being illegally caged and traded.

Ashutosh Anand completed his L.L.B from University of Pune. Since his college days, he actively worked for social cause and imparted free legal aid to the needy. He successfully participated in national and international moot courts. He has worked for various national level seminar organized for Human Rights related issues. At present, he is rendering professional services in the High Court of Jharkhand at Ranchi.

HEALTHS Books

David Servan Schreiber (Guerir)
- The Instinct to Heal — 195.00
  (Curing stress, anxiety and depression without drugs and without talk therapy)

M. Subramaniam
- Unveiling the Secrets of Reiki — 195.00
- Brilliant Light — 195.00
  (Reiki Grand Master Manual)
- At the Feet of the Master (Manal Reiki) — 195.00

Sukhdeepak Malvai
- Natural Healing with Reiki — 100.00

Pt. Rajnikant Upadhayay
- Reiki (For Healthy, Happy & Comfortable Life) — 95.00
- Mudra Vigyan (For Health & Happiness) — 60.00

Sankalpo
- Neo Reiki — 150.00

Dr. Shiv Kumar
- Aroma Therapy — 95.00
- Causes, Cure & Prevention of Nervous Diseases — 75.00
- Diseases of Digestive System — 75.00
- Asthma-Allergies (Causes & Cure) — 75.00
- Eye-Care (Including Better Eye Sight) Without Glassess — 75.00
- Stress (How to Relieve from Stress A Psychological Study) — 75.00

Dr. Satish Goel
- Causes & Cure of Blood Pressure — 75.00
- Causes & Cure of Diabetes — 60.00
- Causes & Cure of Heart Ailments — 75.00
- Pregnancy & Child Care — 95.00
- Ladie's Slimming Course — 95.00
- Acupuncture Guide — 50.00
- Acupressure Guide — 50.00
- Acupuncture & Acupressure Guide — 95.00
- Walking for Better Health — 95.00
- Nature Cure for Health & Happiness — 95.00
- A Beacon of Hope for the Childless Couples — 60.00
- Sex for All — 75.00

Dr. Kanta Gupta
- Be Your Own Doctor — 60.00
  (a Book about Herbs & Their Use)

Dr. B.R. Kishore
- Vatsyana Kamasutra — 95.00
- The Manual of Sex & Tantra — 95.00

Dr. M.K. Gupta
- Causes, Cure & Prevention of High Blood Cholesterol — 60.00

Acharya Bhagwan Dev
- Yoga for Better Health — 95.00
- Pranayam, Kundalini aur Hathyoga — 60.00

Dr. S.K. Sharma
- Add Inches — 60.00
- Shed Weight Add Life — 60.00
- Alternate Therapies — 95.00
- Miracles of Urine Therapy — 60.00
- Meditation & Dhyan Yoga (for Spiritual Discipline) — 95.00
- A Complete Guide to Homeopathic Remedies — 120.00
- A Complete Guide to Biochemic Remedies — 60.00
- Common Diseases of Urinary System — 95.00
- Allopathic Guide for Common Disorders — 125.00
- E.N.T. & Dental Guide (in Press) — 95.00
- Wonders of Magnetotherapy — 95.00
- Family Homeopathic Guide — 95.00
- **Health in Your Hands** — 95.00
- Food for Good Health — 95.00
- Juice Therapy — 75.00
- Tips on Sex — 75.00

Dr. Renu Gupta
- Hair Care (Prevention of Dandruff & Baldness) — 75.00
- Skin Care — 75.00
- Complete Beautician Course (Start a Beauty Parlour at Home) — 95.00
- Common Diseases of Women — 95.00

Dr. Rajiv Sharma
- First Aid (in Press) — 95.00
- Causes, Cure and Prevention of Children's Diseases — 75.00

Dr. R.N. Gupta
- Joys of Parenthood — 40.00

M. Kumaria
- How to Keep Fit — 20.00

Dr. Pushpa Khurana
- Be Young and Healthy for 100 Years — 60.00
- The Awesome Challenge of AIDS — 40.00

Acharya Satyanand
- Surya Chikitsa — 95.00

Dr. Nishtha
- Diseases of Respiratory Tract (Nose, Throat, Chest & Lungs) — 75.00
- Backache (Spondylitis, Cervical Arthritis, Rheumatism) — 95.00

Usha Rai Verma
- Ladies Health Guide (With Make-up Guide) — 75.00

L.R. Chowdhary
- Rajuvenate with Kundalini Mantra Yoga — 95.00

Manoj Kumar
- Diamond Body Building Course — 95.00

Koulacharya Jagdish Sharma
- Body Language — 125.00

G.C. Goyal
- Vitamins for Natural Healing — 95.00

Dr. Vishnu Jain
- Heart to Heart (with Heart Specialist) — 95.00

Asha Pran
- Beauty Guide (With Make-up Guide) — 75.00

Acharya Vipul Rao
- Ayurvedic Treatment for Common Diseases — 95.00
- Herbal Treatment for Common Diseases — 95.00

Dr. Sajiv Adlakha
- Stuttering & Your Child (Question-Answer) — 60.00

Om Gupta
- How to Enjoy Sex (Questions-Answers) — 95.00

Dr. S.K. Sharma
- Tips on Sex — 75.00

Books can be requisitioned by V.P.P. Postage charges will be Rs. 20/- per book.
For orders of three books the postage will be free.

⬥ DIAMOND POCKET BOOKS

X-30, Okhla Industrial Area, Phase-II, New Delhi-110020, Phone : 011-51611861, Fax : 011-51611866
E-mail : sales@diamondpublication.com, Website : www.fusionbooks.com

Religion and Spirituality

Goswami Tulsidas
- Sri Ramcharitmanasa (Doha- Chopai in Hindi, Roman Description in English) 1500.00

Ed. Acharya Bhagwan Dev
- Sanskar Vidhi 125.00

B.K. Chaturvedi
- Gods & Goddesses of India 150.00
- Shiv Purana 95.00
- Vishnu Purana 95.00
- Shrimad Bhagvat Purana 75.00
- Devi Bhagvat Purana 75.00
- Garud Purana 75.00
- Agni Purana 75.00
- Varah Purana 75.00
- Brahamvevart Purana 75.00
- The Hymns & Orisons of Lord Shiva (Roman) 30.00
- Sri Hanuman Chalisa (Roman) 30.00
- Pilgrimage Centres of India 95.00
- Chalisa Sangreh 40.00

S. K. Sharma
- The Brilliance of Hinduism 125.00
- Sanskar Vidhi (Arya Samaj) 125.00

Dr. B.R. Kishore
- Hinduism 95.00
- Rigveda 60.00
- Samveda 60.00
- Yajurveda 60.00
- Atharvveda 60.00
- Mahabharata 60.00
- Ramayana 60.00
- Supreme Mother Goddeses Durga (4 Colour Durga Chalisa) 95.00

Manish Verma
- Fast & Festivals of India 95.00

Prof. Gurpret Singh
- Soul of Sikhism 125.00

Shiv Sharma
- Soul of Jainism 125.00

Pt. Ramesh Tiwari
- Shrimad Bhagavad Gita (Krishna, the Charioteer) (Sanskrit, Hindi, English & Description in English) 400.00

Manan Sharma
- Buddhism (Teachings of Buddha) 150.00
- Universality of Buddha 150.00

Anurag Sharma
- Life Profile & Biography of Buddha 150.00
- Thus Spoke Buddha 150.00

Udit Sharma
- Teachings & Philosophy of Buddha 150.00

S.P. Ojha
- Sri-Ram-Charit Manas 95.00

Chakor Ajgaonkar
- Realm of Sadhana (What Saints & Masters Say) 30.00

K.H. Nagrani
- A Child from the Spirit World Speaks 10.00

F.S. Growse
- Mathura & Vrindavan, The Mystical Land of Lord Krishna (8 Colour photos) 495.00

Dr. Giriraj Shah
- Glory of Indian Culture 95.00

R.P. Hingorani
- Chalisa Sangreh (Roman) 60.00

Acharya Vipul Rao
- Srimad Bhagwat Geeta (Sanskrit & English) 75.00

Dr. Bhavansingh Rana
- 108 Upanishad (In press) 150.00

Eva Bell Barer
- Quiet Talks with the Master 60.00

Joseph J. Ghosh
- Adventures with Evil Spirits 80.00

Dr. S.P. Ruhela
- Fragrant Spiritual Memories of a Karma Yogi 100.00

Yogi M.K. Spencer
- Rishi Ram Ram 100.00
- Oneness with God 90.00

H. Seereeram
- Fundamentals of Hinduism 250.00

Books in Roman
- Bhajan, Lokgeet or Aartiyan (Roman English, Hindi) 95.00
- Hindu Vrat Kathayen (Including Saptvaar Vrat Kathayen) 40.00
- Chalisa Sangreh (Including Aarties in Roman) 60.00
- Shri Satya Narayana Vrat Katha (In English and Hindi) 25.00
- Sanatan Dharm Pooja 95.00
- Sudha Kalp 95.00
- Shiv Abhisek Poojan 25.00
- Daily Prayer (Hindi, English, French, Roman) 25.00
- Sanatan Daily Prayer 25.00
- Durga Chalisa 10.00
- Gaytari Chalisa 10.00
- Shiv Chalisa 10.00
- Hanuman Chalisa 10.00

Acharya Vipul Rao
- Daily Prayer 25.00

Books can be requisitioned by V.P.P. Postage charges will be Rs. 20/- per book. For orders of three books the postage will be free.

◉ DIAMOND POCKET BOOKS

X-30, Okhla Industrial Area, Phase-II, New Delhi-110020, Phone : 011-51611861, Fax : 011-51611866
E-mail : sales@diamondpublication.com, Website : www.fusionbooks.com

DIAMOND POCKET BOOKS
Presents
Osho's illuminating and enlightening discourses

SUFI, THE PEOPLE OF THE PATH
- ☐ *Singing Silence 150.00
- ☐ *A Lotus of Emptiness 150.00
- ☐ *Glory of Freedom 150.00
- ☐ *The Royal Way 150.00

PHILOSOPHY & UPNISHAD
- ☐ * I am the Gate 150.00
- ☐ * The Great Challenge 150.00
- ☐ *A Cup of Tea 150.00
- ☐ The Mystery Beyond Mind 50.00
- ☐ Towards The Unknown 50.00
- ☐ A Taste of the Divine 50.00
- ☐ The Alchemy of Enlightenment 50.00
- ☐ Be Silent & Know 50.00
- ☐ A Song Without Words 50.00
- ☐ Inner Harmony 50.00
- ☐ Sing, Dance, Rejoice 50.00
- ☐ Secret of Disciplehood 50.00
- ☐ The Centre of the Cyclone 50.00
- ☐ The Greatest Gamble 50.00

MEDITATION
- ☐ *Meditation-The Art of Ecstasy ... 150.00
- ☐ Love & Meditation 50.00
- ☐ Meditation- The Ultimate Adventurer 50.00
- ☐ *The Psychology of the Esoteric .. 150.00

PATANJALI YOGA SUTRA
- ☐ *Yoga - The Alpha and The Omega-I (The Birth of Being) 150.00
- ☐ *Yoga - The Alpha and The Omega-II (The Ever Present Flower) 150.00
- ☐ *Yoga - The Alpha and The Omega-III (Moving to the Centre) 150.00

JESUS AND CHRISTIAN MYSTICS
- ☐ * I say unto You - I & II ..... Each 150.00

ZEN & ZEN MASTERS
- ☐ *Zen and the Art of Living 150.00
- ☐ *Zen and the Art of Enlightenment 150.00
- ☐ *Zen : Take it Easy 150.00
- ☐ *Zen and The Art of Meditation 150.00

OSHO ON KABIR
- ☐ *The Divine Melody 150.00
- ☐ Ecstasy : The Language of Existence 50.00

BAUL MYSTICS
- ☐ Bauls : The Dancing, Mystics 50.00
- ☐ Bauls : The Seeker of the Path 50.00
- ☐ Bauls : The Mystics of Celebration 50.00
- ☐ Bauls : The Singing Mystics 50.00

TANTRA
- ☐ Tantra Vision : The Secret of the Inner Experience 50.00
- ☐ Tantra Vision : The Door to Nirvana 50.00
- ☐ Tantra Vision : Beyond the Barriers of Wisdom 50.00
- ☐ Tantra Vision : An Invitation to Silence 50.00

VEDANTA
- ☐ Vedanta : The Ultimae Truth 50.00
- ☐ Vedanta : The First Star in the Evening 50.00
- ☐ Vedanta : An Art of Dying 50.00
- ☐ Vedanta : The Supreme Know 50.00

OSHO'S VISION FOR THE WORLD
- ☐ *And the Flowers Showered 150.00
- ☐ Be Oceanic 50.00
- ☐ One Earth One Humanity 50.00
- ☐ Freedom form the Mind 50.00
- ☐ Life, A Song, A Dance 50.00
- ☐ Meeting the Ultimate 50.00
- ☐ The Master is a Mirror 50.00
- ☐ From Ignorance to Innocence 50.00
- ☐ Eternal Celebration 50.00
- ☐ Laughter is My Message 50.00

BOOKS ABOUT OSHO
Dr. Vasant Joshi, Ma Chetan Unmani
- ☐ *New Vision for the New Millennium 100.00

Swami Chaitanya Keerti
- ☐ *Allah To Zen 150.00

Swami Arvinda Chaithnya
- ☐ Our Beloved Osho 195.00

Ma Dharm Jyoti
- ☐ One Hundred Tales for Ten Thousand Buddha 95.00

Order books by V.P.P. Postage Rs. 20/- per book extra.
Postage free on order of three or more books, Send Rs. 20/--in advance.

DIAMOND POCKET BOOKS (P) LTD.
X-30, Okhla Industrial Area, Phase-II, New Delhi-110020,
Phones : 51611861 - 65, Fax : (0091) -011-51611866, 26386124

OUR BEST SELLERS

WHY WOMEN ARE WHAT THEY ARE
Swati Lodha

This is a stimulating book on women. It is a book for women, of women, by a woman. It is a clarion call for the faceless, oppressed Indian women to wake up from the closets and come to the sprawling new world, where opportunities are beckoning them. **(Available in English & Hindi)**

Price: English–Rs.195/- Hindi–150/-

201 DIET TIPS FOR HEART PATIENTS
Dr. Bimal Chhajer, M.D.

This book is a boon for all heart patients as it answers all their queries concerning the ideal diet. Queries regarding diet–such as calculation of calories, composition and details about the fat content of various food items as well as what is good and bad for the heart– are answered in a lucid style and simple language. **(Available in English & Hindi)**

Price : English–Rs.150/- Hindi–95/-

Other books by Author
- Zero Oil Cook Book • Zero Oil Sweets • Zero Oil 151 Snacks
- Zero Oil South Indian Cook Book

THE INSTINCT TO HEAL

This book by David Servan-Schreiber, himself a scientist and physician, is a wonderful manual to help reconcile our emotional and rational brains. He bases his prescription about how to improve our lives on a profound understanding of how our brain works, on a broad synthesis of the latest knowledge in neuropsychology. (Available in English & Hindi)

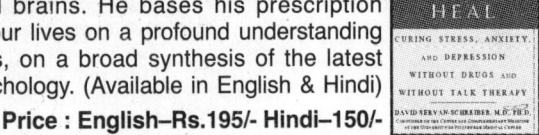

Price : English–Rs.195/- Hindi–150/-

ESSENCE OF VEDAS *Dr. Brij Raj Kishore*

This treatise is a compilation of all the four *Vedas – Rigveda, Samveda, Yajurveda and Atharvaveda –* in an easy-to-understandable language and simple diction for the common reades. It is a well established fact that *'Vedas'* are the oldest form of written books in our literature. *Vedas* contain the priceless teachings to human life.

Pages – 456. Price : Rs. 195/-

Books can be requisitioned by V.P.P. Postage charges will be Rs. 20/- per book. For orders of three books the postage will be free.

ⓕ FUSION BOOKS

X-30, Okhla Industrial Area, Phase-II, New Delhi-110020, Phone : 011-51611861, Fax : 011-51611866
E-mail : sales@diamondpublication.com, Website : www.fusionbooks.com